The Essential Attorney Handbook™ for Internet Marketing, Search Engine Optimization, and Website Development Management

The Essential Attorney Handbook™ for Internet Marketing, Search Engine Optimization, and Website Development by Jeffery W. Lantz

Published by: Esquire Interactive LLC
12112 Rancho Vistoso Blvd. Suite 150-310
Oro Valley, AZ 85755 Website: www.EsquireInteractive.com

Copyright © 2009 by Esquire Interactive LLC, Oro Valley, Arizona.

All rights reserved. The text of this publication, or any part thereof, may not be reproduced in any manner without written permission from the publisher, Esquire Interactive LLC.

Trademarks: Esquire Interactive, Esquire Interactive LLC and The Essential Attorney Handbook are trademarks of Esquire Interactive LLC. All other trademarks contained herein, including Microsoft, Google, Yahoo!, Ask.com, and Joomla, are trademarks of their respective owners.

NO REPRESENTATION IS MADE WITH RESPECT TO THE ACCURACY OR COMPLETENESS OF THE CONTENTS OF THIS WORK OR ANY INFORMATION CONTAINED HEREIN. ANY AND ALL WARRENTIES ARE SPECIFICALLY DISCLAIMED, INCLUDING, WITHOUT LIMITATION, ANY WARRANTIES OF MERCHANTABILITY AND/OR FITNESS FOR A PARTICULAR PURPOSE. THE STRATEGIES AND COMMENTARY SET FORTH HEREIN MAY NOT BE SUITABLE FOR ALL USERS, ATTORNEYS, OR LAW FIRMS. THERE IS NO REPESENTATION OR WARRANTY OF ANY KIND THAT THE MARKETING AND OTHER STRATEGIES SET FORTH HEREIN ARE ALLOWABLE UNDER ANY SPECIFIC JURISDICTIONS GOVERNING THE PRACTICE OF LAW, AND ATTORNEYS AND LAW FIRMS ARE URGED TO CONSULT WITH THE REGULATIONS GOVERNING THEIR PRACTICE OF LAW BEFORE IMPLEMENTING ANY SUCH STRATEGIES. NOTHING CONTAINED HEREIN SHALL BE CONSTRUED AS LEGAL ADVICE FOR ANY PURPOSES WHATSOEVER. IN ADDITION, THE STRATEGIES SET FORTH HEREIN ARE GENERAL IN NATURE, AND USERS SHOULD HIRE PROFESSIONALS BEFORE IMPLEMENTING ANY OF THE STRATEGIES CONTAINED HEREIN. THE PURCHASE OF THIS BOOK SHALL NOT BE DEEMED TO BE A CONTRACT BETWEEN THE PUBLISHER AND/OR AUTHOR AND ANY PURCHASER WITH RESPECT TO ANY SERVICES OR STRATEGIES SET FORTH HEREIN, AND NEITHER OF THEM SHALL HAVE ANY LIABILITY TO ANY PURCHASER ARISING OUT OF OR RELATING TO ANY ACTIONS TAKEN BASED UPON THE INFORMATION CONTAINED HEREIN. THE INFORMATION CONTAINED HEREIN MAY HAVE CHANGED SINCE PUBLICATION OF THE ORIGINAL TEXT.

Printed in the United States of America
ISBN: 9781449540548
Library of Congress Catalog Number: 209939013

DEDICATION

To my parents, Chuck and Joyce; and

To my Wife, Kelly, and my Children, Karlyn and Brayden.

THE ESSENTIAL ATTORNEY HANDBOOK™ FOR INTERNET MARKETING, SEARCH ENGINE OPTIMIZATION, AND WEBSITE DEVELOPMENT

TABLE OF CONTENTS

Dedication iii
Table of Contents iv
Preface xvii
    Disclaimers xvii
    About Me xviii
    Street Cred and Education xx
        About our Publisher Esquire Interactive xx

Part I – Internet Marketing Lessons and the Connected Generation 1

Chapter 1 – Lessons from the Digital Front 3

Chapter 2 – The Changing Nature of Communications and Understanding the New Connected Generation of Clients 6
    What is Internet Marketing? 7
    Why Internet Marketing is Important 8
    The Connected Generation 8
        Who is Included in the Connected Generation? 8
        Why We Should Care About Reaching the Connected Generation 9
        Virtual Companies and Reluctant Entrepreneurs 10

Part II – Strategic Planning, Value Proposition Development, and Branding 12

Chapter 3 – Developing a Value Proposition and Brand for Your Law Firm 13
    What is a Brand? The Differences between Branding, Marketing, and Advertising 13
    Why it's Critical to Develop Your Law Firm's Brand 14
    Branding Example - Soap 15
        What does Soap Branding Have to do with Law Firm Branding? 16
    A Law Firm's Brand Should be Developed from its Strategic Plan 17
    Branding From Strategic Planning – A Conceptual Diagram 18
        Strategic Planning – Charting the Direction of Your Law Firm 19
        Identifying Who Your Clients Are, and the Characteristics of Your Clients ... 19

- Your Firm's Services and Attorney Expertise 21
- A Law Firm's Value Proposition 24
- The Legal Service Component of the Value Proposition 24
- The Non-Legal "Needs" Component of the Value Proposition 24
- The "Cost" Component of the Value Proposition 25
- Satisfaction for Clients and Attorneys Results When the Value Proposition Offered and Delivered by the Firm Matches the Value Proposition Sought by Clients 26
- A Law Firm's Brand Should Be Developed From the Firm's Value Proposition Offered 28
  - The Corporate Firm's Brand – "Great Town's Trusted Business Counsel" 29
  - Logo, Business Cards, and Other Collateral 30
  - Firm Website 30
  - Slogans 30
- Adhering to Your Brand 31
- Get Help to Develop Your Firm's Value Proposition and Brand 31

Part III – Domain Name Registration and Website Hosting 33

Chapter 4 – Domain Name Registration 34

- Domain Name Overview 34
  - What is a Domain Name, and How are Domain Names Issued? 34
  - How Much Does it Cost to Register a Domain Name, and What Rights are Acquired? ... 35
  - Ethical Considerations for Domain Name Registration 35
- What Domain Names Should My Law Firm Register? 35
  - Should I Register www.OurFirmSucks.com? 36
- Domain Name Registration 37
  - Make Sure All Domain Names are Registered In Your Name or in the Name of Your Law Firm 37
  - Where Can I Check to See if the Domain Name that I Want Is Available? 38
  - Private Registration 38
  - How Are Domain Names Associated with A Server? 39
  - How to Acquire the Domain Name You Really Want from the Current Registrant 39
  - Using the WHOIS Database to Find Registrant Information 40
  - Domain Name Auctions 40
  - Using a Domain Escrow Agent 40
  - Using Domain Backorder Feature 41

Chapter 5 – Servers and Website Hosting 42

The Basics of Servers and Hosting 42
- What Is a Server? 42
- Should I Buy or Lease a Server? 43
- Wouldn't It be Cheaper to Buy a Server and Run it From My Firm? Why This is Not a Good Option for Most Firms 43
- Can I Save on Costs by Buying A Server and Sending it to the Hosting Facility? 45

Hosting Company Services 45
- Hosting Company Facilities – Tier 1 Hosting Facility 45
- What Services are Provided By Hosting Companies? 46

Types of Hosting – Shared Servers, Virtual Dedicated Servers, Dedicated Servers, and Cloud Hosting 46
- What is Shared Server Hosting, and What are the Advantages and Disadvantages? 46
- What is a Virtual Dedicated Server or Virtual Private Server? 48
- What Are Dedicated Servers? 48
- What Is Cloud Computing? Should We Have our Server Hosted in a Cloud Environment? ... 48

Understanding Your Firm's Website Traffic Needs 49
- The Difference Between Hits and Visits 49
- How Much Server Storage Does Your Website Require? Understanding Your Website's Server Storage and Internet Traffic Needs 50
- How Much Storage Space and Monthly Transfer are Typically Allowed by Shared Hosting Plans? 50

Other Hosting Considerations 51
- What is an Up-Time Guarantee, and What Happens if the Hosting Company Doesn't Meet Its Guarantee Obligations? 51
- Should I Use My Developer for Hosting? 51
- What are SSL Certificates, and Do I Need One? 52

Website Security 52
- Will the Hosting Company Guarantee that My Website Won't Get Hacked? 52
- What are the Risks if My Website Is Hacked? 53
- Should I Get Insurance to Cover The Risks of Hacking? 54

Chapter 6 – Dedicated Server Hosting – What You Need to Know if a Dedicated Server is Required or Desired 55

Dedicated Servers and Levels of Managed Hosting – Understanding the Combined Nature of These Aspects 55

- What Is Managed Hosting? 56
- If We Choose to Have a Dedicated Server, How Do We Keep It Secure? 56
- How Much Storage and Transfer Are Included in Dedicated Server Hosting 56
- Dedicated Server Recommendations 56
- What if This Plan is Not Enough? 57

Other Server Information 57
- What are the Differences in Server Hardware? 57
- Server and Processor Brands 57
- Server Operating Systems and Set-up Configurations 58
- Costs 59

Part IV – Website Development and Search Engine Optimization 60

Chapter 7 – Communicating Your Firm's Value Proposition Through Your Firm's Website 61

Your Website – Your Continuous Form of Promotion 61

Identifying Website Goals and Communicating Your Firm's Value Proposition Through Your Firm's Website 61
- Take the Challenge – How Well are Your Firm's Key Messages Communicated to Prospective Clients on Your Firm's Website? 62
- The Typical Law Firm Website Development Process 63

Potential Problem # 1 – No Defined Website Goals or Plan for Communicating the Firm's Value Proposition 64

Potential Problem #2 – Over-Promotion of the Firm and Its Credentials 67
- Remember, It's Not All About You or Your Firm's Credentials 67

Potential Problem # 3 – No Meaningful Branding 68
- Make Your Website Blend in with the Crowd or Standout? 68
- Making Your Brand Resonate with Current and Prospective Clients 69

Potential Problem # 4 – No Useful Search Engine Optimization 70

The Call to Action – Encouraging Clients to Contact Your Firm Through Firm Phone Numbers and Contact Information Forms 71
- Firm Telephone Numbers 71
- "Contact Us" Forms 71
- Include the "Contact Us" Form on Practice Area Pages and Attorney Profile Pages 73

Your Firm's Contact Information 74

Prominently Promote Website Content Sections that You Want Users to See 74
    How to Get Prospective Clients and Website Users to Visit Your Key Content Pages 75

Chapter 8 - Website Design Trends – Web 2.0 and Beyond *77*

Web 2.0 and Website Design 77
    What is Web 2.0? 77
    The Standard for Web 2.0 Websites 78
    Before Looking at Elements that Constitute Web 2.0, Let's Look at Web 1.0 –
        What Looks New and What Looks Dated 78

Website 2.0 Design Elements – Current Trends 80

Website Navigation – The Importance of Simple Navigation 82

Bonus Information - Web 3.0. 82

Chapter 9 – Creating the Client-Centered Website *83*

The Typical Law Firm Website Design 83

What Is the Client-Centered Website and How is it Different Than

Traditional Law Firm Websites? 83
    The Client-Centered Website Home Page 84
    Attorney Profile Pages – The Traditional Approach vs. The Client-Centered Approach 86
    Attorney Profile – Joe Blow, Esq. (Traditional Attorney Profile) 88
    Attorney Profile – Joe Blow, Esq. (Client-Centered Attorney Profile) 89
    What are the Differences Between the Traditional Approach and the
        Client-Centered Approach for Attorney Profiles? 90
    Practice Area Profiles – <u>How</u> are Services Delivered? 90

Chapter 10 - Website Development and Content Management Systems *92*

Who Should Develop My Website? Picking the Right Website Developer. 92
    Should I Build My Website Myself? 92
    OK, I Understand, But I Really Want to Learn Website Development 93
    Website Templates – to Use or Not to Use? 93
    Where Can Website Templates Be Found, and what Aspects Should I look For
        in a Template Design? 94

Understanding the Difference between the Design Process and Development Process

– Ensuring that Both Types of Expertise Are Covered 94

What Your Should Look For in a Website Developer 95

Be a Good Client – Take an Active Role in the Development Process 96

Content Management Systems – What Are They, and Why They Should be Included in Law Firm Websites 97

Dynamic vs. Static Web Pages 98
The Difference Between Dynamic and Static Web Pages 98
Dynamic vs. Static Web Pages – Why Should I Care? 98
Custom Content Management Systems 98
Non-Custom Content Management Systems – Open Source Licensed Software and Content Management Systems vs. Proprietary Licensed Software and Content Management Systems 100
PHP and MySQL vs. ASP and SQL – What Are They, and Which Option is Better? 102
A Note about Open Source 103

Joomla 103
The Benefits of Joomla Attorney Websites 103
The Joomla Open Source Platform for Law Firms 104
Creating Websites on Joomla vs. HTML (Non-CMS/Database Websites) 104

Chapter 11 – Search Engine Optimization 105

Search Engines, Search Engine Companies, and Search Engine Rankings – Why It's Important to be on the First Page of the Search Engine Results 105

It's Important to be #1 For the Search Terms Used by Prospective Clients 106
What Words do Prospective Clients Use? Using Wordtracker 107

The Basics of Search Engine Optimization (SEO) 108
The General Factors Used by Search Engines In Rankings 109

The Title Tag 109
Title Tag Size and Placement of Key Words 109
Common Title Tag Mistakes – What Not To Do 110

The Description Tag 111
On-Page or Visible Text 112

Keywords – How Long Will They Last? 112

High Search Engine Rankings Part 1 – Web Page Consistency 113

High Search Engine Rankings Part 2 – Link Power 114
Incoming Links 114

- Anchor Text 114
- Link Power and Oprah 115
- What do Search Engines Value? 116

Designing a Website for High Search Engine Optimization – Getting it Right from the Beginning 117

Chapter Bonus – Google Bombs 117

Chapter 12 - Search Engine Optimization Companies and Search Engine Optimization Plans 118

The Goals of Search Engine Optimization 118

The Elements of an Effective Search Engine Optimization Plan 120
- A Baseline Analysis Report 120
- Recommendations Report 120
- Search Engine Optimization Plan 121
- Measurement Reports 121
- Search Engine Optimization Timetable for Improvements 121

Search Engine Ethics 122

Part V – Internet Marketing and Networking 123

Chapter 13 - Launching Your Website – Now That Your Site is Live, What Should Be Done Next? 124

Is Kevin Federline a Search Engine Guru, and If So, Why Did Britney Leave Him? 124

How to Get Your Site Indexed by the Search Engines – The Site Submission Process 125
- Google Site Submission 125
- Yahoo! Site Submission 126
- Ask.com Site Submission 126
- Bing Site Submission 126

What is the Google Sandbox, and How Do I Get Out? 126

Improving Your Website Rankings – Where to List your Website. 127
- Google Maps 127
- Yahoo! Local 127
- City Search 127
- Yelp 128
- Local.com 128

xi | Page

Chapter 14 - Law Firm Marketing Metrics – How Should Our Marketing Spend be Allocated? 129

How Do Our Clients Find Us? 129

Calculating and Understanding Your Client Acquisition Cost and Average Client Value 129

The Components of an Effective Marketing Program 130
    Where do Prospective Clients Look for You Firm's Services? 131

The Types of Marketing Opportunities Available to Law Firms to Reach Prospective Clients 133

Measuring The effectiveness of Marketing Opportunities 133
    Phone Number and E-mail Account Measurement for Non-Internet Campaigns 134
    Measuring Internet Campaigns and Marketing 135

Webalizer and Google Analytics 135
    Google Analytics 142
    Other Statistics Programs 143
    Measuring the Effectiveness of Directory and Online Program Inclusion 143

Re-Allocating Marketing Spend 145

Chapter 15 – Search Engine Marketing (or Pay-Per-Click Advertising) on Google, Bing, and Yahoo! 146

Overview of Search Engine Marketing – Google PPC Example 146
    How Much Will You Be Charged Per Click? 147
    The minimum ad bid does not mean that your ads will be displayed 148

The Analytics Dashboard/Administration Panel 148

The Benefits to Law Firms of Pay-Per-Click Advertising 149

Pay-Per-Click Advertising on Google, Bing, and Yahoo! 150

Pay-Per-Click Campaign Creation – Determining a Consistent Structure to be Used 150

Determining the Keywords to be Used 151

Creating Mutiple Ads for the Same Campaign on Google 151

Limiting the Geographic Scope of Where Your Ads Will Be Shown 152

Beyond Search Engine Marketing – How to Get Your Ads Displayed on Specific Websites and Cost Per Thousand Impressions (CPM) Billing 153

The Google Search Network and the Google Content Network 154

Importing Campaigns to Bing and Yahoo! from Google 156
- Yahoo! 156
- Bing 156

More Information about Search Engine Marketing 157

Chapter 16 – Promoting Your Firm and Future Services Through E-Newsletters 158

What are Electronic Newsletters? 158

The Reasons Firms Avoid E-Newsletters 158

E-Newsletter Value to Clients and Call to Action 159

Two things Kenney Chesney Won't Do 160

E-Newsletters and Legal Obligations 160

E-Newsletter Feedback – Advantages Over Printed Newsletters 161

Dropping Off Subscribers – Where Are You Taking Them, and What Do You Want Them To Do After You've Dropped Them Off? 161

How to Get Started with an E-Newsletter 162

E-Newsletters and Spam Filters 163

Blacklisting 164

Chapter 17 – Blogging 166

Blogging Overview and FAQ's 166
- What are Blogs? 166
- Why Should I Blog – Who Would be Interested in What I'm Doing Every Day? 166
- The Blog Purpose 166
- What Should I Blog About? 167
- The Elements of A Good Blog 167
- How Often Should I Blog? 168
- Blog Categories versus Blog Tags – What is the Difference, and How Should Each Be Used? 168
- Can Categories and Tags Be Added After a Posting is Published? 169
- Creating a Blog Title 169

Creating My First Posting – How Do I Do It Right? 169
Hold the Presses – Can I Change a Posting After It's Been Published? 170

Blog Hosting 171
What Blog Platform Should I Use? 171
Where Should My Blog Be Hosted – On the Firm's Website or Somewhere Else? 171

Who uses WordPress? 172
A Note About Open Source, PHP, and MySQL 172
Installing WordPress 173
Choosing and Customizing Your WordPress Theme 173

Understanding the WordPress Control Panel 174
Blog Options 174

Hello, Is there Anybody Out There? - Promoting Your Blog 174
Syndicating Your Blog Through RSS Feeds 175
Submitting Your Blog to Blog Search Engines 176
Using a Separate Free E-mail Account for Blog Submission 177
Should I Let Search Engines Ping Me, and Does it Hurt Much? 177
What's a "Trackback", and What Type of Animal Are We Hunting? 178
Widgets for Blogs 178
Blogging About Your Practice Area(s) 179
Comments – To Allow, or Not to Allow – That is the Question 179
Attribution and Other Blogging Etiquette 180
Will Blogging Help With Search Engine Optimization and Website Rankings? 181
Other Ways to Get People to Your Blog and to Make Comments 181
Adding RSS to Your Facebook Business Page 182
Post Links on Twitter & Facebook 182
How Blog Comments Help Your Image for Prospective Clients 182
Blogging and the Potential For Lawsuits 182

Chapter 18 – Facebook, Twitter, LinkedIn, and Other Internet Social Promotion and Networking Opportunities *184*

Social Networking on the Internet – The Big Picture 184

Facebook – Will You Be My Friend? 187
Why has Facebook Become so Popular? 187

Facebook – Initial Impressions and Getting Started 188
Recommendations for Facebook 188
Keeping Connected – How to Encourage Others to Write on Your Wall 189

I'm No Longer Your [Friend, Fan, Group Member] 189

Adding Your Blog Postings To Facebook 190

Linking Your Facebook Updates to Twitter "Tweets" 190

Twitter – Should I Tweet? 191
The Twitter Sign-Up Process 191
Getting Followers of Your Tweets 191
How Twitter May Be Used to Promote an Attorney's Blog 192

MySpace 192

LinkedIn 192

Plaxo 193

Yelp 194

Social Networking Etiquette 194

Chapter 19 – Public Relations Plans and PR Firms 196

What's So Important for Law Firms about Public Relations Efforts? 196

Hiring a Public Relations Firm and Developing a PR Plan 196
PR Proposals and PR Plans 196

Becoming a Media Expert 197

Press Releases 198
Issue Press Releases on a Regular Schedule; Preferably with News that Will Benefit Others 198
Make Sure Your Press Releases are Optimized for Search Engines 198
Targeting Industries 199
Press Release Formatting 199
Press Release Distribution 200

Appendix 1 - Registering Your Firm's Domain Names 202

The Domain Registration Process 202

Appendix 2 – Changing The Nameserver for Your Domain Name (For Godaddy or Esquire Interactive Domain Accounts) 206

Appendix 3 – Creating a Pay-Per-Click Account with Google 210
Create an Account 211
Structure Your Advertising 213

xv | Page

Ad Creation 216
　　Create Campaigns 217
　　Create Compelling Ads 226
　　Create Keywords to Trigger Display of Ads 229
　　Enter Billing Information & Activate Ads 230
　　Manage and Revise Ads 231

Appendix 4 – Creating a Pay-Per-Click Account with Yahoo! Search Marketing 233
　　Target Customers by Geographic Location 235
　　Choose Keywords 236
　　Tell Us How Much You'd Like to Spend 237
　　Create Your Ad 237
　　Review and Activate Your Ad 238

Appendix 5 – Creating a Pay-Per-Click Account with Microsoft Bing 240
　　Targeting Your Clients 242
　　Creating Your Ad 243
　　Enter Your Keywords 244
　　Set Your Budget 245
　　Confirm Your Ad Campaign Details 246
　　Activating Your Ad Campaign 247
　　Making Changes to Your Account 247
　　Changing Ad Group Settings 248
　　Importing Campaigns from Google 249

Appendix 6 – Creating Your Facebook Business Page 250
　　Advertising on Facebook 254

Appendix 7 – Creating a Twitter Account 256
　　Changes to Facebook / Twitter Link 260

PREFACE

Thank you for purchasing this book. I hope it proves to be a great resource for your law firm's marketing program.

A few notes - While this book provides a fairly detailed discussion of Internet marketing, it's also designed to be specific to the needs of law firms. For this reason, some aspects of Internet marketing, such as e-commerce programs and affiliate advertising, are not addressed.

Second, this book assumes that you don't have any website coding knowledge. While a few coding issues are mentioned (such as the importance of Meta tags in search engine optimization), coding for the most part is not discussed.

Third, periodically I'll provide my opinions on various matters and recommendations based upon my experience as an Internet entrepreneur. I hope these opinions/recommendations will prove useful, but certainly others may disagree or have their own preferences.

Lastly, like the law, Internet marketing is continuously changing. If you have any suggestions or comments about this book, please do not hesitate to send me an e-mail at Jeff.Lantz@EsquireInteractive.com.

DISCLAIMERS

No book written for attorneys would be appropriate without at least one legal disclaimer. So, please note the following:

> This book does not provide legal services or legal advice. Because the rules and regulations of state bar associations and other attorney governing bodies vary from state to state, no warranty is expressed that the marketing suggestions provided herein are allowed under the rules or regulations of any specific jurisdictions.
>
> Further, such rules and regulations will likely change and become further defined over time in response to new marketing opportunities. Therefore, as with all legal marketing, please ensure that your website and marketing efforts are done strictly in compliance with any rules and regulations governing your practice as an attorney. Before engaging in any of the strategies described herein, also

consider engaging a professional in the appropriate area, particularly as search engine marketing and similar areas are continuously changing.

ABOUT ME

I've been an Internet entrepreneur since 2004, and was a practicing corporate attorney from 1991-2004.

My first Internet venture – RetirementLifeToday.com, now known as 55-Alive! (www.55-Alive.com) - was aimed at providing a "MySpace" / News website for those over age 55, way back in the days when it was commonly assumed that no one over age 55 used a computer (that would be 2004). Shortly thereafter, I launched two related websites – www.RVListingsOnline.com and www.RetirementCommunitiesOnline.com. It was 2004 and I was well on my way to Internet riches and fortune!

While the huge Internet acceptance by those over age 55 was realized, the following year traditional media and other start-up companies entered the "55+" market. Several of these companies invested millions in their websites, with one company receiving venture capital financing of over $30 million. These amounts were far in excess of the limited personal savings that I had invested in my companies.

55-Alive! managed to hold its own through this process, and was featured on *CNBC's Power Lunch* and in the "Elevator Pitch" column in *Inc. Magazine*. Several competing companies have since folded or have significantly cut back from their initial business plan.

Over the course of building these companies, I've had a tremendous opportunity to learn firsthand both what it takes to attract website users and how Internet marketing and search engine optimization can be used effectively. My Internet education was earned the old-fashioned way – through making mistakes and learning from others. A number of these "learnings" are set forth in "Chapter 1 – Lessons from the Digital Front", and are discussed throughout this book. Perhaps the most important of these lessons is "Because You Built it, Doesn't Mean They Will Come (or even find you)."

With respect to marketing in general, and Internet marketing specifically, law firms have lagged behind most other industries in a number of critical areas, including brand development, effective marketing strategy creation, and the development of solid value propositions that resonate with current and prospective clients. As will be discussed, a brand is much more than a logo – a brand is developed from the value proposition *offered* by the firm, and arises from careful strategic planning. Once developed, the brand and value proposition should be incorporated into the firm's only form of continuous advertising – its website.

Following the branding/value proposition discussion, the steps associated with having a website developed are discussed. Chapter 4 discusses the process of securing a domain name or names for your law firm's website, Chapters 5 and 6 provide information on important hosting considerations, and Chapters 7, 8, 9, and 10 provide the critical information necessary for having an effective website built that can be easily managed.

How can a law firm connect with potential clients searching for its services? Chapter 11 discusses the importance of search engine optimization (or SEO), and what can be done to turn a website into an effective marketing tool for prospective clients actively looking for the services provided by a law firm, and Chapter 12 discusses SEO companies and the elements of SEO Plans.

After your website is "live" there are a number of opportunities available to increase your firm's Internet presence, ranging from inclusion in free and paid directories, to pay-per-click advertising (also called search engine marketing) on the three major search engines - Google, Microsoft Bing, and Yahoo! Chapter 13 discusses ways to promote your website on the Internet, Chapter 15 discusses search engine marketing, and the appendices to this book go over the step-by-step details for creating accounts and advertising on these search engines.

How can you measure the effectiveness of your website's Internet marketing programs? Are prospective clients actually finding your firm's website? Should you pay to advertise with law firm directories and companies that promise to produce clients? Chapter 14 discusses measuring marketing spend, and provides an overview of website statistics and analytics programs that provide comprehensive information of how users find your website.

How can you use interactive social media (such as blogs, Facebook, and Twitter) to reach prospective clients? Chapter 17 discusses blogging, and Chapter 18 discusses ways to enhance your Internet presence on these social networking websites. Thereafter, Chapter 19 discusses effective public relations strategies.

Before getting into the details of Internet marketing, it's important to understand the changing nature of communications. Chapter 2 examines these changes in light of the current business, social, and technology changes, and includes a description of the new "Connected Generation."

In this book, boxes that have a scroll with an "E" in them [E] signify ethics matters, and boxes with a ⚡ signify other important matters.

STREET CRED AND EDUCATION

Prior to becoming an Internet entrepreneur, I was a "large firm" corporate finance and securities attorney in Phoenix, Arizona (Snell & Wilmer LLP) for five years, served as senior counsel for an international resources company (BHP Billiton) for seven years, and served as VP, General Counsel, and Corporate Secretary for an aerospace and defense contractor in St. Louis (Westar Aerospace and Defense Group, Inc.). In addition to founding the companies previously noted and our publisher Esquire Interactive, I also served as President, CEO, and a Director of a publicly-held mining exploration company (War Eagle Mining Company, Inc. – TSX:V:WAR), and was a co-Founder and the President of Widget Realm, Inc., a company devoted to developing communication widgets on the Yahoo! widget platform.

I graduated from Indiana University's Maurer School of Law *cum laude* and was a member of Law Journal/Law Review, and received an M.B.A. in Finance from Indiana University's Kelley Graduate School of Business, both in December, 1990. I also received a B.B.A. in Business Administration (Finance & Marketing) from The University of Iowa in 1987.

ABOUT OUR PUBLISHER ESQUIRE INTERACTIVE

Esquire Interactive is a leading provider of website development, branding, and Internet marketing services for law firms. Esquire Interactive serves its clients through brand creation, website development, search engine optimization programs, search engine marketing programs, and newsletter campaign creation. Esquire Interactive additionally partners with other companies to provide its clients with public relations services and video development, and offers domain name registration services, and is also available for direct consultation and speaking engagements.

Esquire Interactive can be reached at www.EsquireInteractive.com, and can also be seen on Facebook at http://www.facebook.com/pages/manage/#/pages/Esquire-Interactive-Law-Firm-Attorney-Website-Development-SEO/153105772903 (shorter url to be forthcoming) and Twitter at EsqInteractiveLLC. For more information on law firm Internet marketing, please see the Attorney Library and the Esquire Interactive blog at www.EsquireInteractive.com.

THE ESSENTIAL ATTORNEY HANDBOOK™ FOR INTERNET MARKETING, SEARCH ENGINE OPTIMIZATION, AND WEBSITE DEVELOPMENT

PART I – INTERNET MARKETING LESSONS AND THE CONNECTED GENERATION

There has been tremendous publicity this decade regarding Internet millionaires, search engine optimization, website development, and Internet marketing in general. As a result, many misperceptions about the Internet have been created. Chapter 1 provides a short list of some of the more prevalent of these misperceptions. Chapter 2 provides an overview of the Connected Generation of clients, and how law firms need to focus their marketing efforts so that they reach the Connected Generation; particularly since the Connected Generation is influencing the way we all act.

CHAPTER 1 – LESSONS FROM THE DIGITAL FRONT

One of the reasons for this book is to share lessons learned from starting and operating several Internet companies. Like the practice of law, Internet marketing continues to evolve; therefore there is not one specific "plan" that will guaranty success every time. There are, however, many tested marketing opportunities that work, such as search engine optimization. Similarly, there are a number of misperceptions about Internet marketing (and website development in particular). The following is a short list of both of these items.

1. **If you build it, they will come**. This is **by far** the biggest misperception regarding the Internet. The theory is that now that you're "on the Internet", everyone (including prospective clients) will (1) see your website, and (2) use your services, (3) buy your products, and (4) make your website the most popular thing ever. It's like hanging out a shingle and assuming that now that your law firm is in business, clients will be beating a path to your door. Unless your website is on the first page of Google and other search engines in response to search queries by prospective clients, chances are your website will not be seen (and thus your firm won't be considered) by prospective clients.

2. **Everyone knows that our firm is the best in (pick a practice area); therefore Google will rank us #1 in the search results.** Search engine rankings are based upon complicated and proprietary algorithms concerning page content, Meta tags, incoming link "power", and other technology factors. **The rankings have nothing to do with how good you or your firm are at practicing law, how long you've been practicing law, or any "best firm / best lawyer" rankings**. One attorney with whom I consulted couldn't believe his firm's website was listed on the third page of Google for the term "DUI attorneys" (he had been practicing for over twenty years and had several hundred DUI trials), while another attorney's website who recently graduated from law school (and had no DUI trials) was on the first page of the search results.

   First page placement on search engines usually doesn't happen by accident; it takes creating a carefully optimized website and implementing an effective search engine optimization plan.

3. **Money spent on law firm branding, effective search engine optimization, and good public relations campaigns can be far more effective in generating clients than spending an equal amount of money on advertising.**

4. **We don't need a website.** Message to prospective clients – "We don't care about keeping up with technology." Response from prospective clients – "How else isn't the firm conducting business effectively? Don't they get it?" Today, all companies, including law firms, are expected to have an Internet presence.

5. **Everyone knows where to find us on the Internet.** Those who are specifically looking for your firm's website will be able to find it through search engines such as Google. Those who are looking for an attorney to represent them won't find your firm unless your firm's website is listed on the first page of the search results in response to the prospective client's search query.

6. **Our website looks great.** Chances are if your firm's website is more than a few years old, it probably looks outdated. See Chapter 8 which discusses Web 2.0. More importantly, if your website doesn't provide a clear value proposition for prospective clients and an effective call to action, it likely won't be very effective in generating clients.

7. **Prospective clients love lots of information about the law.** Actually, they really don't want to know a lot about the law. They like short, simple explanations to their legal questions – "will I lose my house or car if I file for bankruptcy? What is likely going to happen to me if I'm found guilty of DUI?" If you're going to provide information about the law, write to answer the questions that your clients are likely to have. Of course, you can provide all of the disclaimers you want, but at least try to give them some real information.

8. **If I provide great legal information about specific areas of law for prospective clients, they will call me to represent them.** Don't make this assumption. **Prospective clients don't hire the attorney who has the most information on a website, they hire the attorney whose message best resonates with them.** The website with great information remains a terrific resource for prospective clients, but that attorney may not be the one who gets hired.

The lesson is this – first and foremost, your firm's website should be built around communicating your firm's value proposition to prospective clients in a manner that will resonate with them.

9. **We need to spend thousands of dollars per year to be in [name of directory], because [we've always done it, every other prestigious firm is listed in the directory, we're really not sure but they tell us prospective clients go there to look for attorneys].** Prior to the Internet, the choices for law firm advertising were relatively few and generally expensive. With the Internet, marketing opportunities have significantly increased, and many of these opportunities cost much less than the more traditional forms of marketing. As a result, law firms should consider the full suite of marketing opportunities available, especially ones that may be less costly and more effective than traditional marketing opportunities.

10. **There is no way to easily measure marketing campaign effectiveness.** Website statistics and other programs can be used to get a clear understanding of Internet marketing campaign performance. Many of the statistics programs are free, and provide comprehensive details about how website visitors "find" a law firm's website (such as through a search on Google or from a link in a law firm directory). Similarly, offline advertising (such as phone book advertising) can also be measured using techniques such as alternative phone numbers and e-mail addresses. Using these simple tools, firms can better allocate their marketing spend to the areas that are generating the best results, and (in many instances) reduce marketing spend on areas that are extremely costly but generate few clients.

Before discussing some of these items in detail, it's important to first understand the new connected generation of clients.

CHAPTER 2 – THE CHANGING NATURE OF COMMUNICATIONS AND UNDERSTANDING THE NEW CONNECTED GENERATION OF CLIENTS

In order to stay competitive, law firms must embrace the changing nature of communications and understand the underlying market forces influencing the ways in which business is being conducted, as well as the personal views and motivations of clients. The increasing lack of job security, the many new business opportunities resulting from the Internet and other technologies, and the increase in social networking are at the heart of the business revolution.

Once, not too long ago in a galaxy that seems far, far away, the nature of attorney-client communication was simple. Communication was done face-to-face, by telephone, or by mail.

Then came faxes, cell phones, and e-mail, which were soon followed by instant messaging, Skype (with free video chat!), texting, Facebook, and Twitter. Undoubtedly new and faster forms of communication will continue to emerge.

Even voice communication methods are changing. Cell phone ownership continues to increase and land line usage continues to decrease.[1] Skype allows users to chat via computer by voice and video with users around the globe.

Other trends are also changing the way we communicate. According to a Nielsen Company 2008 Report, high-speed Internet access is now the norm rather than the exception, as more than half of American households now have high-speed Internet access.[2]

Further, according to Pew Research Center for the People & the Press, people are increasingly relying on the Internet as the primary source of information for national and

---

[1] The Birth of a Cellular Nation, Mediamark Research Inc., October 9, 2007, http://www.mediamark.com/PDF/WP%20The%20Birth%20of%20a%20Cellular%20Nation%20Revised.pdf

[2] http://blog.nielsen.com/nielsenwire/wp-content/uploads/2009/03/overview-of-home-internet-access-in-the-us-jan-6.pdf

international news.[3] Printed newspaper readership is shrinking in favor of online readership,[4] and "non-traditional" media (such as blogs, discussion boards, and online groups) are becoming increasingly important.

The changing communication landscape is an important area that must be addressed by law firms not only to <u>communicate with current clients</u> in the manner(s) preferred by them, but also to <u>reach prospective clients effectively.</u> Will it continue to make sense for firms to pay high costs for telephone book ads if many clients aren't using phone books to find an attorney? Should more advertising dollars be diverted to Internet marketing? If so, what types of Internet marketing are the most effective? Oh, by the way, what exactly is Internet marketing?

WHAT IS INTERNET MARKETING?

This question can often be asked in a number of ways – out of curiosity (I want to know more about it), confusion (I don't understand the terminology or how it works); even out of contempt (I don't want to learn about Internet marketing, thank you).

> IN SIMPLE TERMS, INTERNET MARKETING FOR LAW FIRMS CAN BE THOUGHT OF AS ANY TYPE OF COMMUNICATION ON THE INTERNET THAT LEADS POTENTIAL CLIENTS TO THE LAW FIRM'S WEBSITE OR OTHERWISE PROVIDES INFORMATION ABOUT THE LAW FIRM, IN EITHER CASE WHICH RESULTS FROM EFFORTS BY THE LAW FIRM TO POSITIVELY INFLUENCE THE FIRM'S IMAGE.

Using this definition, Internet marketing is comprised of many items: the firm's website, blogs written by the firm or its attorneys (and postings made by firm attorneys on the blogs or social networking pages of others), pay-per-click advertising on Google and other search engines, advertising on websites, inclusion of the firm in online directories, search engine optimization designed to achieve higher rankings for the firm in response to search engine queries by prospective clients, press releases, Facebook, MySpace, and other social networking sites (in the name of the firm or by firm attorneys), YouTube videos, and Twitter "tweets".

---

[3] Pew Research Center for the People & the Press, *Internet Overtakes Newspapers As News Outlet*, 2008, http://people-press.org/report/479/internet-overtakes-newspapers-as-news-source.

[4] NPR, *Chronicling the Death of American Newspapers*, by Linton Weeks, March 2, 2009, http://www.npr.org/templates/story/story.PHP?storyId=101237069.

This list is not exclusive, and new forms of advertising opportunities continue to emerge. Additionally, some of these existing opportunities are continuing to evolve. Google, for instance, allows companies to advertise directly on the websites of others (through its AdWords/AdSense programs) not just with text links, but also with banner ads (including animated ads) and video. Remarkably, advertisers can target their advertising to specific participating websites, and no website/advertiser direct interaction is required.

WHY INTERNET MARKETING IS IMPORTANT

Internet marketing is important for a number of reasons: it's likely where your current and prospective clients are spending a significant amount of time, it's where your prospective clients are searching for your firm's services, and, if done correctly, it's likely much more cost effective than almost any other form of marketing. Where else, for instance, is it possible to reach prospective clients actively searching for your firm's services for a quarter? (See Chapter 15 for more information about search engine/pay-per-click advertising).

The Internet is here to stay. As attorneys interested in law firm marketing we can embrace it and determine how to make it work for our law firm or face being left behind by the Internet marketing efforts of other firms. To be effective, however, we need to understand how the Connected Generation operates and communicates.

THE CONNECTED GENERATION

Who is Included in the Connected Generation?

I would suggest that the Connected Generation be thought of as those graduating from college after 1995. This generation has never been without computers, and, since graduation, is now rarely without an Internet connection through a notebook computer or cell phone.

In addition to abandoning land lines, the Connected Generation is forging new ways to stay in constant contact with friends and to conduct business networking. Initially websites such as MySpace and Facebook were used to keep connected with friends, and other websites such as LinkedIn were used for professional networking. This is no longer the case, as a Facebook presence, for instance, is quickly becoming a "must have" for professionals.

WHY WE SHOULD CARE ABOUT REACHING THE CONNECTED GENERATION

Those in the Connected Generation are becoming our clients for both personal legal matters and as business executives and owners.

To some extent the Connected Generation is like previous generations. Following graduation from college they followed many of the traditional paths: starting a career, getting married, starting a family, advancing in career, and, over time, joining executive management. Their legal needs followed a similar path – few and primarily personal needs following college, and more complex legal needs later – both personal (such as divorce or bankruptcy) and business (needing to retain counsel on behalf of a corporation).

To another extent, the Connected Generation is not like previous generations. As the first decade of the new millennia draws to a close, the economy is bleak, unemployment has risen dramatically, and the financial stability offered by large employers in previous decades has vanished. Those in the Connected Generation understand that job stability, pensions, and even 401(k) matching plans have become a thing of the past for most companies. Working a lifetime for only one company no longer seems realistic. Conversely, the chance that a given company will go out of business or be merged (leading to layoffs) seems to be increasing each year.

Those fortunate enough to find jobs during the economic downturn did so knowing that they, or their company, may not be there tomorrow, resulting in an increased importance upon networking and keeping a resume current. As a result, attitudes about corporate employers are much different than those held by previous generations. Realizing that an employment relationship is likely to last only three to five years,[5] those in the Connected

---

[5] Individuals born from 1957 to 1964 held an average of 10.8 jobs from ages 18 to 42. These baby boomers held an average of 4.4 jobs while ages 18 to 22. The average fell to 3.3 jobs while ages 23 to 27 and to 1.9 jobs from ages 38 to 42. Jobs that span more than one age group were counted once in each age group, so the overall average number of jobs held from age 18 to age 42 is less than the sum of the number of jobs across the individual age groups.

Although job duration tends to be longer the older a worker is when starting the job, these baby boomers continued to have large numbers of short-duration jobs even as they approached middle age. Among jobs started by workers when they were ages 38 to 42, 31 percent ended in less than a year, and 65 percent ended in fewer than 5 years.

United States Department of Labor, Bureau of Labor Statistics, Economic News Release - *Number of Jobs Held, Labor Market Activity, and Earnings Growth Among the Youngest Baby Boomers:*

Generation may be less willing to put in long work weeks or cancel important personal events to get company work done.

In light of corporate job insecurity and wanting a lifestyle with more job control, many in the Connected Generation have opted to start businesses, either while working for a company or instead of working for a company. Technology is largely responsible for enabling this growing trend.

VIRTUAL COMPANIES AND RELUCTANT ENTREPRENEURS

The Connected Generation doesn't need to have high overheads on rent and fixed salaries to operate their businesses, especially virtual companies, which can be started easily. Virtual companies are companies that tend to focus on one core product or service and outsource almost all of the functions not directly related to the core product or service (often to other companies using the same business model), instead of employing people to fill the "non-core" business needs.[6] Even secretaries and phone receptionists may be outsourced instead of physically being located in the same office as the business principals.

Results From a Longitudinal Survey Summary, June 27, 2008, http://www.bls.gov/news.release/nlsoy.nr0.htm.

[6] Specifically, BusinessDictionary.com defines a "virtual enterprise" (often called a "virtual company") as an:

> Ad hoc alliance of independent experts (consultants, designers, developers, producers, suppliers, etc.) who join to pursue a particular business opportunity. Virtual enterprises have little or no physical presence or infrastructure, rely heavily on telecommunications and networks such as internet, and usually disband when their purpose is fulfilled or the opportunity passes. Agile, flexible, and fluid, they are extremely focused and goal driven, and succeed on the basis of little investment requirements, low startup and overhead costs, and fast response time. Geographically dispersed members of a virtual enterprise collaborate on the basis of their core strengths from wherever they are and whenever they are able to do so, and may become competitors in pursuit of another opportunity.

http://www.businessdictionary.com/definition/virtual-enterprise.html. The term "virtual company" is now being used for companies that have adopted the low overhead, high outsourcing, heavy use of technology business model. For instance, see Fast Company, *"This 'Virtual' Company Is for Real"*, December 18, 2007, http://www.fastcompany.com/magazine/12/monorail.html?page=0%2C0. Proposed legislation in Vermont would make it a haven for virtual companies. See Inc. Magazine, *"A Haven For Virtual Companies"*, July 1, 2008, http://www.inc.com/magazine/20080701/a-haven-for-virtual-companies.html.

Virtual companies have legal issues, especially as they grow. Because many of the owners have little or no experience working for large corporations, they often have no experience with corporate attorneys. And, because the owners may operate out of their house or a small office space instead of a large, prominent building, their companies are largely invisible to business attorneys. The challenge will be for corporate law firms to find and connect with these business owners.

Further, as large numbers of 40, 50, and 60 year olds are finding themselves downsized and unable to find work quickly in the current recession, many in this group are starting their own businesses. My prediction is that the number of these "reluctant entrepreneurs" will continue to increase as a result of the current recession, fundamental shifts in job outsourcing and production to overseas companies, and the decline in job security that once existed with big companies. Like their younger counterparts, these reluctant entrepreneurs are embracing technology, forming virtual companies, and actively engaging in social networking.

Thus while the Connected Generation may have started in an age-specific demographic, the core beliefs of the Connected Generation are being embraced by those of all ages. Ultimately, as attorneys, we need to embrace and understand the Connected Generation because it is we who are becoming more like them.

The good news is that law firms that understand Connected Generation values and communication methods can effectively use the Internet to reach prospective clients at a lower cost than ever before. The difficulty for some may be learning and embracing new marketing forms, especially those forms that might make us somewhat uncomfortable (such as blogging), instead of outright dismissing the new marketing opportunities available. The following chapters in this book discuss these opportunities.

PART II – STRATEGIC PLANNING, VALUE PROPOSITION DEVELOPMENT, AND BRANDING

Before discussing website development and Internet marketing, it's necessary to understand and create the fundamental value proposition that your firm will offer, and to develop branding that will resonate with prospective clients. Without understanding and creating marketing around these fundamentals, it's unlikely that a firm's marketing – in particular its website – will be effective to the extent desired. An attractive website, for example, may not be effective if it's not designed in a way or contains a message that resonates with clients. The next chapter discusses strategic planning and the fundamentals of creating value propositions and branding upon which an effective website and Internet marketing program can be built.

CHAPTER 3 – DEVELOPING A VALUE PROPOSITION AND BRAND FOR YOUR LAW FIRM

By default, one law firm is indistinguishable from another firm in the minds of most prospective clients. Differentiating a firm from its competitors requires carefully developing a strategic plan. From this plan a firm's value proposition and brand can be developed and communicated to the firm's targeted clientele. The more effective that the firm is in communicating its brand, the more likely it is that the firm will be perceived as the best choice by prospective clients. Conversely, firms that don't differentiate themselves from competitors will compete for clients by out-spending competition or relying on non-media factors to reach clients.

WHAT IS A BRAND? THE DIFFERENCES BETWEEN BRANDING, MARKETING, AND ADVERTISING

A brand is much more than a logo. A brand embodies the central theme around which your law firm provides services. Marketing consists of the processes employed to present your brand to your targeted clientele, which might consist of advertising, client development functions, and writing industry articles. Advertising is one form of marketing, and involves the use of media to display a firm's message for a specified time period, usually in consideration for a payment made by the law firm advertiser.

Successful branding encompasses a number of aspects: *who* your clients are, the *characteristics* of your clients, the *services* your firm provides, and the *expertise* of your firm's attorneys. These four elements combine to form the *value proposition* offered by your firm.

The goal of branding is to clearly communicate your firm's value proposition to your intended audience (current and prospective clients, as well as the general public) in such a way that significantly differentiates your firm from others offering the same types of legal services.

The more your firm can be differentiated in the minds of prospective clients from other law firms offering the same legal services, the more your firm will be established in the minds of prospective clients that it is the clear choice for their legal needs.

Once the brand for a law firm is developed, an effective Internet marketing and advertising program can be built around the brand. The process for Internet marketing is straightforward:

> Reach prospective clients *before* and *at the time* they are looking for your firm's services;

> Distinguish your law firm from other firms by *branding* and *establishing the value proposition* offered by your firm to prospective clients; and

> Encourage prospective clients to *contact you or your firm* so that you will be the first attorney called by prospective clients (which will hopefully give you the opportunity to convince prospective clients to choose your firm before contacting other firms).

WHY IT'S CRITICAL TO DEVELOP YOUR LAW FIRM'S BRAND

In order to effectively engage in Internet marketing (or any type of marketing), a firm must develop its brand. Branding is especially important if there's no opportunity to speak directly with potential clients (such as when a potential client conducts a search on Google to find an attorney or visits a law firm's website after seeing a phone book ad).

There is a strong tendency for attorneys and law firms to disregard branding entirely other than to have a logo and business cards developed. There may be a several reasons for disregarding branding: other pressing billable work, a belief that it's simply not necessary for law firms, or uncertainty about how to develop a brand.

I suspect that to some extent we attorneys – in our local practices – have branded ourselves and each other in the sense that we know which attorneys are experienced and proficient in various legal matters. We might therefore assume that the public (and specifically potential clients) also have this same knowledge (which seldom is the case).

It's much more likely, for example, that potential clients won't know whether Smith and Jones is a leading multi-national law firm, or two attorneys just out of law school. Similarly, while Smith and Jones might be a two person law firm, they may be the leading attorneys in a particular area of law being sought by a potential client. Branding is how Smith and Jones distinguish their law practice and the value proposition they offer clients from the services and value propositions offered by other firms.

To understand better why it's critical for law firms to develop an effective brand, let's examine the consequences of failing to create a unique brand.

At a basic level, your firm will by default be considered the same as other firms offering the same legal services in the minds of prospective clients. One general practice firm will be viewed as fungible with another general practice firm. Even if you don't perceive your firm to be similar to other law firms, and even if your firm is considered by those in the legal community to be the top firm, *prospective clients (who aren't familiar with your firm or other firms) will perceive your firm and the other firms as being indistinguishable.* Unless this perception is changed, it will remain.

> **WHILE THIS SITUATION EXISTS, THE COST TO ACQUIRE CLIENTS IS HIGH, PRIMARILY BECAUSE DOLLARS ARE BEING SPENT ON <u>ADVERTISING</u> AS OPPOSED TO <u>BRANDING</u>.**

In simple terms, firms that have failed to distinguish their services from others compete against other firms by outspending the other firms. Bigger yellow page ads. More billboards and television commercials. Essentially non-branded firms offering the same legal services tend to have exactly the same message: "we represent accident victims and bring justice", for example. How will prospective clients choose which law firm to use when there might be a dozen or more firms with the same message?

BRANDING EXAMPLE - SOAP

The retail product giants of our generation are experts in branding. Take soap, a fairly fungible product in terms of product utility. Most types of soap work well for the intended purpose of getting one clean. Do the soap companies focus their advertising on saying the same thing – "our soap will get you clean"? Why should we care about purchasing a particular brand of soap if they all accomplish the same functional purpose, and, more importantly, why should we pay more for one brand of soap than another?

Soap companies don't compete against each other by telling us that their soap will get us clean. Instead, they carefully brand their soaps around specific ideas and concepts to match our particular needs, and then direct advertising to the intended audience about how their soap fulfills these identified needs.

UNDERSTAND THAT THE NEEDS BEING SOUGHT BY CLIENTS MAY BE MORE THAN THE OBVIOUS LEGAL SERVICES BEING PROVIDED

Soap companies identify the *specific need in a target audience* to be fulfilled, and then develop a *brand based on fulfilling that need*. The "need" is not necessarily the obvious, functional need that the product will provide. For soap, the "need" to be fulfilled may be to become "Irish" clean (Irish Spring), to use a "trusted, pure" soap (Ivory), to use a "hard-working" soap capable of getting a working person clean (Lava), or to use a gentle, moisturizing soap (Neutrogena). Once the need and brand are developed, marketing and advertising are done to communicate the brand *to* the targeted audience.

By concentrating on a specific "need", soap companies are much more effective (and profitable) with branding and marketing. As a result, even the large soap companies offer a number of different types of soap rather than marketing one "super soap" that is all things to all people.

Once a soap company has successfully developed its brand in the minds of the targeted audience, it no longer has to outspend its competitors to generate sales. Irish Spring, for instance, doesn't compete directly against Neutrogena. Instead, once the brand is created and communicated, the targeted audience will buy the brand based on the imputed characteristics that have been associated with the brand. Marketing and advertising serve to reinforce the brand's image ("you'll feel Irish fresh in the morning") rather than back-tracking to the basic functionality of the product (i.e. "Our soap will get you clean. Really, it will.").

Similar to soap companies, **law firms should understand that clients seek to have needs fulfilled beyond simply the legal services to be provided.** These non-legal needs may or may not be readily identifiable, even by the clients themselves. Just as we don't go into a store with the specific intention of finding a soap to get us "Irish clean", a corporate client representative might not be aware that what she really wants is to retain a "high-powered" law firm that will validate her personal success in business.

WHAT DOES SOAP BRANDING HAVE TO DO WITH LAW FIRM BRANDING?

The way in which soap is branded is illustrative of an important concept. If companies can develop strong consumer affinities around products such as soap that are much the same, we, who provide very individualized services and vary greatly in terms of experience in different legal areas, should be able to successfully develop a brand that will set our firm apart from our competitors based not only on the legal services we provide, *but also for the non-legal client needs that our firm fulfills*.

A LAW FIRM'S BRAND SHOULD BE DEVELOPED FROM ITS STRATEGIC PLAN

The following diagram illustrates a process for developing a brand and value proposition for a law firm. At the heart of the process is developing a strategic plan, which involves carefully identifying the clients to be targeted, the legal services to be provided to clients, and the legal expertise required.

The strategic plan should not be static in the sense that only current clients and staff are considered. Instead, the firm should develop the strategic plan around answering the questions "Where do we want to be in three (or five) years, and what does it take for us to get there?" It might be that additional attorneys need to be hired and new practice areas need to be developed. If this is the case, the strategic plan should include specific actions such as identifying possible lateral partners to join the firm and a time frame for completing these actions.

The next few sections discuss the diagram in detail. For illustration purposes, let's consider a firm of about 15 attorneys with a variety of different practice areas in the city of Great Town. Currently the firm does not have any specific brand other than its logo, and the firm more or less operates as individual attorneys who enjoy working together, and who sometimes work together in client development. They now wish to develop a strategic plan aimed at representing the business community, and would like to be known as "Great Town's Trusted Business Counsel." We'll call this firm "The Corporate Firm", and the remaining sections of this chapter discuss how the firm might go through each of the steps shown in the diagram.

BRANDING FROM STRATEGIC PLANNING – A CONCEPTUAL DIAGRAM

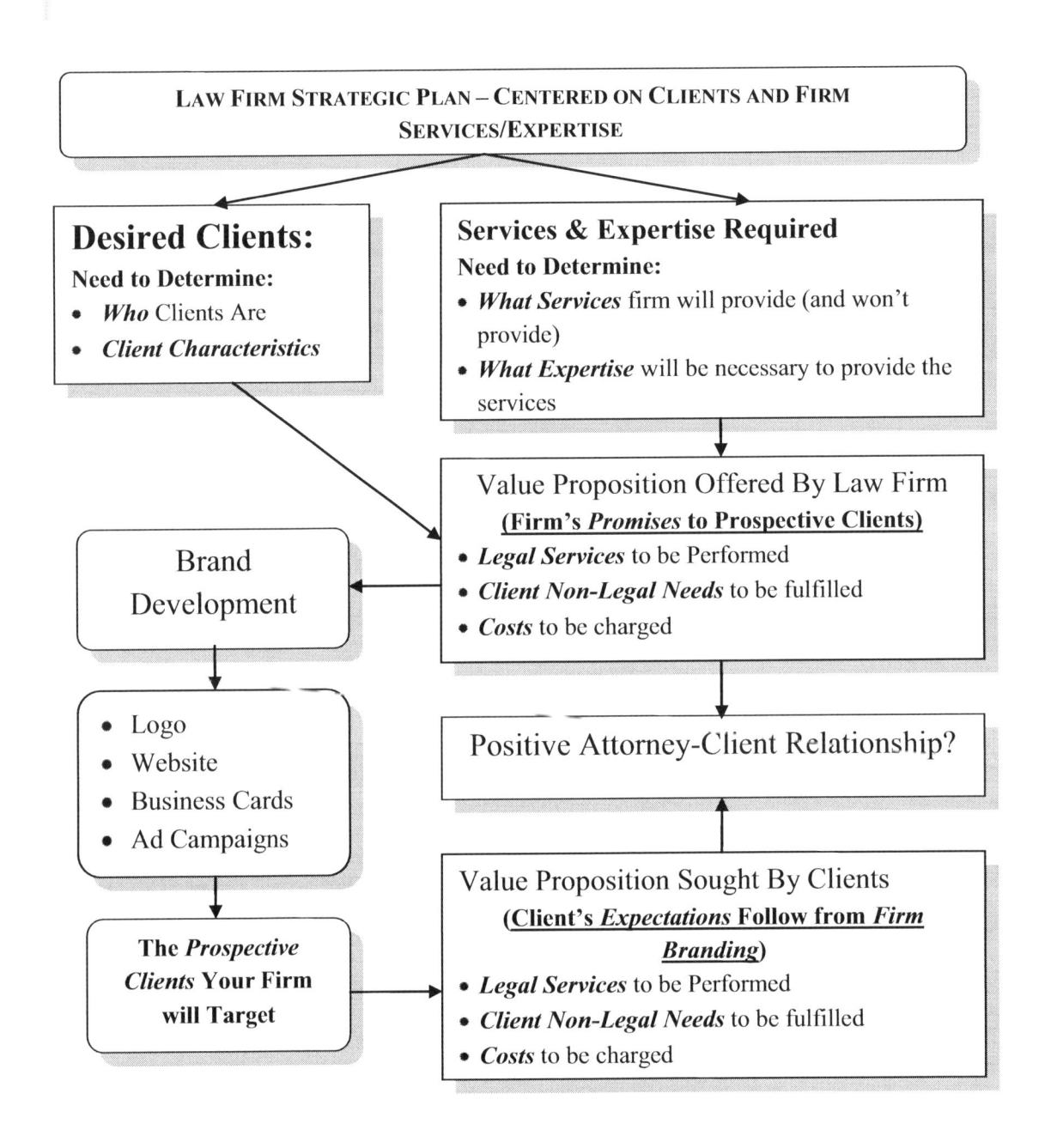

LAW FIRM STRATEGIC PLAN – CENTERED ON CLIENTS AND FIRM SERVICES/EXPERTISE

Desired Clients:
Need to Determine:
- *Who* Clients Are
- *Client Characteristics*

Services & Expertise Required
Need to Determine:
- *What Services* firm will provide (and won't provide)
- *What Expertise* will be necessary to provide the services

Value Proposition Offered By Law Firm
(Firm's *Promises* to Prospective Clients)
- *Legal Services* to be Performed
- *Client Non-Legal Needs* to be fulfilled
- *Costs* to be charged

Brand Development

- Logo
- Website
- Business Cards
- Ad Campaigns

The *Prospective Clients* Your Firm will Target

Positive Attorney-Client Relationship?

Value Proposition Sought By Clients
(Client's *Expectations* Follow from *Firm Branding*)
- *Legal Services* to be Performed
- *Client Non-Legal Needs* to be fulfilled
- *Costs* to be charged

Strategic Planning – Charting the Direction of Your Law Firm

The diagram sets forth a process for developing a value proposition and brand for a law firm. As the diagram suggests, a firm must first consider the clients that it seeks to target and the services it intends to provide so that the value proposition (its promise to prospective clients) can be developed. Then, the brand is developed around the value proposition, and the brand is translated into tangible and electronic (website, Internet) messages directed to the target clientele.

At the same time, prospective clients have their own value proposition that they are seeking to have fulfilled. In determining whether a firm is right for them, they seek information from the law firm brands in the marketplace. Often, because most law firms haven't developed a brand, prospective clients must go through lists of services offered by firms and try to determine if a given firm will meet their needs instead of going directly to "Great Town's Trusted Business Counsel", for instance.

If they are able to find a firm that has developed a brand, prospective clients develop expectations based upon the brands which may shape their value proposition when a firm is retained. Ultimately, a beneficial attorney-client relationship exists when the value proposition offered by the firm matches the value proposition expected by clients.

Identifying Who Your Clients Are, and the Characteristics of Your Clients

The first part of strategic planning focuses on two aspects: identifying the clients your firm will serve, and determining the services and expertise required. To some extent there is overlap between these two areas, but for the sake of this section they will be treated separately.

Client identification can be broken down into identifying the specific types of clients the firm is seeking that will require the firm's services. The firm's intended clientele may or may not be reflected by the firm's current clientele.

To expand on the example above, "Great Town's Trusted Business Counsel" is committed to transforming itself into primarily a corporate business and business litigation firm. The targeted clients are identified as businesses, community and non-profit organizations, and similar entities. As part of this transformation, the firm is going to phase out the acceptance of personal injury cases and divorce matters, but has decided that estate planning will still be offered, as this area is seen as supporting the small business owners who are expected to make up much of the firm's clientele.

Once the desired clientele has been determined, it's necessary to identify the **characteristics** commonly possessed by the desired clientele. <u>The goal of identifying client characteristics is that ultimately your firm's brand, which is communicated through marketing, should encompass these characteristics.</u> These characteristics consist not only of general characteristics about the clients (such as income level, job status, etc.) but also characteristics common to the legal matters for which they need your firm's services.

The characteristics of the corporate clients (or more accurately, those acting on behalf of the corporate clients) are then determined. Here, for instance, The Corporate Firm has determined that those representing both the established large businesses and the usually smaller family-owned businesses in the community tend to be middle or upper class in income level, and care deeply about the community's perception of their business. They tend to make legal decisions based upon the long-term consequences, even to the extent of short-term profits, and generally are adverse to litigation (perhaps even willing to write-off losses in situations where they would clearly prevail in litigation). They also have a strong sense of community and are actively involved in civic activities of Great Town. Most of these people were born and/or raised in Great Town, and therefore have a strong feeling of community pride. They also tend to be firmly rooted in the community, and not simply workers passing through Great Town on the way to bigger opportunities in larger cities.

The "Desired Clients" box for the corporate firm may be illustrated by the following diagram:

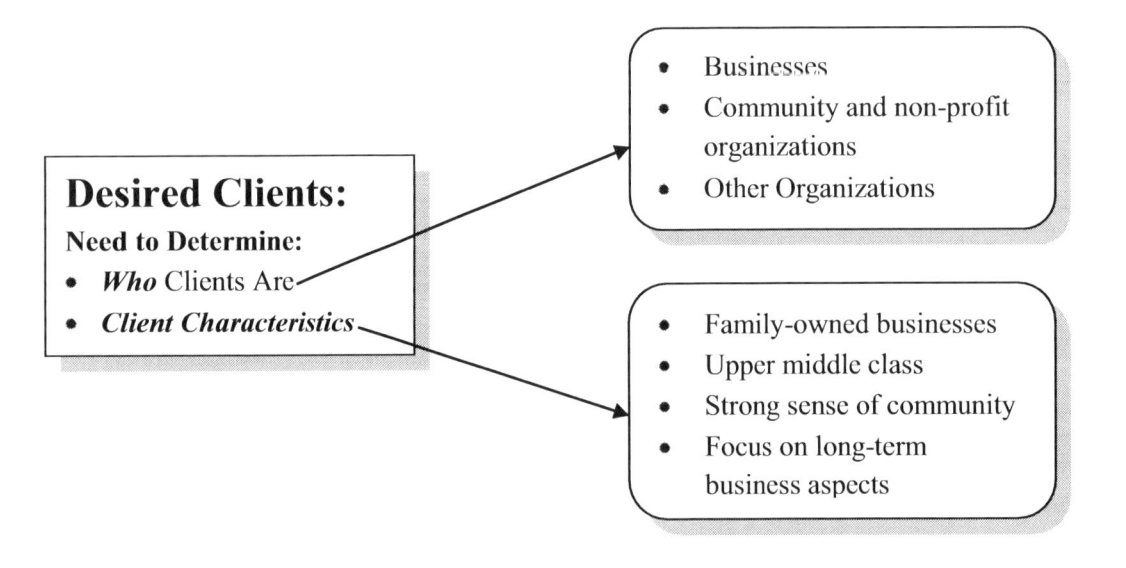

Desired Clients:
Need to Determine:
- *Who* Clients Are
- *Client Characteristics*

- Businesses
- Community and non-profit organizations
- Other Organizations

- Family-owned businesses
- Upper middle class
- Strong sense of community
- Focus on long-term business aspects

YOUR FIRM'S SERVICES AND ATTORNEY EXPERTISE

The second part of strategic planning is to determine the *services* required by the intended clientele and developing a plan for having the attorney *expertise* available to provide such services.

For The Corporate Firm, the services to be provided and the expertise necessary may look like the following:

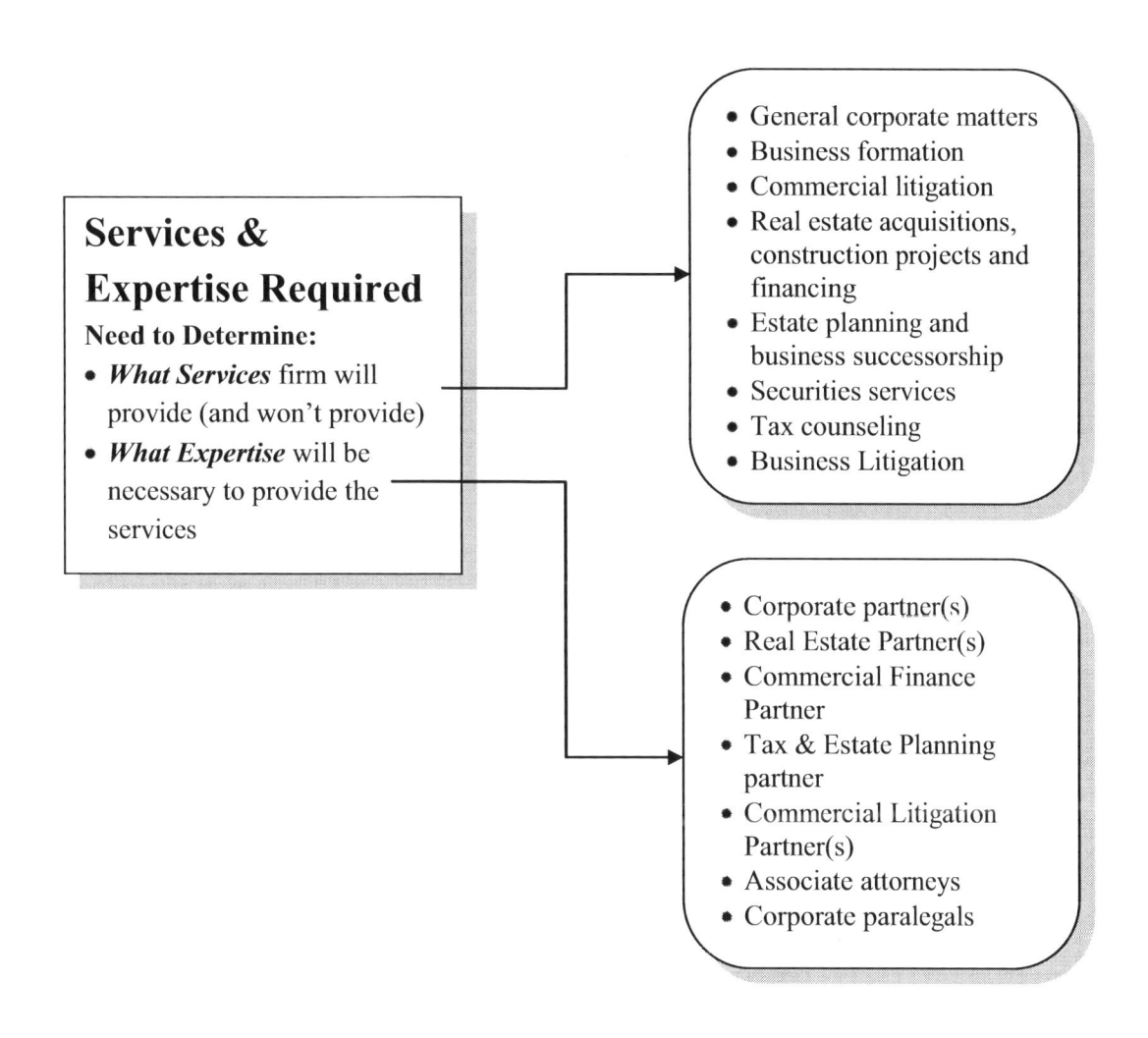

Services & Expertise Required

Need to Determine:
- *What Services* firm will provide (and won't provide)
- *What Expertise* will be necessary to provide the services

- General corporate matters
- Business formation
- Commercial litigation
- Real estate acquisitions, construction projects and financing
- Estate planning and business successorship
- Securities services
- Tax counseling
- Business Litigation

- Corporate partner(s)
- Real Estate Partner(s)
- Commercial Finance Partner
- Tax & Estate Planning partner
- Commercial Litigation Partner(s)
- Associate attorneys
- Corporate paralegals

In The Corporate Firm example, successful branding requires not only assessing the needs of the corporate clientele, <u>but also identifying what services are *not* core needs of the corporate clientele</u> (and would detract from the brand). For instance, if several of its partners practice high-profile criminal defense law, will this practice over-shadow the firm's corporate practice? When a potential corporate client visits the firm's website and finds much of it is devoted to criminal defense, will this turn-off the prospective client? How will the corporate client representative feel about having her company use the same firm that may also be representing those charged with serious crimes? Should the firm stop practicing criminal defense work completely?

These are important strategic decisions that must be addressed by The Corporate Firm. In a depressed economy, developing a strong brand can become even more difficult, as there will be an increased tendency to accept any matters that will help pay the bills, even if doing so does not promote long-term brand development. <u>While a firm may still take on matters that may not be consistent with its long-term strategy, it can minimize the focus of its website devoted to these types of matters so that its brand is not undermined.</u>

Returning to our example, the combined "Desired Clients" and "Services and Expertise" boxes for The Corporate Firm may be illustrated by the following diagram:

Desired Clients:

Need to Determine:
- *Who* Clients Are
- *Client Characteristics*

- Businesses
- Community and non-profit organizations
- Other Organizations

- Family-owned businesses
- Upper middle class
- Strong sense of community
- Focus on long-term business

Services & Expertise Required

Need to Determine:
- *What Services* firm will provide (and won't provide)
- *What Expertise* will be necessary to provide the services

- General corporate matters
- Business formation
- Commercial litigation
- Real estate acquisitions, construction projects and financing
- Estate planning and business successorship
- Securities services
- Tax counseling
- Business Litigation

- Corporate partner(s)
- Real Estate Partner(s)
- Commercial Finance Partner
- Tax & Estate Planning partner
- Commercial Litigation Partner(s)
- Associate attorneys
- Corporate paralegals
- Secretaries

Now that these areas have been determined, the next step is to build The Corporate Firm's value proposition.

A LAW FIRM'S VALUE PROPOSITION

> **THE VALUE PROPOSITION FOR LEGAL SERVICES CONCERNS THREE ASPECTS: THE <u>LEGAL SERVICES</u> TO BE PREFORMED, THE <u>NON-LEGAL NEEDS</u> THAT ARE TO BE FULFILLED, AND THE <u>COSTS</u> TO BE CHARGED.**

Correspondingly, clients seeking legal services have value proposition expectations. *<u>Ideally, satisfied clients (and attorneys) result when the value proposition expected by clients matches the value proposition promised and delivered by the law firm.</u>*

THE LEGAL SERVICE COMPONENT OF THE VALUE PROPOSITION

The legal service component of the value proposition is relatively straightforward. A client needs to retain counsel for a specific legal need, and requires an attorney having expertise in a particular legal area. A law firm holds itself out as having such expertise. Usually the services component of the value proposition will be consistent for both the law firm and the potential client.

THE NON-LEGAL "NEEDS" COMPONENT OF THE VALUE PROPOSITION

The non-legal "needs" component of the value proposition goes beyond the specific legal services provided by the law firm, much like the non-legal "needs" of soap consumers goes beyond the functional utility of soap in getting one clean. *<u>In some instances, the non-legal needs may be more important than the legal needs for the client in the sense that the perceived ability to satisfy the non-legal needs may be the reason for choosing one law firm over another.</u>*

Very few firms, however, address non-legal needs in their website or other marketing materials. ***<u>As a result, firms that can successfully create a brand which encompasses the non-legal needs sought by prospective clients will be able to significantly differentiate themselves from their competition.</u>***

Here are a few examples of the "non-legal" needs that clients might seek to have fulfilled.

Legal Matter	Client Non-Legal Needs
Divorce	Reassurance that custody matters will be resolved
	As much as it hurts now, soon things will be much better
	I won't lose all of my assets (or I will get a fair settlement)
DUI	Everyone makes mistakes
	This will not harm me permanently
	Need to have an "expert" tell me that everything will be ok
Corporate	I feel good about retaining the most high-powered firm in town
	I am always treated like a VIP by the firm and its staff
	I feel more comfortable about the legal decisions I need to make when these decisions are affirmed by legal experts.

The better a firm does with identifying the non-legal needs of its clientele and incorporating how they will fulfill such needs into their brand and marketing, the more the firm's message will resonate with prospective clients. It's important, therefore, for a firm to identify these non-legal needs in order to better connect with potential clients.

THE "COST" COMPONENT OF THE VALUE PROPOSITION

The cost component of the value proposition centers on the fees charged by the firm for fulfillment of the legal services and non-legal needs to be fulfilled. The cost component does not necessarily mean low fees. A high cost might have been charged by the firm relative to the prices charged by competing firms; however, if the client was seeking to have intrinsic needs fulfilled (retaining the firm that she believes to be the most powerful firm in the city), then a higher fee may be acceptable. The client in this case may feel reassured when she visits the firm's impressive office, and is handled like a VIP by both the firm's staff and attorneys, and that the firm shows attention to every detail in how she is treated.

Similarly, firms can also succeed on the low end of the cost spectrum by providing quality legal services for lower fees. Clients may understand that the firm does not have the most expensive office space in town, and that their attorneys have many other similarly-situated clients (and thus might not always be able to speak with the client whenever the client calls). If the price being charged by the firm reflects these aspects, clients may be willing to put up with these inconveniences.

SATISFACTION FOR CLIENTS AND ATTORNEYS RESULTS WHEN THE VALUE PROPOSITION OFFERED AND DELIVERED BY THE FIRM MATCHES THE VALUE PROPOSITION SOUGHT BY CLIENTS

The Corporate Law Firm's Value Proposition and the Value Proposition being sought by its targeted clients might look like this:

The Corporate Firm's Value Proposition (to be delivered)	Identified Clients' Value Proposition (being sought)
Legal Services: • Corporate formation • Contracts • Real Estate • Estate Planning • Securities law • Tax • Business Litigation	**Legal Services:** • Corporate formation • Contracts • Real Estate • Estate Planning • Securities law • Tax • Business Litigation

The Corporate Firm's Value Proposition (to be delivered)	Identified Clients' Value Proposition (being sought)
Non-legal Needs (firm's understanding of the non-legal needs that its target clients seek to have fulfilled): • Firm realizes the significant role of its clients in the community, and understands that often clients may be interested in not pursuing legal matters, even if the clients would be likely to prevail • Firm understands that client officers and staff regularly interact with other parties (or their counsel) in contract, litigation, and on other matters. As a representative of the clients, the firm understands the clients' concern with being ethical and conducting itself with the highest professional regard. • The firm is ready to handle all of the clients' needs, and will treat each corporate client as a VIP • The firm will generally not handle criminal defense matters or other matters that may be perceived as highly controversial in the community	**Non-legal Needs (that clients are seeking to have fulfilled):** • Understanding of our company's role as a pillar of the community, and that the company takes a long-term view in making business decisions • Understanding that company officers and staff regularly interact in social settings and community functions with company clients, and thus our company needs to be seen as ethical in all business relationships, even those that may be adversarial • Seeking one "business" law firm to represent the company in most of the company's legal business needs • Do not want a firm that represents clients or interests that may be viewed negatively by the community • The company officers want to deal with a "high-powered" business law firm as it seeks to confirm their decisions to seek the best legal counsel in the community.

The Corporate Firm's Value Proposition (to be delivered)	Identified Clients' Value Proposition (being sought)
Cost: The firm has committed itself to working with corporate clients, and is one of the few local firms that is well-positioned to handle almost all legal needs for business clients. The firm can add value to corporate clients based on the cross-functionality of its practice areas, and, as a firm client, the firm offers one-stop shop expertise on corporate matters. As a result of the firm's focused brand and full team of business attorneys, the firm is able to charge fees at the higher end of the cost spectrum.	**Cost:** The company seeks to have one firm that can handle all of the company's legal needs, if possible. The company wants to develop a long-term relationship with the firm, as it values the time and efficiency aspects that can arise with "one-stop" shopping. The company recognizes that it may have to pay higher fees than otherwise might be charged if it instead used a number of different law firms, but is willing to pay higher fees so long as they are reasonable.

Stated simply, if the clients expect a lot, and your firm promises a lot, clients usually won't mind paying a higher price if your firm delivers. Problems for both clients and their attorneys arise when some aspect of the value proposition expected by the clients doesn't match with the value proposition delivered by the law firm. The disconnect could occur for a number of reasons – costs being higher than the clients expected, or client needs that were overlooked, for example.

A LAW FIRM'S BRAND SHOULD BE DEVELOPED FROM THE FIRM'S VALUE PROPOSITION OFFERED

A firm's brand should be developed around the firm's value proposition – the legal services to be provided, the non-legal needs to be fulfilled, and the costs to be charged. Branding consists of tangible items (such as logos, business cards, and other collateral), electronic information (firm website and Internet marketing), and intangible items (such as slogans). Before discussing these items, let's develop a logo that would encompass a brand for The Corporate Firm.

THE CORPORATE FIRM'S BRAND – "GREAT TOWN'S TRUSTED BUSINESS COUNSEL"

There are an endless number of nice logos that can be created for The Corporate Firm; however, the firm is concerned not with having a nice-looking logo, but rather a *logo that promotes and extends its brand* so that the logo will resonate with current and prospective clients.

The Corporate Firm has identified a number of characteristics common to its targeted clientele. One of the characteristics that stands out (and that the firm would like to use) is "having strong roots in the community." The firm also wants to incorporate into its logo and branding the concept that it is a modern firm; thus it does not care for having traditional elements in its brand that would conjure images of large oak-paneled board rooms. It does not want to be perceived as a stuffy old-style firm.

As a result, the firm wishes to create its image around an oak tree with roots symbolizing the firm's strong roots in the community. The design incorporates a very modern depiction and concept of an oak tree, and the font used is also considered modern. The firm believes that this logo will communicate the ideas that the firm is deeply rooted in the community and strong, but yet takes a very modern approach in how it provides legal services. The following is the design to be used:

THE CORPORATE FIRM

"Great Town's Trusted Business Counsel"

Now that the logo concept has been developed, The Corporate Firm will need to finalize the logo colors and create business cards and other collateral, and incorporate the branding into its other marketing materials.

LOGO, BUSINESS CARDS, AND OTHER COLLATERAL

There's no right or wrong logo concept or colors that a firm should use, nor is there any right or wrong business card concept. The logo should be appealing to the intended clientele, and should be used in all of the firm's collateral, including business cards, stationery, the firm's website, and marketing any other materials.

The marketing materials should be internally consistent, such that the same fonts, colors, and other artistic aspects should be used. Old-style fonts, for instance, shouldn't be used on business cards, while a modern-type font is used on firm brochures. Similarly, if the firm's website is developed around a "cutting-edge" theme, brochures with oak paneling and large leather chairs might detract from the firm's image.

FIRM WEBSITE

Once the logo and brand have been developed, the more difficult step is to translate the firm's brand and value proposition to the firm's website. For this process, working with a professional website designer who can help develop the right look and feel for the firm's website that will appeal to the firm's intended clientele is highly recommended.

Website development is discussed later in this book, and thus won't be repeated here. The important part of this discussion is making sure that the website is firmly focused on the firm's value proposition, and centered specifically on communicating how the firm will fulfill the legal and non-legal needs of the targeted clientele. In designing a firm's website, including the layout, navigation, practice area descriptions, and text, the constant question that should be asked (from the perspective of a potential client) is "***What is the law firm going to do for me***?" Every aspect of the firm's website should be built around answering this question. This idea is discussed further in Chapter 9 – ***The Client-Centered Website***.

SLOGANS

Slogans can be a great way to differentiate one law firm from its competitors, particularly if the slogan is especially memorable. For a slogan to be effective it should be used often in advertising and marketing materials and it should enhance the brand of the firm. The value of a good slogan is built up over time; therefore, once chosen, a slogan should not quickly be changed. It's probably not wise to be "the accident lawyers" this year, "the personal injury shop" next year, and "the DUI guys" the following year. Likewise, having a slogan like "Crazy Phil's Law Firm – I'll Sue Anybody", while memorable, may not send the best message.

The Corporate Firm wishes to use the slogan and build its brand around being "Great Town's Trusted Business Counsel". Based upon their value proposition, this seems to be a slogan that will resonate well with the firm's targeted clientele.

ADHERING TO YOUR BRAND

Suppose The Corporate Firm created an advertising campaign around its message of being "Great Town's Trusted Business Counsel," and was successful in communicating this message to the local business leaders. However, when these same business leaders visited the firm's website to learn more about The Corporate Firm, few of the listed practice areas and profiles of the firm's attorneys reflect the firm's message of being "Great Town's Trusted Business Counsel."

Instead, the practice areas consist of a range of non-corporate practice areas, such as divorce, estate planning, personal injury, etc. The profiles of most of the firm's attorneys reflect these diverse practice areas; it seems that only a few of the attorneys at The Corporate Firm concentrate on business law matters. As a result, the business leaders in the community may not believe that The Corporate Firm really is "Great Town's Trusted Business Counsel", and other clientele for whom the firm is providing divorce, estate planning, personal injury, and other services may be dissuaded from using a "business" law firm and instead seek a firm focused more on their needs.

The message – once a brand has been developed, it's important that all aspects of a firm's marketing program – especially its website – be consistent with the brand.

GET HELP TO DEVELOP YOUR FIRM'S VALUE PROPOSITION AND BRAND

As a group, attorneys are smart. While we may be highly educated, and may even be experts in areas outside law, most of us still recognize the wisdom in the old adage about an attorney who represents himself.

Get professional marketing help to develop your law firm's value proposition and brand. First, an outside professional can provide an objective view, and will be able to ask the right questions and be valuable at coming up with (and helping your firm develop) creative ideas throughout the process. Second, an outside professional can lead the firm through the strategic planning process, which has the potential to get complicated, especially if there is a significant difference in views in the partnership about the direction of the firm.

While it may seem unnecessary to some to engage an external facilitator, and undoubtedly will take up billable time, the benefits of creating a solid strategy, value proposition, and firm brand will pay off tremendously in the long run.

PART III – DOMAIN NAME REGISTRATION AND WEBSITE HOSTING

In order to establish an Internet presence, a law firm must register a domain where the law firm's website can be seen, and determine whether to host the website in-house or at a hosting company. The next three chapters address the specifics of domain registration and website hosting.

CHAPTER 4 – DOMAIN NAME REGISTRATION

A domain name (or URL) is the address where a website can be accessed. Domain names are registered for a certain number of years, and must be re-registered prior to expiration, otherwise they again become available to anyone. Because domain name registration is cheap (about $8-$20 per year), consider registering your law firm's domain name for an extended period, such as ten years. Also consider registering domain names with the ".net" extension, and any common misspellings of names included in the primary domain name.

DOMAIN NAME OVERVIEW

WHAT IS A DOMAIN NAME, AND HOW ARE DOMAIN NAMES ISSUED?

In order to establish an Internet presence, a law firm must first register a domain name. Domain names (sometimes also referred to as the URL, which stands for Uniform Resource Locator) are much like a website address for the Internet. All domain names must consist of an allowed ending, such as ".com".

Specific extensions are applicable to different types of companies or organizations. The extensions ".com" and ".net" may be used by virtually anyone, while ".gov" is for government agencies and ".edu" is for educational institutions. Many extensions are based upon where the registrant is based, such as ".us" for the United States, or ".ca" for Canada. The ".pro" extension may also be used by law firms, as this extension is available to credentialed professionals and related entities. The portion of the domain name to the left of the period is referred to as a subdomain. Thus "EsquireInteractive" is a subdomain for www.EsquireInteractive.com. The extensions following the period (such as ".com") are referred to as "top-level domains" (or "TLD's"), but they will be referred to herein as simply "extensions".

> **E** *The Bar Associations of some states prohibit the registration of domain names ending in ".org".*

All domain names are issued by the Internet Assigned Numbers Authority (IANA, www.iana.org), which is operated through the Internet Corporation for Assigned Names and Numbers (ICANN, www.icann.org), and are registered through accredited registrars and resellers (such as GoDaddy and Esquire Interactive). IANA/ICANN *do not* register domain names directly to end users.

HOW MUCH DOES IT COST TO REGISTER A DOMAIN NAME, AND WHAT RIGHTS ARE ACQUIRED?

Basic domain registration of a ".com" name typically costs $8-$12 per year, but some companies in the past have charged significantly higher registration fees (approximately $35). The accredited registrar must then pass along a portion of the fees to IANA/ICANN, and any amount remaining is revenue for the registration company. Domain registrations for extensions other than ".com" can be more or less than the ".com" registration.

> **The $8-$10 domain registration fee is for one domain for one year. Different domain extensions (such as ".net") are considered a different domain name, and thus require an additional registration fee.**

Registration of the domain name allows the registrant to have exclusive control over the domain name for the period of time in which the domain name is registered. If the domain name is not timely renewed by the registrant, it then becomes available for registration to anyone.

ETHICAL CONSIDERATIONS FOR DOMAIN NAME REGISTRATION

Before settling on a domain name, consider any applicable ethics rules governing domain name registration. In some jurisdictions the domain name may need to include the name of at least one partner, or contain abbreviations for the name of at least one partner.

Other ethics domain name prohibitions may exist that might, for instance, prevent use of domain names such as *www.TheBestLawFirmEver.com*, or *www.WeWinBigEverytime4You.com*. Additionally, the ".org" extension may not be permitted under applicable ethics rules.

WHAT DOMAIN NAMES SHOULD MY LAW FIRM REGISTER?

The short answer is that registration should be undertaken for the primary domain name and any other common misspellings or variations that clients might use.

Let's consider the law firm of "Zollo & Lantz". The firm "Zollo & Lantz" might want to register www.zollolantz.com (to be used as the primary domain name), www.zollolance.com, www.zolloandlantz.com, and www.zolloandlance.com, as well as the ".net" extensions. The "primary" domain name would be where the website could be seen, and the firm would "point" the other URL's to the primary domain name. Then, if www.zollolance.com were entered, the user would automatically be re-directed to www.zollolantz.com, which would display the firm's website.

> **E** *Before registering firm name misspellings, ensure that such misspellings are permissible under the ethics rules of your jurisdiction.*

> **E** *Interestingly, in some jurisdictions it appears that a domain name that would violate ethics rules to be used as the firm's primary domain name (such as www.WeWinBigEverTime4You.com), may not violate ethics rules if it is used as a "redirect" domain name. In this case, a person entering the domain name www.WeWinBigEverTtime4You.com would automatically be re-directed to www.zololantz.com.*

In addition to registering the ".com" extension(s), firms should also consider registering the ".net" extensions. Law firms may also wish to register ".us" and/or ".pro" extensions, but these extensions are far less important from a marketing perspective than the ".com" extension.

> *If the desired ".com" domain name is not available, see Appendix 1 for ideas on other ".com" registration possibilities. If a ".com" registration is not done, clients and others may inadvertently be directed to another company or law firm if they forget that your primary domain name is not a ".com".*

SHOULD I REGISTER WWW.OURFIRMSUCKS.COM?

A number of prominent companies have been the subject of certain groups registering the name of the company followed by the word "sucks" – i.e. www.OurFirmSucks.com. Typically such registrants then create websites devoted to the hatred of the targeted company.

The more sophisticated groups then use search engine optimization (SEO) techniques to enhance the web visibility for the "sucks" domain name. Their goal is to have *their* website listed at the top of the search engine results *before* the website of the target. The really nasty of these groups take their scheme one step further – once they've achieved high search engine rankings, they may contact the target company and offer search engine optimization services to increase the search engine rankings of the target company, so that the target (real) company will appear higher in the search results than the company with the "sucks" domain name. For a price, of course.

As a result, some Internet marketing companies recommend that companies and firms also register the name of their company (or firm) and the word "sucks". Presumably this would prevent dissatisfied third parties from registering the name of the firm + "sucks" and creating a website about how bad the firm is.

Should the "sucks" registration be done? Does it prevent the potential problem?

My suggestion is that such registration not be undertaken. First and foremost, it's expensive to try to acquire all potentially offensive domain names. For instance, if a firm wants to cover all concerns, it would also need to register other extensions, such as the ".net", ".org", ".us", etc. for the domain www.OurFirmSucks.com. Renewals would also need to be done for each of these domain names every year.

Second, no matter how many registrations are undertaken, other words or the inclusion of dashes can easily be used to achieve the same effect. For example, the domain names www.Our-Firm-Sucks.com, www.OurFirmBites.com, or www.OurFirmSux.com could be registered.

The domain name variations on the "sucks" theme that can be registered are virtually unlimited. It's impossible to stop all of the negative potential domain name registrations.

DOMAIN NAME REGISTRATION

MAKE SURE ALL DOMAIN NAMES ARE REGISTERED IN YOUR NAME OR IN THE NAME OF YOUR LAW FIRM

It's important that you or your law firm have legal control over the domain name. Beware – some website developers register the domain names of clients in their name. After the website is live, these developers charge high hosting fees. When the client decides to host its website with another hosting company, the developer may refuse to allow the domain name to be transferred to the new hosting company. If this happens, the client might need to register a new domain name, which could be a significant issue.

Worse, the developer may forget to have the domain name renewed, or may go out of business. In this case, it may become extremely difficult to renew the domain name, and, if timely renewal cannot be effectuated, the domain name may lapse and be registered by someone else.

WHERE CAN I CHECK TO SEE IF THE DOMAIN NAME THAT I WANT IS AVAILABLE?

Once you've determined the domain name(s) to be registered, the next step is to determine whether it or they are available. There are a number of websites that can be used to check availability, such as www.EsquireInteractive.com (shameless promotion here), or our other favorite domain registration site, www.GoDaddy.com. We'll assume GoDaddy will be used for the registration process, and thus won't suggest going to www.EsquireInteractive.com for registering your firm's domain name (and possibly picking up another copy of this book for a colleague).

GoDaddy is the largest domain name registrant in the United States. (Esquire Interactive is a domain name reseller under a GoDaddy affiliate.) GoDaddy is popular because it offers a fairly simple registration process (if you ignore the add-on products) the registration cost is low (around $8 per domain name), and it's reliable (it provides several reminder e-mails prior to the expiration of domain names). The steps for registering domain names are set forth in **Appendix 1.**

PRIVATE REGISTRATION

One aspect to consider during the registration process is private registration. With GoDaddy (or Esquire Interactive) private registration, the domain name is registered in the name of a GoDaddy affiliate (called Domains by Proxy), although the person or firm making the registration still controls the domain name. With a private registration, the Domains by Proxy contact information is publicly displayed in the WHOIS information, not your registrant information, which may reduce spam. (See *"Using the WHOIS Database to Find Registrant Information"* below for more information about domain name registrant information.) Private registration usually costs about $10 extra per domain name per year.

HOW ARE DOMAIN NAMES ASSOCIATED WITH A SERVER?

After registering your domain name(s), the domain name(s) must be associated with a specific server. Think of it this way – a domain name is like a cell phone number; once the number has been provided, it must be associated with a specific cell phone.

While the process to make this association is fairly straightforward, it can take about 24 hours to take effect. Fortunately, unlike cell phone registration, you won't have to stand in a store line.

When your domain name is registered, it will be "parked" with the registration company. Often the registration company will post a "page under construction" message to users visiting your domain. This message and your domain name are being hosted on one of the servers of the registration company. Once you've selected a website hosting provider, you (or your website developer) will need to access your account at the registration company (GoDaddy for example) and change the domain nameserver to the appropriate nameserver at your hosting company. The steps to make this change are set forth in **Appendix 2**.

HOW TO ACQUIRE THE DOMAIN NAME YOU REALLY WANT FROM THE CURRENT REGISTRANT

Suppose you simply have to have a certain domain, such as www.TheLawOfficesofJohnathonRandolphsonPumpernickelsmithJr.com. After checking, you find that this name has already been registered to someone else (perhaps another Johnathon Randolphson Pumpernickelsmith Jr.). Should you let your dreams for this domain name be shattered?

Perhaps not. First, type the domain name into an Internet browser to see whether it's being used as an active website, or if it is simply parked (meaning that a website has not yet been built or associated with the domain name). Perhaps a speculator acquired the domain name on the hunch that it could be re-sold at an exorbitant profit.

If there's already a website associated with the domain name, chances are good that they may not be willing to "sell" it to you, especially if they've built up substantial goodwill with the name. But, if the price is right, they may be willing to transfer the name. (It doesn't hurt to make an offer, right?).

USING THE WHOIS DATABASE TO FIND REGISTRANT INFORMATION

If there isn't a website associated with the domain name (other than a "parked" or "under construction" page), it's possible to check what is known as the WHOIS record for registrant information.

The WHOIS record is a record of the registered "owner" of a domain name. WHOIS records can be checked on the websites of virtually every accredited registrar and domain name reseller. For instance, at either GoDaddy or Esquire Interactive, enter a domain name in the domain search box. If the domain name is already registered, the next page will provide a message to this effect, and will provide a link that may be clicked to get more information about the registrant. Click this link, and you'll be provided with the WHOIS record for the domain name.

The WHOIS record for the domain name will provide information such as the administrative and technical contacts, and other contact information such as the telephone number, which will hopefully allow you to contact the registrant directly should you be interested in acquiring the domain name.

In looking at the WHOIS record for the domain that you want, you may find that the domain registration contact is Domains by Proxy, or a similar name. Domains by Proxy is GoDaddy's private registration company, which, as previously discussed, does not allow users to see the underlying registrant information. In this case, you might wish to try sending an e-mail that will hopefully reach the right person, such as to webmaster@[thedomainyouwant].com

DOMAIN NAME AUCTIONS

Another possibility of acquiring a specific domain name is to see if it's available through a domain name auction. Three websites to check for domain name availability through auctions are www.Sedo.com, www.GoDaddy.com, and www.BuyDomains.com. These companies also have options for using an agent to assist in the domain name acquisition, and an escrow agent to make sure the transfer process is handled correctly.

USING A DOMAIN ESCROW AGENT

There are a number of companies that offer negotiation, transfer, and escrow services, including Godaddy. You can use these companies for any or all of the services that you might need. These companies all charge different fees for their services, with some fees being based upon a set amount plus and certain percentage of the sales price. Like any other commercial transaction, obtaining the domain name you wish to have will likely be determined by how much you're willing to pay, and the price at which the seller is willing to "sell" (have transferred the seller's interest in) the domain name.

It's worth noting briefly that there are remedies available under the ICANN rules if a law firm legitimately believes that the registrant is misappropriating the firm's intellectual property. In general, these cases are difficult to win, as many companies may have legitimate uses for the same words or abbreviations. To find out more about challenging another registrant's use of a domain name, please see http://www.icann.org/en/udrp/. Of course you should also consider consulting with an attorney who has experience in these matters.

USING DOMAIN BACKORDER FEATURE

Both GoDaddy and Esquire Interactive provide another service for acquiring domain names through Backordering. Backordering costs approximately $18 per domain name, and consists of an automated attempt to acquire the domain name as soon as it becomes available (which would happen only if the current registrant fails to renew the domain name registration). There is no refund of the $18 fee if the name cannot be acquired. Certainly this is not the ideal option to use, and you'll want to check the WHOIS record to see the current expiration date of the domain name to determine whether it's worthwhile to pay the $18 cost (probably not if the registration lasts another ten years).

Once you've acquired the domain names to be used for your law firm's website, the next step is to select a hosting provider.

CHAPTER 5 – SERVERS AND WEBSITE HOSTING

Have your website hosted on a shared server at a Tier 1-type hosting facility. Don't consider hosting your website at your firm or buying a server; the time and effort to manage a server and operating system updates far outweigh any benefits. If (1) your website is less than 100 pages, (2) you're not streaming video from your server, and (3) you're not likely to be receiving more than a couple of thousand visits (not hits) per day, a package with 15 GB of storage and 150 GB of monthly bandwidth transfer should be more than adequate, and should cost approximately $5-$25 per month. Additional storage and bandwidth transfer plans can be easily added for a small increase in the monthly hosting fee (perhaps $10-$20 more per month). If you need or want a dedicated server, plan on spending $200-$500/month for server hosting and managed services.

THE BASICS OF SERVERS AND HOSTING

In order to have your website seen by others on the Internet, your website (consisting of code, files, images, and possibly databases) must be hosted on a server that is connected to the Internet. In order to be hosted, your domain name must be associated with a server, so that when a user types your firm's website address into an Internet browser (such as Internet Explorer), the browser will contact the server where your firm's website is hosted. This server will then serve up your web pages based upon links that may be clicked by the user. The server can reside at your firm, with a hosting company, or anywhere else that has an Internet connection.

WHAT IS A SERVER?

A server is essentially a computer that is included in a network environment. The computer/server often has specific software on it depending upon how it will be used. The network environment can consist of linking together other computers at a law firm (often called "network servers"), or to handle a specific type of function, such as printing jobs (a "print server"), or to deliver website code and information to users accessing the server through a browser over the Internet (a "web server"). [7] For purposes of this book the term "server" will refer only to a web server.

---

[7] See Webopedia, *Server*, http://www.webopedia/TERM/S/Server.html

The primary functions of a server are to store website code, images, databases, and related information and to deliver web page content to users through an Internet connection. The process consists of a user entering a website address in an Internet browser, and the browser then connecting with the server on which the website is located and making a request for page content. The server then returns the information for the web page, and the web page is displayed through the Internet browser on the user's computer (or cell phone or other similar device).

> ***Details - Because web browsers are not uniform in how they handle the display of information, the same website can look different depending upon the particular browser used. For instance, a web page opened with Internet Explorer might look different than if the same page is opened using a Firefox or Safari browser. Usually the differences are small but annoying: text doesn't quite line up, section edges aren't straight, etc. Because of the possibility of these differences, website developers need to test the website code using the major browsers to ensure that any such differences are fixed before the website goes live. You should also view your firm's website in different Internet browsers to ensure that no such problems exist.***

SHOULD I BUY OR LEASE A SERVER?

The decision to buy or lease a server fundamentally revolves around the question of whether to host your website at your firm or use a hosting company. In the case of the vast majority of firms, the best decision is almost always to lease a server from a hosting facility, either through a shared hosting plan or by leasing a dedicated (or virtual dedicated) server. ***The server buy/lease decision is really not a hardware issue (as would be the case if a firm is considering purchasing computers), but rather a service issue (who will be ensuring Internet connectivity, installing software patches, and maintaining firewalls).***

WOULDN'T IT BE CHEAPER TO BUY A SERVER AND RUN IT FROM MY FIRM? WHY THIS IS NOT A GOOD OPTION FOR MOST FIRMS

Running and maintaining a server is more complex than running a computer. Because servers are connected to the Internet, they can easily become subject to hacking attempts and all sorts of other malicious activities. Not only will evil-doers try to hack into your server, they may also try to use your server to launch mass spam, phishing, and other activities from your server. If these activities occur, other Internet service providers

(ISP's) may blacklist your server, in which case your firm's website may not be shown to users at that ISP trying to access your firm's website.[8]

To minimize malicious activities, firewalls, anti-virus software, and operating system patches need to be installed and updated. These activities usually require human intervention; it's not simply the case that once they're installed, they take care of themselves.

At a more fundamental level, purchasing (or even leasing) a server and operating it from your firm doesn't make sense financially compared to a shared hosting plan. A simple shared hosting plan that would be sufficient for the vast majority of firms will likely cost about $5-$25 per month, which includes firewall, software updates and patch installation, Internet connection, and guarantees for 99% or more uptime. Compare this option with purchasing a server, which might cost $1,000 or more upfront, and thereafter costs to install the server, Internet connectivity costs, maintenance and installation of software updates and firewalls, and associated problems if the server goes down. It's expensive to ensure that these patches and updates are installed; a couple of hours of time over the course of a year for these issues alone likely costs more than hosting costs for an entire year.

---

[8] Wikipedia defines a "blacklist" or DNSBL (DNS Blacklist) as:

> a list of IP addresses published through the Internet Domain Name Service in a particular format. DNSBLs are most often used to publish the addresses of computers or networks linked to spamming; most mail server software can be configured to reject or flag messages which have been sent from a site listed on one or more such lists.
>
> "DNSBL" is a software mechanism, rather than a specific list or policy. There are dozens of DNSBLs in existence, which use a wide array of standards for listing and delisting of addresses. These may include listing the addresses of zombie computers or other machines being used to send spam, listing the addresses of ISPs who willingly host spammers, or listing addresses which have sent spam to a honeypot system. (links included in original text not included here)

http://en.wikipedia.org/wiki/DNSBL.

CAN I SAVE ON COSTS BY BUYING A SERVER AND SENDING IT TO THE HOSTING FACILITY?

Buying a server and sending it to a hosting company to operate is referred to as "co-location". While some hosting companies allow this practice, many do not, and for good reason.

First, while it would seem that this arrangement might save on costs, important issues can arise. What happens if the server goes down? The hosting company will not have any spare servers or products on hand. Your website will then be down until a new server can be acquired (bought or leased) and the website code can be added to the new server. With leased servers, this is generally not an issue, as reputable hosting companies have both spare servers and equipment on hand, and can usually quickly swap out a server or parts as necessary.

Also, there are practical equipment management and liability issues. Where should the hosting company place the server so that it doesn't get mixed in with other leased servers? Whose fault is it if a server is damaged or simply stops working correctly?

While server co-location is possible, in most situations it's not advantageous based on the same financial economics discussed above. Co-location is usually a better option for companies requiring a number of servers with multiple redundancies.

HOSTING COMPANY SERVICES

HOSTING COMPANY FACILITIES – TIER 1 HOSTING FACILITY

While there are not any specific rules about what constitutes a Tier 1 Hosting Facility, the common notion is that a Tier 1 hosting facility has a professional staff onsite 24/7, and that the facility itself often will have multiple and redundant network backbone connections to the Internet grid and to power grids, backup power generators, fire suppression systems, and advanced security systems (both in terms of accessing the facility itself and also accessing servers maintained at the facility). In addition, in the event of a hardware (server) failure, the facility should have trained staff and excess servers and parts on hand 24/7 so that server replacements can be made quickly (especially for dedicated servers).

Most of the larger hosting companies have facilities that meet most or all of the above requirements; nevertheless it's a good idea to check with the hosting company to learn a little more about exactly what they offer, especially in terms of 24/7 onsite professional staff and network connections. If it appears that the hosting company has most of these features, they will probably be an acceptable hosting provider; what you really want to avoid is becoming dependent upon a single person responsible for all of your hosting needs at either your firm or an external hosting company.

WHAT SERVICES ARE PROVIDED BY HOSTING COMPANIES?

The types of services provided by a hosting company depend first on whether the website will be hosted on a shared server, a virtual dedicated server, or a dedicated server. Because the hosting company's services and your responsibilities vary greatly between these server options, let's go over the types of server hosting options and the level of services that usually come with each of the options.

TYPES OF HOSTING – SHARED SERVERS, VIRTUAL DEDICATED SERVERS, DEDICATED SERVERS, AND CLOUD HOSTING

WHAT IS SHARED SERVER HOSTING, AND WHAT ARE THE ADVANTAGES AND DISADVANTAGES?

As the name implies, a shared server is a server that hosts websites controlled by a number of unrelated companies. **For most law firm websites, a shared server will be the best hosting option**.

Shared server hosting has a number of advantages.

- Hosting is cheap, often less than $10/month.

- The hosting company is responsible for installing operating system patches and other software updates.

- The hosting company is responsible for implementing and maintaining firewalls and other security aspects.

- The hosting company is responsible for all hardware issues.

- The hosting company is responsible for maintaining connections to the Internet and up-time.

The disadvantages of shared hosting are few, but can include the following:

➢ The hosting company can cram dozens or more websites onto a single server that may not be powerful enough to efficiently handle all of the associated website traffic. If this happens, website visitors can experience web pages that load slowly, and in some instances users may experience problems accessing the website.

➢ If there is a disreputable website company hosted on the same server as your firm's website, your website IP address or server could be "blacklisted" by ISP's, in which case users on the ISP might not be able to access your website. You'll then need to transfer your website to another server or perhaps even to another hosting company.

➢ If your website is hosted with a reputable hosting company, the risk of being blacklisted is small, and certainly should not be the sole determining factor for not using shared hosting. Remember – blacklisting may affect the other websites hosted on the server and potentially other servers at the hosting company. Therefore, hosting companies have strong incentives to quickly remove any websites that are being used for malicious activities.

➢ If your firm intends on streaming a significant amount of video, a shared server may not be the best choice unless the video will be streamed from another server (such as a video hosting company). A short video clip on your server should be fine, showing long, high definition videos to many simultaneous users or turning your site into the next YouTube will likely pose a problem.

➢ In some instances, your website (or software related to your website, such as advanced website statistics software) may require what is referred to as "root level access". Root level access refers to the ability to modify server settings at the operating system level in order to use certain programs or functions. Hosting companies will not allow website owners to have root level access on a shared server, as modifications to the operating system settings could affect other websites hosted on the server. *Generally, law firms do not need this type of access for their websites, so having root level access is not a concern.* Ask your website developer whether root level access is required; if your website does require root level access you'll likely need to have a virtual dedicated server or a dedicated server.

WHAT IS A VIRTUAL DEDICATED SERVER OR VIRTUAL PRIVATE SERVER?

A virtual dedicated server (or virtual private server) refers to a server that has been "partitioned" into more than one area. Each area has a separate operating system and can function much like a dedicated server. Server partitioning has advantages over a shared server, as clients can be given root level access to make changes and install programs requiring core-level installation (Note that not all programs requiring root level access will work in the virtual environment; if root level access is necessary a dedicated server may be required. Check with your developer).

WHAT ARE DEDICATED SERVERS?

As the name suggests, with a dedicated server you control the entire server. There are no other websites hosted on the server other than yours (and any other websites that you choose).

As previously noted, the vast majority of firms don't require dedicated servers. The primary reasons for having a dedicated server is for firms that have extremely high traffic needs (either because they have tens of thousands of visits (not hits) per day), or that they are streaming a significant amount of video, or because they require root level access.

Because dedicated servers have a number of technical and server management issues that do not need to be considered in a shared hosting environment, dedicated servers will be addressed separately in the following chapter, which may be skipped completely by firms utilizing shared website hosting.

WHAT IS CLOUD COMPUTING? SHOULD WE HAVE OUR SERVER HOSTED IN A CLOUD ENVIRONMENT?

Another emerging hosting environment is cloud computing. Cloud computing essentially separates various computing tasks across networked servers. Cloud computing can also link together infrastructures, platforms, and software, all as services that are scalable depending upon the needs of the client. The whole linked process is referred to as the "Cloud".[9]

Don't worry if you don't understand this explanation – you don't need to. What you should know is that unless a firm is implementing an over-all cloud technology plan, a cloud computing environment for website hosting does not offer any advantages over a simple shared hosting environment. Additionally, some concern has been expressed about

---

[9] http://searchcloudcomputing.techtarget.com/sDefinition/0,,sid201_gci1287881,00.html#

whether database interaction will work consistently as intended in a cloud environment, although these concerns may not be well-founded. For these reasons I would suggest not considering cloud computing as a hosting option.

UNDERSTANDING YOUR FIRM'S WEBSITE TRAFFIC NEEDS

THE DIFFERENCE BETWEEN HITS AND VISITS

Before reviewing website hosting packages, it's worthwhile to discuss the meaning of common website terms – hits and visits – that are often confused. A "hit" is a request by an Internet browser to a server for a particular chunk of information; a "hit" is NOT the same thing as a visit. Displaying web pages may consist of several hits (depending upon how the web page is coded). So, one visit in which a user accesses 10 web pages might result in 30 hits.

It's important to note this distinction, as often hits are mistaken for visits (such as "our website received 30,000 hits last month", instead of "our website received 1,000 visits last month"). At one time, a "hit" was the equivalent of one page view, but this is no longer the case, as web pages have become much more sophisticated. "Hits" really are more of a historical term, and provide little useful information, especially because the number of hits is tied to the way in which a page is coded. The more important numbers (especially for websites selling advertising) are the following:

1. Visits – A visit starts when a user accesses a website, and continues while the user browses pages on the website, and ends when either the user leaves the website, or a certain period of time elapses with no user activity on the website (usually 30 minutes).

2. Unique visitors - this essentially is the number of different users that access a website during a specified period.

3. Page Views – this is the number of web pages that are viewed by visitors. With websites that utilize framing, the page views reported may be more than the page views seen by users, as what would appear to be one page may in reality be two pages.

4. Page views per visitor. This number is important to advertisers, as it reflects somewhat on the user's experience when visiting a website. Some websites have extremely low average page views per visitor, such as 2. What this means is that on

average users don't stay long or interact much with the website, they go to one page, click on another page, and then move on to another website or close their browser window.

HOW MUCH SERVER STORAGE DOES YOUR WEBSITE REQUIRE? UNDERSTANDING YOUR WEBSITE'S SERVER STORAGE AND INTERNET TRAFFIC NEEDS

Website hosting plans have both a "storage" aspect, which is the amount of storage space required on a server to store a website's code, images, content, and database(s), and a "transfer" aspect, which is the amount of information, expressed in megabytes (MB) or gigabytes (GB), associated with showing your firm's web pages to Internet users. Transfer is analogous to monthly cell phone minutes – the more visitors your firm's website receives, and the more web pages displayed, the more monthly transfer will be required. If your firm's website includes video, significant additional transfer will be required.

For storage, let's assume that your firm's website is less than 100 pages in total. Your website has pictures on most of the pages, but doesn't include any video other than perhaps a couple of short videos about your firm. Depending upon whether your website uses databases for a content management system, blogs, or other functionality, the total storage required for your website will likely be in the order of 25 MB to 500 MB. A video that is approximately 3 minutes in length may also have a storage need of approximately 20 MB.

For transfer, let's assume your site's web pages average 250 kilobytes (or .25MB) in size, your site receives 1,000 visits per day, and an average of 10 pages are viewed each visit. Your website's monthly transfer is calculated by multiplying these numbers (.25 MB X 1,000 visits x 10 pages), or 2,500 MB (or 2.5 GB) of transfer.

In addition, let's assume that your firm has a three minute video that is shown 1,000 times each month, and that the transfer required to show the video each time is approximately 20 MB. Thus the video portion of the transfer would include 20,000 MB (or 20 GB). In this instance, your monthly transfer would increase from 2.5 GB to 22.5 GB.

HOW MUCH STORAGE SPACE AND MONTHLY TRANSFER ARE TYPICALLY ALLOWED BY SHARED HOSTING PLANS?

Basic shared hosting plans often allow 15 GB or so of storage, and monthly transfer of 250 GB (with an add-on cost if this monthly transfer rate is exceeded), and typically cost about $5-25 per month. For a slightly higher cost (perhaps an additional $10/month), both storage and transfer can be significantly increased.

As a result, even basic shared website hosting plans will likely be sufficient for the needs of most law firm websites.

OTHER HOSTING CONSIDERATIONS

What is an Up-Time Guarantee, and What Happens if the Hosting Company Doesn't Meet Its Guarantee Obligations?

Most hosting companies have up up-time guarantees of 99% of more; you'll be hard-pressed to find a hosting company with a lower number. What this number means is that your website will be available 99% of the time (other than planned down-time, which is relatively rare). The guarantee is usually backed by a reduction in hosting charges for any given month if there is more down time than allowed. As an example, if downtime exceeds 3 hours in any month, a credit of 10% of the monthly hosting amount might be applied, up to a 100% refund if more than 24 hours of downtime occurs. Major company hosting plans typically disclaim any liability for any and all other damages that might occur (including consequential damages) for downtime, specifically limiting the damages to a reduction in the monthly hosting fee.

Should I Use My Developer for Hosting?

Sure, so long as the actual hosting is done in a Tier 1 – type facility.

Many developers have hosting relationships with large hosting companies, and then re-sell hosting to clients. There are two primary forms of re-sale: (1) a developer-leased server (the developer leases a server and then provides and manages space on his server), or (2) the developer acts as an agent of the hosting company to re-sell hosting services. In either case your website will be hosted on a server at the same hosting facility.

The hosting fees charged by developers are often slightly higher than the rock-bottom shared hosting fees charged by the hosting company. For example, the hosting company might charge $8 per month, while your developer might charge $20 per month.

Is it worth paying the extra $12 per month to go through your developer? In my admittedly-biased opinion – you betchya. Here's a few of the reasons to spend the extra $12 or so (assuming a developer-leased server is used):

1. Your developer is going to have a strong incentive to monitor the server and to make sure that the server isn't overcrowded with websites in order to keep you happy. The hosting company isn't going to have this same incentive.

2. Your developer knows what other websites are on your server, and will make sure that there are no malicious websites that might get you blacklisted.

3. Because your developer controls the server, you'll be able to get root level access to the operating system to make configuration changes if needed. This won't be the case in a shared hosting environment.

4. Most importantly, if there are issues that arise (your server crashes, for instance), your developer will likely have a strong relationship with the hosting company (and will probably know the names of at least some of the dedicated support staff), and will be in a good position to get any problems resolved quickly. Also, if any coding issues arise, your developer will understand the specifics of the platform and operating system better than if your website is hosted on another platform.

So, my advice is to pay the minimal extra money and host through your developer (assuming that a reputable hosting company is involved). It will pay off in the long run.

What are SSL Certificates, and Do I Need One?

An SSL (Secure Sockets Layer) Certificate is used for the secure transfer of information between a user and the website's server. It does NOT prevent the server from being hacked; instead it only keeps the information secure while it is being transferred over the Internet, such as during the transfer of credit card information. Unless your firm is going to be utilizing its website to transfer confidential information submitted by website users, an SSL certificate is not required.

WEBSITE SECURITY

Will the Hosting Company Guarantee that My Website Won't Get Hacked?

The short answer is that hosting companies won't take on potentially huge liability for hosting your site for $15 per month. (This is particularly true with e-commerce sites that could lose significant business in a short time.)

Hacking consists of an unauthorized access to a server, often for the purpose of modifying software settings or coding or gaining access to database information in order to further some malicious activity. The protection you need really comes from the reputation of the hosting company. Large hosting companies with hundreds or thousands of servers usually have sophisticated systems to continuously monitor hacking attempts, and employ staff to make sure that firewall systems are in place, and that operating system patches are implemented as soon as they are available.

Hackers have become extremely sophisticated, and have been able to successfully steal millions of pieces of credit card information from highly protected data processing and server facilities. Thus there can be no guaranty that your website won't be hacked. In addition to accessing data, hackers also employ other methods to shut down websites. For example, one scheme (called a Denial of Service attack), involves first infecting hundreds or thousands of servers (called zombies), which then seek to access the same website repeatedly at the same time. The simultaneous overload of the servers causes the website to go down.

WHAT ARE THE RISKS IF MY WEBSITE IS HACKED?

If only your website is hacked, the risk to your firm is relatively low. Let's look at the possible risks.

You're most likely not collecting any financial information through your website, so there is no risk that thieves could use credit card information for identity theft purposes.

You may have a newsletter list that includes names and e-mail addresses of current or prospective clients, as well as others who have subscribed to your newsletter. You may also have information relating to contact forms completed by potential clients. As will be discussed in Chapter 7, it's best to have the information that can be completed in the contact forms to be limited for ethical reasons; this is an additional reason for limiting such information.

As a result, it's really the information collected through your website that is the biggest risk of a server being compromised, not the website code. Fortunately, though, it would appear that stealing this type of information would be of limited financial value, at least compared to credit card, social security numbers, and similar types of information.

SHOULD I GET INSURANCE TO COVER THE RISKS OF HACKING?

Sure, assuming that the price is acceptable. Talk to your insurance agent about what the cost might be, and whether your firm is already covered under a current policy (or if it's possible to be covered under a rider for no additional cost). You'll be asked to complete an application describing your Internet usage and hosting arrangements.

The biggest factor in pricing these policies are (1) Whether your firm provides hosting services for others, and (2) Whether you are collecting financial information (such as credit card numbers). Since neither of these items will apply to your firm, your premium should be relatively low.

The next chapter discusses dedicated server hosting.

CHAPTER 6 – DEDICATED SERVER HOSTING – WHAT YOU NEED TO KNOW IF A DEDICATED SERVER IS REQUIRED OR DESIRED

The vast majority of law firm websites will function perfectly in a shared hosting environment. Not only is a shared hosting environment preferred from a cost perspective, but it also eliminates the need for a firm to actively manage (or pay someone else to actively manage) the server, including the installation of important updates and security patches. A minority of law firms will want or need to have dedicated website servers, either because they need root level server access in order to run programs, or for some other reason. If your firm doesn't require a dedicated server, you can skip this chapter entirely.

DEDICATED SERVERS AND LEVELS OF MANAGED HOSTING – UNDERSTANDING THE COMBINED NATURE OF THESE ASPECTS

The following section discusses dedicated servers and levels of managed hosting and assumes a leased server at a third party hosting facility. As noted in the previous chapter, leasing a dedicated server also requires making a related decision – how to manage the server with respect to firewalls, operating system updates and patches, and security software. In general, the level of services provided by the hosting company can range from relatively few services being provided (not much more than keeping the sever functioning) to fully managed services.

The specific services included in a "fully-managed" plan vary from one hosting company to another, so you'll want to see the specific list of services provided. In most cases fully-managed services will include installing software updates and patches, monitoring server usage to identify potential server threats, email and messaging, security audits, and other domain services.

A dedicated server is a server controlled by a single client. The client decides which website(s) to host on the server, and the specific software to be included on the server (including operating software, security software, and software related to various other types of programs).

What Is Managed Hosting?

Managed Hosting is usually only applicable in a dedicated server environment, as the hosting company should be providing firewall, anti-virus, and operating system updates in a shared hosting environment. (Remember – in a shared environment, in which a number of websites of unrelated companies are all hosted on the same server, it's not possible for only one of the website companies to manage these aspects).

If We Choose to Have a Dedicated Server, How Do We Keep It Secure?

Companies that offer dedicated server hosting typically offer different levels of support regarding server management.

At one extreme, the hosting company may do little more than offer firewall and basic anti-virus prevention to prevent attacks in general, but nothing specific for your server. While this provides some level of protection, it's not ideal. At the other extreme the hosting company may provide a number of services, including operating systems, security patches, sophisticated firewalls, monitoring for server attacks, and more. If you wish to save money, you can also manage updates, patches, and other server changes yourself.

How Much Storage and Transfer Are Included in Dedicated Server Hosting

While storage and transfer vary, a typical dedicated server plan usually has at least 200 GB of storage space and 500 GB to 2,000 GB (2 Terabytes) of monthly Transfer. Pricing for dedicated server plans typically range from about $100 per month (at the very low end, which does not include any server management) to $500 per month depending upon the level of managed hosting included in the plan.

Dedicated Server Recommendations

Unless your website is serving up huge amounts of streaming video, my suggestion would be to purchase a middle of the road option – perhaps something like a 2x Xeon 2.4 GHz server with 2 GB of Ram, 250 GB hard drive storage and 1,000 GB (or 1 TB) of transfer bandwidth should be plenty sufficient. This type of server configuration should cost around $100-$225/month (not including server management fees, which will add another $50-$200/month, depending upon the hosting provider). Upgrades to Ram, hard drive capacity, and transfer can be added if required. The hosting plan should also include automatic back-up on a set schedule.

WHAT IF THIS PLAN IS NOT ENOUGH?

In all likelihood, this configuration will be more than enough to suit your firm. Most law firm websites simply don't need huge amounts of bandwidth or computing capacity because (a) there is usually little "high-resource" information served (specifically, streaming video), and (b) most law firm websites typically aren't quite as popular as Facebook. In any event, if these resources are not sufficient, you may have to pay very small overage charges, just like cell phone plans, for extra storage or bandwidth.

OTHER SERVER INFORMATION

WHAT ARE THE DIFFERENCES IN SERVER HARDWARE?

Like computers, servers have a number of options that determine speed, memory and processing capabilities. The key server terms are as follows:

Single Core – this is a processing system composed of one core (or CPU) where only one operation can be started at a time.

Multi-Core – this is a processing system composed a single processor system with two or more independent cores. Multiple cores allow computers to leverage processing through performing multiple tasks.

Confusingly, there are also multiprocessor systems, which contain two or more physical processors. A multi-core processor system generally will do what a multiprocessor system will do, but since a multi-core system functions around the single processor, a multi-core system does not have the additional hardware (motherboard) configurations required by multiprocessor. Note that multiple multi-core processors can be incorporated into a single server. A 2x Xeon server processor therefore would contain 2 Xeon cores, while a 2x Xeon Quad core process configuration would have 2 processors, with each processor having 4 independent cores.

SERVER AND PROCESSOR BRANDS

Both servers and processors are made by the same major companies that serve the PC industry. Dell and HP account for a fair share of the server market, and Intel has a commanding presence in the server processor chip market.

Assuming that your firm will be leasing a server, you may not have much choice regarding the server brand being used, nor should you really care. After all, you're never going to see the server. So, whatever brand the hosting company prefers likely will be fine.

Choosing server processor chip(s) is much like choosing a computer processor chip for a PC, and the terminology is just as confusing. At the low end of the price spectrum are servers with Celeron and Pentium chips. At the high end of the price spectrum with Intel are the Xeon chips, which are often configured in multiple core and multiple processor configurations (such as Xeon Quad Core, or 2x Xeon Quad Core), and which have incredible amounts of processing capability.

SERVER OPERATING SYSTEMS AND SET-UP CONFIGURATIONS[10]

Servers require an operating system and web server to run the server (a web server is a type of software that interacts with the operating system of a server to serve web pages). Two of the most popular operating systems/web servers are: (1) Microsoft Windows and Microsoft IIS (Internet Information Services), and (2) Linux/Apache.

In addition to the operating systems and web servers, website coding generally requires scripting code that interacts with a database. Two of the most popular scripting codes are ASP.NET (a Microsoft product) and PHP (an open source product), and two of the most popular databases are SQL (Microsoft database, sometimes written as MS SQL) and MySQL (open source database).

The most popular server, software, scripting code and database configurations are: (1) a Microsoft system (Microsoft Windows, Microsoft IIS, SQL, and ASP.NET), and (2) an Open Source system (LAMP - Linux, Apache, MySQL, and PHP).

The system that will be best for your website will be dependent in part upon the scripting code and databases used for your website. Because of (i) the cost savings, (ii) the huge amount of development and applications built of PHP/MySQL, and (iii) the ability to use powerful and free Open Source content management systems (such as Joomla), my preference would be build a website to run on the LAMP configuration. For more information about these options – particularly concerning content management systems (CMS) – please see Chapter 10 – *Website Development and Content Management Systems*.

---

[10] http://webhostingrating.com/

Costs

The LAMP Open Source configuration on a dedicated server should not have any additional monthly costs, as all of the software components are open source and thus do not require a license fee.

The Microsoft system will require additional license fees, and possibly additional set-up fees. The operating system (assuming Microsoft 2008 Web Edition) will likely cost around $15-$30 per month. The database (assuming Microsoft MS SQL 2008 Web Edition) will likely cost another $40-$60 per month. Thus over the course of a year a Microsoft-based system will likely run an extra $660-$1,080 in addition to the basic hosting plan. Check with your developer and hosting company about prices, as prices can vary significantly among hosting companies.

PART IV – WEBSITE DEVELOPMENT AND SEARCH ENGINE OPTIMIZATION

Websites are becoming one of the main vehicles for reaching prospective clients and conveying a law firm's branding and value proposition. It's critical, therefore, that a law firm's website be professionally designed. The website design should encompass current design standards, and should be created around how the firm serves clients. In addition to the look and feel of the website, the website content should serve as a call to action for prospective clients, and should be "optimized" for high search engine rankings. Law firms should strongly consider having their website built around a content management system (CMS), so that changes and additions to the website can be easily made without developer assistance.

CHAPTER 7 – COMMUNICATING YOUR FIRM'S VALUE PROPOSITION THROUGH YOUR FIRM'S WEBSITE

Because your firm's website is the one form of marketing that is on display continuously, invest the time and expense to make the website resonate with your targeted clientele. Your website should clearly convey the value proposition offered by your firm to show that it matches the needs of prospective clients. Your website should also be an effective marketing tool for developing clients, and should serve as a call to action for prospective clients to contact you - today. Having a simple "contact us" page is not enough; actively promote the idea for prospective clients to contact your firm.

YOUR WEBSITE – YOUR CONTINUOUS FORM OF PROMOTION

Your website is likely the most public form of marketing for your law firm. It's functioning 24 hours a day, 7 days a week, available for potential and current clients, the media, your firm's competitors, and others who may be interested in finding our more about your firm.

Many firms, however, invest little time and money in website development. Often, website development is seen as a non- revenue-producing task, much like getting a telephone number. The less time and money spent to accomplish the task, the better (according to this line of thinking).

This chapter focuses on one theme – communicating your firm's value proposition in a way that will resonate with prospective clients so that prospective clients will call your firm. This is the single largest area in which most law firm websites fail. If you haven't done so already, please read Chapter 3 on developing a brand and value proposition for your law firm, as the items discussed there will be applicable to this chapter.

IDENTIFYING WEBSITE GOALS AND COMMUNICATING YOUR FIRM'S VALUE PROPOSITION THROUGH YOUR FIRM'S WEBSITE

A law firm's website should be developed around one or more goals, including communicating the firm's value proposition to current and prospective clients. The website should also be centered on how the firm serves clients. To the extent possible, every aspect of the law firm's website should answer one question posed from the perspective of a prospective client – "What are you going to do to help me?" To be effective, the answer to this question must resonate with prospective clients.

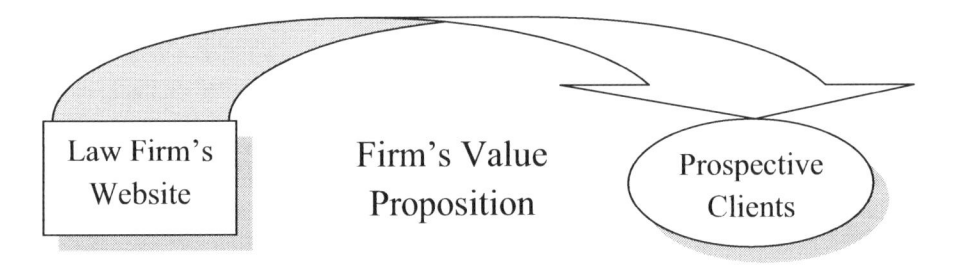

```
[Law Firm's Website] ──→ Firm's Value Proposition ──→ (Prospective Clients)
```

TAKE THE CHALLENGE – HOW WELL ARE YOUR FIRM'S KEY MESSAGES COMMUNICATED TO PROSPECTIVE CLIENTS ON YOUR FIRM'S WEBSITE?

If your firm currently has a website, take out a sheet of paper and write down the three most important messages that your firm wants to communicate to prospective clients. These messages should be specific (messages like "we care" or "we'll handle your legal needs" are not specific enough for this exercise), and the messages should be client-centered ("we have the largest legal team in town" isn't client-centered, as it doesn't focus on benefits to clients).

Here's an example of such a message:

> We understand that the bankruptcy process involves not only legal issues, but also a wide range of emotional and basic lifestyle issues that can have a dramatic impact upon the person or couple filing for bankruptcy, as well as family and loved ones. We know that you have important questions about how bankruptcy will affect your housing, personal belongings, vehicles, debt obligations, and other aspects of your life. We're here to represent you, to answer your questions, to stop creditors and debt collection agencies from contacting you, and to help you get through the bankruptcy process as quickly as possible so that you can start anew.

Now for the challenge – take the messages that you've written and carefully go through your firm's website. Are the messages communicated to prospective clients as clearly as you've written them?

Unless your messages are conveyed almost exactly as you've written them, the messages won't get through to prospective clients. In other words, prospective clients won't infer these key messages simply by statements that your firm practices bankruptcy law, or even stating that creditors are prevented from contacting them once the bankruptcy process is filed.

> ***Important - Your key messages (which are part of your firm's value proposition and branding) need to be clearly communicated to prospective clients throughout your firm's website, and should be reinforced with images and other design aspects. <u>Simply presenting your firm's practice areas isn't good enough – prospective clients won't "get it".</u>***

Now, let's take a few minutes to go over the typical law firm website development process to see how it might be improved.

THE TYPICAL LAW FIRM WEBSITE DEVELOPMENT PROCESS

A law firm needs a website. Perhaps the firm has postponed developing a website for years, or maybe the firm is brand new. In either case, the responsibility for managing the development of the firm's website is often delegated to one person, perhaps an attorney or firm staff member.

The responsible person usually has much more "important" tasks to accomplish, and thus can't spend 100% of her time on the website project. So, she focuses on finding a website developer who is inexpensive and who produces websites that look good.

The website to be developed is fairly simple, consisting of attorney profiles (including a detailed list of credentials, articles authored, and speaking engagements), a few pages about the firm's practice areas, and the firm's contact information. The requisite pictures of law books, scales of justice, courtrooms, gavels and other legal objects are also included. The result is a nice-looking website that presents a powerful image of the law firm.

> <u>Checklist for Law Firm Websites</u>
> ✓ Website has detailed information about all attorneys, their education, credentials, publications, major cases, significant transactions, and speaking engagements
> ✓ Website has great law pictures of impressive courthouses, scales of justice, etc.
> ✓ Website looks very nice
> ✓ <u>Firm image is very powerful</u>
> = **Effective Website??**

What, then, could possibly be wrong with this process?

The following are four significant problems that may arise from this process:

1. **NO DEFINED WEBSITE GOALS OR PLAN FOR COMMUNICATING THE FIRM'S VALUE PROPOSITION**. *The website is not created around a purpose* other than to establish an Internet presence for the firm with a website that looks good. *A website's purpose should be to communicate the firm's value proposition to current and prospective clients.* Other purposes may also be desired, such as communicating that the firm is a good corporate citizen, that it doesn't discriminate, or even that it is environmentally responsible, but if the website does not communicate the fundamentals of the firm's value proposition (services, non-legal needs to be satisfied, and cost) there is little chance that it will resonate with potential clients.

2. **OVER-PROMOTION OF THE FIRM AND ITS CREDENTIALS**. The website likely focuses on the firm and its credentials, *not* on how it *delivers services* or satisfies the *needs* (particularly the non-legal needs) of prospective clients.

3. **NO MEANINGFUL BRANDING**. There will likely not be any meaningful firm branding included, other than the firm's logo. *The firm's website therefore fails to distinguish the firm from other law firms offering the same services.*

4. **NO USEFUL SEARCH ENGINE OPTIMIZATION**. No useful search engine optimization will have been done. As a result, the website will not be effective for connecting prospective clients using Google and other search engines to find the legal services provided by the firm.

Each of these four items is discussed in separate sections below. Before continuing, did the developer do a poor job developing the website? No. He was hired to develop a simple, attractive website; he wasn't hired for branding, search engine optimization, or law firm marketing purposes.

POTENTIAL PROBLEM # 1 – NO DEFINED WEBSITE GOALS OR PLAN FOR COMMUNICATING THE FIRM'S VALUE PROPOSITION

Developing a website should be viewed much like implementing a marketing campaign, not just a way to establish an Internet presence. Like a marketing campaign, goals should be established, a plan to achieve the goals should be developed, a budget set, and the return on investment should be measured to the extent possible.

First, remember the three components of the value proposition: the *legal services* to be performed, the *non-legal needs* to be fulfilled, and the *costs* to be charged. Most law firm websites describe (or at least list) the legal services to be performed; a few mention cost and fee details (usually the "no fee if you don't win" part of litigation), and very few focus on the non-legal needs to be fulfilled.

Let's look at how The Corporate Firm might communicate the components of its value proposition to prospective clients through its website:

The Corporate Firm's Value Proposition	Website Communication
Legal Services: • Corporate formation • Contracts • Real Estate • Estate Planning • Securities law • Tax • Business Litigation	**Legal Services:** • Instead of simply listing all of the firm's different practice areas and expecting prospective clients to know what is encompassed by each practice area, the firm's website discusses specific examples of exactly how each practice area serves the needs of clients. • The firm's website also discusses cross-functionality of practice groups and how teams are created to handle the wide range of needs of corporate clients. For example, the "New Business Formations" group encompasses corporate, tax, estate planning, securities, and intellectual property attorneys make sure that all aspects of a new business has all of its needs addressed at the outset of formation. • The Corporate Firm wishes to distinguish itself from other law firm websites that simply list practice areas on an individual attorney's bio page, or even a specific practice area page, both of which give the impression that it's up to the prospective client to determine their legal needs.

The Corporate Firm's Value Proposition	Website Communication
Non-Legal Needs that Clients Seek to Have Fulfilled: • The firm realizes the significant role of its clients in the community, and understands that often clients may be interested in not pursuing legal matters, even if the clients would be likely to prevail. • The firm understands that that targeted corporate clients are concerned with their attorneys being ethical and conducting themselves with the highest professional regard. • The firm is ready to handle all of the clients' needs, and will treat each corporate client as a VIP. • The firm generally will not handle criminal defense matters or other matters that may be perceived as highly controversial in the community	**Non-Legal Needs that Clients Seek to Have Fulfilled:** • The firm's website will make use of pictures showing community landmarks, parks, community buildings, and historical monuments and places. • The firm will communicate "traditional values" through pictures such as two "typical" men (perhaps neighbors) shaking hands in a non-business setting. • Firm will discuss ethics, and use images make clear its commitment to acting ethically in all aspects of representing corporate clients. • The website will use pictures depicting people being given a VIP-type of treatment. • The firm will note that it does not handle criminal defense work.

The Corporate Firm's Value Proposition	Website Communication
Cost: The firm has committed itself to working with corporate clients, and is one of the few local firms well-positioned to handle almost all legal needs of its business clients. The firm can add value to corporate clients based on the cross-functionality of its practice areas, and, as a "firm client", the firm offers "one-shop" expertise on corporate matters. As a result of the firm's focused brand and full team of business attorneys, the firm is able to charge fees at the higher end of the cost spectrum.	**Cost:** Instead of omitting any mention of fees and costs, the firm's website is going to highlight its policy on clearly communicating fees and costs to clients. **As part of the message the firm will note that fees and costs are a concern to all of us as consumers, irrespective of whether we are purchasing legal services or groceries.** The message will be that we all want to know to the extent possible what the costs and fees will be, and to ensure that only the legal services that are approved by the client are billed. Pictures will be added that reinforce the firm's understanding of the concern of clients about costs.

As noted in the chart above, The Corporate Firm has carefully identified each of the components of its value proposition, and has developed ideas around how these components will be translated to prospective clients through its website. This type of chart can then be used to further develop the exact text (such as the bankruptcy message shown prior to the chart) to be used on the website, images can be found and licensed to depict the messages, and a website developer will have an understanding for exactly what the firm wishes to achieve for its website.

POTENTIAL PROBLEM #2 – OVER-PROMOTION OF THE FIRM AND ITS CREDENTIALS

REMEMBER, IT'S NOT ALL ABOUT YOU OR YOUR FIRM'S CREDENTIALS

A colleague has just told you about how wonderful this book is. Because you want to buy it immediately, you search the Internet to find a bookstore that has this book in stock. After searching Google, you find what appears to be the perfect bookstore – www.TheBiggestBookSellerEver.com (or BigBooks) – that advertises having every book ever printed in stock (and at 50% off with free overnight shipping!).

Now you're really excited. Tomorrow night you'll have the book in hand, learning everything worth knowing about Internet marketing.

But after arriving at the Big Books website what do you find? Articles about the history of BigBooks, video of how BigBooks crushed every other bookseller on the planet, and testimonials from BigBook's impressive client list. There's also the promise that through the BigBook's website you can order any book ever printed, but after ten minutes of going through the website you still can't find how to order the book that you want.

Does this hypothetical seem unrealistic? Take a look at a few law firm websites from the perspective of a client. How much of the website is devoted to telling prospective clients how the firm is going to handle their needs, and how much is devoted to the firm advocating their credentials and impressive client list? Does the firm's website even communicate that they understand needs of the client, or does it instead simply list the legal services provided?

Ideally, a law firm's website should be ***client-focused***, which means that ***the website should be more focused on how the firm will handle the needs of clients and less focused on the credentials of the firm's attorneys***. The philosophy behind this idea - Creating the Client-Oriented Website - is discussed in detail in Chapter 9.

POTENTIAL PROBLEM # 3 – NO MEANINGFUL BRANDING

MAKE YOUR WEBSITE BLEND IN WITH THE CROWD OR STANDOUT?

As noted in Chapter 3, a firm's brand is more than just a logo. It's the sum of the value proposition that a firm communicates to the public, including current and prospective clients. Unless a brand is first developed, it's impossible to create a website around the firm's brand.

In the typical website development process little attention is given to developing or extending a firm's brand, other than to perhaps use colors that might be in the firm's logo. As a result, law firm websites tend to look very similar.

For those who like to blend in with the crowd, I've undertaken an unscientific survey of law firm websites and found the following:

- 90% of all law firm websites have pictures of the scales of justice, marble courthouse columns, court rooms, or law books.
- 45% of all law firm websites have multiple pictures of all of the foregoing.
- 2% of all law firm websites have pictures of a scale of justice sitting next to marble courthouse columns with an open door showing a court room filled with law books.

It seems that we, as attorneys, have a difficult time being creative when it comes to pictorially portraying our profession, at least in a manner that might be appealing to prospective clients.

While we ethically may not be able to show a client celebrating with a wheel barrow of money after winning a court case, or a thumb pushing down on one side of the scales of justice tipping in favor of our client, perhaps there are other themes that we might be able to use, such as trust, competence, teamwork, listening, or caring.

How, then, can you make your website stand out?

Making Your Brand Resonate with Current and Prospective Clients

Consider that you're a DUI defense attorney, and your typical client has little or no involvement with the legal profession. Your new client, Jane, has no close friends or family members who are attorneys, and doesn't know any attorneys well.

When Jane went out for happy hour last night she had no desire to retain an attorney. Unfortunately, her drive home didn't go well, and today Jane needs legal help for her DUI charge. After a quick Internet search, Jane found your firm's website.

Your firm's website prominently features images of the hallmarks of the legal profession – great court rooms, majestic marble columns, law books, and an impressive-looking scales of justice. Do these images resonate well with Jane?

Perhaps not. Jane may have just been released from a holding cell, so in all likelihood pictures of courtrooms are probably the last thing she wants to see.

Same thing for the scales of justice. Jane doesn't want justice; she wants you to keep her out of jail and to avoid having her driver's license suspended, which would cost her a job. So a "scales of justice" picture may have the opposite of the intended effect by scaring Jane even more.

What concepts would resonate with Jane? Perhaps reassurance that her life is not coming to an end because she's been charged with a DUI. She may be concerned about losing her license (and her job), as well as how much legal defense and possible fines may cost. While you may not want to definitively respond to these concerns on your website, you can convey (through text and images) that you ***know and understand*** the issues that she's going through, and urge her to call you so that you might be able to explain the process to her.

POTENTIAL PROBLEM # 4 – NO USEFUL SEARCH ENGINE OPTIMIZATION

When a potential client conducts a Google search and types in a search term such as "Chicago divorce lawyer", it's critical for your firm to be listed on the first page of the search results if you're a divorce attorney in Chicago. In approximately 68% of the searches users don't go past the first page of the search results, and in about 92% of time they don't go past the first three pages.[11] ***Thus if your firm is to be considered by prospective clients, your firm's website needs to be listed high in the search results for the search terms used by prospective clients to find an attorney***.

The process of designing and making changes to web pages so that the page will receive high search engine rankings for specific keywords is known as search engine optimization (or "SEO"). SEO encompasses a number of aspects, including what are known as meta tags. Meta tags provide information to search engines (such as Google) about the content of the page.

The most important meta tags are the Title and Description tags, and to a lesser extent, the Keywords tag (Google no longer considers the keywords tag, other search engines still take into account the keywords tag).

Surprisingly, many website developers have no concept about the importance of search engine optimization. As a result, many websites don't include even simple title meta tags,

---

[11] Iprospect/Jupiter Research Study, April, 2008, http://www.iprospect.com/about/researchstudy_2008_blendedsearchresults.htm.

or if they do contain title meta tags, the words used have little or no SEO value. Only in rare cases is a firm's website developed around good search engine optimization methodology.

The importance of search engine optimization is discussed in detail in Chapter 11 of this book, and thus won't be repeated here. What should be noted is that without a website that's been optimized for search engines, it's difficult to get high search engine rankings. And, as noted above, if your website doesn't rank highly in the search engine results pages, your firm won't be found (or considered) by prospective clients searching for the legal services offered by your firm.

THE CALL TO ACTION – ENCOURAGING CLIENTS TO CONTACT YOUR FIRM THROUGH FIRM PHONE NUMBERS AND CONTACT INFORMATION FORMS

Law firms are in business to make money. To make money, most firms are in a continuous process of client development. Many firm websites, however, don't convey that the firm is even interested in new clients. Instead, it's difficult to find firm contact information such as phone numbers or a "contact us" page.

The message in this section is simple – if you wish for your firm's website to be a marketing tool to engage prospective clients, make it clear that your firm _wants and is interested in_ having website visitors contact the firm and becoming firm clients.

FIRM TELEPHONE NUMBERS

A firm's telephone number should be clearly displayed on all pages, preferably at the top right hand corner of the page (which is where users commonly search for such information). De-emphasizing your firm's telephone number doesn't detract from the firm's message and "prestige" of the firm, but it does send the message that your firm may not be all that interested in hearing from website users.

"CONTACT US" FORMS

There should be a link to the firm's "contact us" page in the main navigation, and at the bottom of every page.

Encourage users that might have questions or need the types of services described to contact you. "Contact us" forms for law firm websites should be relatively simple and short, not only to make it easy for prospective clients to complete, but also so that prospective clients don't reveal too much information about the nature of their legal matters before you've had an opportunity to conduct a conflicts check. Thus I would suggest that the "contact us" form consist of the following:

- The person's first and last name
- The person's telephone number
- A non-work e-mail address (if they have one)
- The best time to call

The firm should decide whether they want to get any more information on the type of legal matter that the person may have. If this is desirable, two options to consider are (1) a drop-down box for the person to choose the matter (if this is done, be sure to include an "other" category), or (2) a fill-in box that is very limited as to how much information can be provided by the prospective client.

For the second option, the box might be limited to 30 characters (including spacing). This will severely limit what information the person might be able to communicate. "Info about filing bankruptcy", for instance, is 28 characters long. While using this type of limited information box reduces potential conflicts and attorney-client issues, even a limited information box could still create issues ("Embezzled company's money", for instance, might be problematic).

Alternatively, it might be preferable to not include an information box and instead to include a short message about client confidentiality, such as the following:

> Thank you in advance for contacting our firm, and one of our attorneys will be contacting you by the end of the next business day. If your matter is urgent and you need to speak with an attorney before then, please call us at 555-555-5555.
>
> Please note that completing and sending to us your information does not constitute an attorney-client relationship, and no such relationship can exist until we have agreed in writing to serve as your legal counsel. As we are concerned with not inadvertently receiving any information that might jeopardize our ability to represent you, we have not included an information box regarding the nature of your matter.

You'll also want to provide any other information required under the rules and regulations governing your practice as an attorney.

INCLUDE THE "CONTACT US" FORM ON PRACTICE AREA PAGES AND ATTORNEY PROFILE PAGES

Firms often include web pages containing descriptions of their practice areas, but in the descriptions themselves, they fail to encourage potential clients to contact them.

If your firm is seeking clients, practice area and attorney profile pages should be constructed as a call to action, *not* simply as a source of information. Therefore, the "contact us" form *should not* be buried in a link at the bottom of a page, but instead should be *promoted on the page*.

Here's an example to be used on an attorney profile page:

How may I assist you?
Please call me at 555-555-5555 or complete this short form and I will call you.

Your Name _____
Your E-mail Address _____
Your Telephone Number _____
Best Time to Call You: _____

[Submit]

Joe Blow, Esq.
Corporate Practice Group
555-555-5555
Joe.Blow@MyFirm.com

Below or near the contact form, you'll also want to include the caveat about attorney-client privilege noted above. Keep in mind the following:

> ➤ Many clients might feel hesitant to call an attorney directly because attorneys make them uncomfortable, they might be embarrassed about a legal problem, or they may feel that "my matter may not be that important" compared to other matters that the attorney is working on.
> ➤ One of the goals of the website (and the profile pages for the individual attorneys) should be to break down these barriers to *encourage communication*. So, while it's helpful to list your credentials and describe your expertise, be

careful not to do it in such a way that you may be viewed as too important for the legal needs of the clients that you are seeking.

YOUR FIRM'S CONTACT INFORMATION

Each of the articles on your firm's website should also have a call to action. For instance, an article about bankruptcy should not stop at describing the elements of a bankruptcy filing. Speak to the user – "Are you wondering whether bankruptcy is right for you? Call me at 555-555-5555 today or send me a message [add simple contact form] and we can discuss your personal situation."

Don't lose the attention of the potential client after you've provided information. You want her to call or contact you *today*, right now if possible, not to go off and think about the information you've provided and then visit other websites (and potentially use another firm for her legal needs).

> *Having a website that is a great resource for information is not worth much if it's not helping to convert prospective clients into actual clients. Make it easy and encourage prospective clients to contact you at every stage in your website.*

PROMINENTLY PROMOTE WEBSITE CONTENT SECTIONS THAT YOU WANT USERS TO SEE

A common mistake made in website development is not prominently promoting important "inner page" website content on the home page. Instead, there is the tendency to think that because an important item **can be** accessed by a navigation link, that such link **is sufficient** to get users to the desired page(s). It's not.

Think of your home page not only as a way to introduce users to your firm and to help brand your firm, but also to as a way to *highlight the areas of the website that you want users to visit.*

Let's consider your firm's blog. You've spent a lot of time and effort on your blog, and believe that it's become an effective way of getting potential clients to call you. Should you leave it up to users to see and click on the small "My Blog" link on your website's navigation bar?

Probably not. Instead, promote your blog prominently on your home page, and on other pages of your firm's website (such as practice area pages and profile pages). Use an image that will encourage users to click on your blog, add the first sentence or two of your latest posting, or, better yet, do both.

Don't assume that because you have a link to a particular section (such as a blog), users will click on the link and find the information that you want them to you find. The lesson - ***If you want users to visit a particular section, you MUST HIGHLIGHT AND PROMOTE THAT SECTION; navigation links are not sufficient.***

HOW TO GET PROSPECTIVE CLIENTS AND WEBSITE USERS TO VISIT YOUR KEY CONTENT PAGES

Now that the importance of promoting key website content is clear, let's go over *how* to effectively promote this content so that users will click the links to the content you wish them to see. Almost no one promotes link-clicks better than AOL.

AOL constantly features a number of articles flashed across the home page. AOL makes money by displaying ads; the more pages that users visit, the more ads that are displayed, and the more ad revenue that is generated.

In order to entice users to click on the featured articles, AOL employs a number of catchy headline gimmicks that revolve around common themes: fear, ways to make you rich (slimmer, healthier, etc.), celebrity gossip (who divorced, died, is dating Britney), and (my personal favorite) news of the bizarre. In almost all of the headlines, important information is missing, thus encouraging users to click on the articles to read more.

Here are examples of some headlines (all of these were taken from the same day):

- Eclipse Raises Fears for Some. Rare Solar Event Will Darken Part Of the World: Ominous Predictions.
- Lost Love Letter Reunites Couple – It Was "Hiding" in Very Unlikely Place
- Tasered Man Bursts Into Flames
- 2 Things Kenney Chesney Won't Do
- Woman Did Her Own Plastic Surgery – Now Regrets Very Botched Results
- 11 Names Likeliest to Be In Trouble

> Car Dealers' Biggest Secret – "Business Manager" Is Just Another Salesman: How to Avoid His Tricks

AOL could have simply listed the two things that Kenney won't do (He won't wear a wig or use a fake name like Garth Brooks did with his "Chris Gaines" one album alter-ego), or the 11 names likeliest to be in trouble (sorry about all of you named Alec, Ernest, Garland, Ivan, Kareen, Luke, Malcom, Preston, Tyrell, or Walter (only ten names were listed)).

AOL knows if it had provided the missing key information with a link to the more detailed article, far less click-throughs would have been generated (and, correspondingly less ad revenue would be received).

What does that mean for your law firm's website?

I'm not suggesting including articles about Elvis sightings, alien attacks or celebrity dating matters. Instead, promote your blogs, articles - even practice areas - in a way that encourages users to visit these and other important sections of your firm's website. If a recent court case might help those charged with DUI, a headline like "Court Reverses Smith Decision" is much less likely to generate user clicks than "Some Phoenix Motorists May Have DUI Cases Dismissed Based on New Court Ruling." **_Keep in mind - it doesn't do much good to develop great content if users won't go the page you want them to see._**

The second reason that it's important to promote your inner page content is a little less obvious – **_the more a user interacts with your website, the more likely it is that your firm's message will resonate with the user._** After reading your firm's blog and seeing some of the profiles of your firm's attorneys, users begin to feel comfortable with the firm. The more comfortable they feel, the more likely they are to contact your firm instead of another firm.

In marketing parlance this is known as user interaction or user experience. In general, companies prefer to advertise on websites that have higher average page views than websites with low page views because it is believed that users will have a more positive experience (and thus be more receptive to buying products) on the "high page view" websites. I believe that the same concept holds true for law firm websites. The more website pages prospective clients view, the more likely they are to call your firm.

The next chapter discusses website design trends.

CHAPTER 8 - WEBSITE DESIGN TRENDS – WEB 2.0 AND BEYOND

Like fashion styles, website design continues to evolve. Website design popular a few years ago consisting of dark backgrounds and content laid out in a box or grid –type format are considered outdated. Current design usually includes light or white backgrounds and "floating" boxes for content (or even the absence of box lines and simply formatted text and images on a page). Because a website is the public face for a firm, it's important that a firm's website communicates clearly not only the firm's value proposition, but also that it is current with the times.

WEB 2.0 AND WEBSITE DESIGN

Web 2.0 is an often-used phrase to describe websites, Internet technology, the connection between users and information, types of communications, and a host of other things. If you've been around some circles of advertising (such as at a conference), you'll hear the phrase Web 2.0 (and maybe even Web 3.0) thrown around often. You may even come to the conclusion that the term "Web 2.0" doesn't necessarily have a real meaning, it's more of a term that's tossed around casually to make the user seem educated. You may be right.

Fortunately, and inevitably, Web 3.0 may be just around the corner, so if you want to appear *really* smart, talk about Web 3.0 at your next cocktail party when the topic of Web 2.0 arises. More about Web 3.0 in a moment; for now let's look at Web 2.0 with respect to website design.

WHAT IS WEB 2.0?

According to Wikipedia,

> "**Web 2.0**" refers to the second generation of web development and web design. It is characterized as facilitating communication, information sharing, interoperability, user-centered design and collaboration on the World Wide Web. It has led to the development and evolution of web-based communities, hosted services, and web applications. Examples include social-networking sites, video-sharing sites, wikis, blogs, mashups and folksonomies.

The term is now closely associated with Tim O'Reilly because of the O'Reilly Media Web 2.0 conference in 2004. Although the term suggests a new version of the World Wide Web, it does not refer to an update to any technical specifications, but rather to cumulative changes in the ways software developers and end-users utilize the Web. According to Tim O'Reilly:

> *Web 2.0 is the business revolution in the computer industry caused by the move to the Internet as a platform, and an attempt to understand the rules for success on that new platform.*

However, whether it is qualitatively different from prior web technologies has been challenged. For example, World Wide Web inventor Tim Berners-Lee called the term a "piece of jargon"[12]. (citations included in original text omitted here)

OK, so now we're all completely clear on what Web 2.0 means (not). Fortunately, we don't have to choose who's right – the media guy or the guy who invented the Web (not Al Gore); what's critical for us is to understand what works as far as website layout, and what looks tired and dated.

THE STANDARD FOR WEB 2.0 WEBSITES

Our US Supreme Court set the standard that should be applied to determining what constitutes a Web 2.0 website – the "you know it when you see it" standard. Web 2.0 encompasses the latest style trends. It looks cool and inviting. Even the people on Web 2.0 websites look smarter and more attractive. Unlike Web 1.0 (which is to be avoided), you'll want your firm's website to be as much like Web 2.0 as possible. (Is this beginning to sound like high school?)

BEFORE LOOKING AT ELEMENTS THAT CONSTITUTE WEB 2.0, LET'S LOOK AT WEB 1.0 – WHAT LOOKS NEW AND WHAT LOOKS DATED

Some of the elements that look dated (or Web 1.0) include the following:

1. **Dark websites, often with no light-colored background.** While this isn't necessarily a killer for Web 2.0, it's really got to be done right to work. Most of the time it doesn't work.

---

[12] http://en.wikipedia.org/wiki/Web_2.0

2. *Websites that use clip art images from the '90s.* Don't use these types of clip art on your law firm's website – ever. This is a killer. Again – this is the "you know it when you see it" standard.

3. *Using one wide column of unformatted text.*

4. *Having web pages look like a bunch of rectangles stuck together, with text and pictures plugged into the boxes.* Website coding (at a basic level) typically uses box-type layouts. Text and/or pictures are then placed in the boxed areas. Although boxed layouts may be used in the backend coding, it doesn't mean that the "boxiness" needs to be shown on the web page.

5. *Boring Text Formatting - Using text that is all formatted exactly the same.* Same font, type size, and color.

6. *Using light blue as the primary color in the website.* It's not really clear why light blue became widely used for websites in the first place; perhaps because Microsoft Office used it in Word and Outlook and there was a tendency to make this a "unifying" color. Be courageous and break the tradition.

7. *Lots of links on a web page.* Usually underlined like this. Some websites have dozens or more links on a single page, not including the navigation. Users can't determine what's important and what's not important. Maybe, instead of figuring out what's important, it might be easier to go to another website. Does this make sense?

8. *No (or few) pictures, or pictures that look very "homemade".* All law firms should have pictures of their attorneys included in their website. Prospective clients want to know who their attorney is and what their attorney looks like.

    Have a professional photographer take pictures of your firm's attorneys. A professional photographer will ensure not only high-quality images, but also consistency in terms of picture resolution and background settings, which would not be the result if the firm's attorneys simply submitted their favorite picture of themselves.

WEBSITE 2.0 DESIGN ELEMENTS – CURRENT TRENDS

Here's a list of Web 2.0 trends –

1. ***Keep Your Website Bright***. Web 2.0 websites typically have white or light colored backgrounds, or otherwise do not use heavy colors for the entire web page. Your website should not look like a painting by one of the Masters of the Renaissance. Also, unless you're an attorney representing skateboarders or heavy metal bands, avoid the dark Goth look.

2. ***Don't be afraid to use colors (even vivid colors), but make sure there is plenty of white background to off-set the colors***.

3. ***Choose colors carefully***. Some colors are much better relegated to accent colors, especially very light colors and yellows and greens. Yellows and light greens in particular can look very different on different monitors. What might look great on one monitor might look terrible on another monitor.

4. ***Use "Floating" Sections on Pages instead of having a website "boxed out"***. Floating sections are rectangular boxes with curved corners that appear to be "floating" on a (usually) white or light grey background. In other words, page section boxes aren't all connected to each other; boxes (and often content such as text) appears to "float" on the page. In some instances pages don't have borders on the side to separate content from the background – which is fine.

5. ***Avoid introductory pages (which are usually done in using Flash)***. Flash elements are OK, but build them into a *small part* of the page itself, not as the main page feature. If you want to have a Flash animation to promote your firm, great – have it included somewhere on the home page but make sure it's not a dominant feature of the page.

6. ***Simplicity – The 10 Second Rule and Avoiding Page Overload***. Here's another of my rules – if it takes an average 5th grader more than ten seconds to look and understand what is on a web page, the page needs to be simplified. This does ***not*** mean that it only takes ten seconds to ***read and understand all of the content on the page***, only that it takes ten seconds for a user to understand what the page is about, such as the topics or information on the page.

As an example of what not to do, look at the websites of television and news media companies. The home pages of CNN.com, MSNBC.com, and USAToday.com, for instance, often contain more than 100 links, and this number doesn't include drop-down (or subcategory) navigation links or "boiler-plate" links at the bottom of a page. The 100+ links are conveniently located under dozens of topic headers.

These websites would all be deemed Web 2.0 websites, but they also clearly violate the ten second rule test. However, as a "destination" website (one that will be visited often, usually because the content is frequently and significantly changed), these websites can get away with what might otherwise be information overload because their readers return often to these websites, and, more importantly, will spend time becoming familiar with the layout and organization.

Clients seeking legal services, on the other hand, likely won't take this time if the website has information overload, especially information overload on the home page. If there's so much information on the home page that it makes their head hurt, they'll simply move on to another firm's website. Having a complicated website may also reflect poorly on your firm – will you be as complicated as your website?

The message here is that you've GOT to keep page content simple or you will quickly alienate potential clients, <u>especially</u> if a page is overloaded with legal content.

7. ***Simple, Easy-to-Understand Navigation***. Minimize the number of main-category links on your firm's website to 7 or fewer topics if possible. You can, however, have more than 7 topics under one main navigation item. The difference in this principle is that when sub-topics are opened it is the *user* initiating the action to see the information; it's not thrust upon the user. Users have a higher tolerance looking at information that *they initiate* then they do for having to wade through information established by someone else.

8. ***Building a website entirely in Flash***. Flash is a type of animated coding. Websites built in Flash can look great, and can have a strong impact if done correctly. However, because search engines have difficulty "reading" Flash content, it's more difficult to get high search engine rankings. Additionally, it's often more difficult to change content in Flash, although there are some content management systems that make it easier.

WEBSITE NAVIGATION – THE IMPORTANCE OF SIMPLE NAVIGATION

Because simple navigation is so important, it's worth spending a little more time discussing.

1. ***Limiting the Number of Topics and Sub-topics and the 3-Click Rule*** – In general, information should not be more than 3 clicks away from the home page, and preferably not more than two clicks away. This is often called the 3-Click Rule.

2. ***Multiple Paths to Access Key Information*** – There should be multiple paths to access information that users may readily need, such as your firm's contact information and a "contact us" form. For example, to get to a firm's "contact us" page, there might be a link at the top of the page, a link in the navigation, and a link at the bottom of the page.

3. ***Consistent Navigation on All Pages*** – Don't have horizontal navigation on the home page and vertical navigation on the other pages, or change the order of the navigation topics.

4. ***Promote Key Content*** – If there is content on your website that you want users to see, you must prominently promote it on your home page. Navigation links are not sufficient to generate link clicks.

BONUS INFORMATION - WEB 3.0.[13]

Web 3.0, sometimes also referred to as the "semantic web" or the "intelligent web", has been described as a fundamental change in the way information is organized so that it will enable users to extract more meaningful data. The goal is that users will be able to ask questions and get responses much like they would in a normal conversation. For instance, you might type in a question like "what should I do this weekend for fun?", and a list of activities and events from different websites might be displayed. In order to make this possible, fundamental ways in which information is gathered (and likely also stored) would need to take place. In the interim, the next chapter discusses a fundamental change in the way law firm websites are designed from a firm-centered to client-centered websites.

---

[13] http://computer.howstuffworks.com/web-30.htm.

CHAPTER 9 – CREATING THE CLIENT-CENTERED WEBSITE

Nearly all law firm websites are focused on one aspect – promoting the firm and its attorneys. This chapter suggests a fundamentally different approach to law firm website development – the Client-Centered Website. The Client-Centered Website is designed around one theme – answering the question "How will the firm serve me?" from the view of prospective clients. With the Client-Centered Website each aspect of the website, including attorney profiles and practice areas, are centered on how the firm serves clients.

THE TYPICAL LAW FIRM WEBSITE DESIGN

Nearly all law firm websites are designed around promoting the firm and its attorneys; usually with the concept of "the more impressive we appear, the more likely we are to generate clients."

The view seems to be that if a firm can convince prospective clients that they have more attorneys who went to better law schools and who published more legal articles and who won more trials, clients will choose their firm over the firm down the street that scores slightly lower in these areas. As a result, attorney profiles are loaded with information about articles authored, speaking engagements, significant trials, major transactions, and legal awards.

This concept is not entirely without merit; most clients would rather have an impressive firm representing them than undistinguished attorneys from less-than-stellar firms. But do law firms get hired simply because they have more credentials than another firm? Does a list of trials won and articles authored resonate with prospective clients more than an explanation of how the firm will serve their needs? Are these two approaches mutually exclusive?

WHAT IS THE CLIENT-CENTERED WEBSITE AND HOW IS IT DIFFERENT THAN TRADITIONAL LAW FIRM WEBSITES?

The client-centered website is designed around one theme – answering the question "How will the firm serve me?" from the view of prospective clients. Instead of focusing on quantitative lists of great legal achievements of the firm and its attorneys, the client-centered website focuses on creating and developing a relationship with prospective clients around how the needs of clients will be served by the firm. Attorney and firm achievements are carefully presented in a manner suggesting value to be provided to clients, not as a tribute to the attorneys or firm. *The goal of the client-centered website is to convey the firm's value proposition and messages in a way that will resonate with clients.*

As attorneys we're often focused on applying logic and quantitative solutions to problem-solving. We understand how to successfully string together arguments in order to win cases and prove that our side should win. Some of us may even be considered a little competitive. All of the forgoing may be reasons why we feel the need to have long lists of our accomplishments prominently displayed on our websites and profile pages. We can't let the guys down the street list more accomplishments on their website than we have on ours; after all we're much better than they are, and the public has the right to know it.

Despite the well-intentioned public service goal, consider for a moment that prospective clients might be more interested in what you're going to do for them, that you care about their matters and helping them be successful, and that you're not some lawyer with an overblown ego who will be difficult to work with (like the guys down the street).

The next sections of this chapter discuss how we can create a Client-Centered Website while still discussing our skills and accomplishments.

THE CLIENT-CENTERED WEBSITE HOME PAGE

A good client-centered website home page will do several things:

1. It will be focused on sending a specific message as to how the firm serves clients (let's call this the **Client Service Statement**). The Client Service Statement does not need to be detailed – in fact, it shouldn't be overly-complicated, and it shouldn't be a mission statement or core values statement. By definition, mission statements focus on the company or organization and the reason for its existence, and core values statements focus on central beliefs of the firm. While either a mission statement or a core values statement might concern clients, clients do not necessarily need to be included.

    Here's an example of a Client Service Statement that might be used for The Corporate Firm:

> **We serve corporate clients through a team-based approach by providing pro-active legal advice, helping clients understand the many laws and regulations that affect their business, and representing clients in negotiations, litigation, financings, and other matters.**

2. It will include a message that will be designed to <u>resonate with prospective clients by making the prospective clients want to retain the firm</u>; NOT serve as an argument for the firm being better than the guys down the street.

3. To be powerful, *the message should consist of pictures, colors and graphics; not just text.* As attorneys, most of us are good writers; however, few of us are good at selecting images, color combinations, and other aesthetically-pleasing web pages that will resonate with prospective clients. To maximize the effectiveness of a firm's message, images, color combinations, and creative art should be used; *the actual text is only part of the message.*

4. The home page <u>should not</u> be filled with awards that the firm or its attorneys have recently won, or a list of speaking engagements firm attorneys have given, <u>unless these aspects are presented as a benefit to prospective clients</u>. For instance, if a new legal decision was announced that affects employment, a speaking engagement announcement shouldn't say:

> Joe Blow spoke at the Great Town Club last week about his recent article on the <u>Smith</u> decision and employment

; instead, the caption might read

> The <u>Smith</u> Decision limits the ability of employees to sue employers. <u>Read more about new employee limitations</u> written by firm partner Joe Blow, who spoke last week at the Great Town Club about what actions employers can take to receive the benefits of the <u>Smith</u> decision.

The first caption is self-serving for the firm; it seeks to validate how good Joe Blow is because he spoke at the Great Town Club. The second caption provides *value* to prospective clients; it informs them that there is a new court decision that may affect employment relationships, and hints that there is something that companies might need to do to gain a potential benefit. While it also mentions that Mr. Blow authored a paper and spoke last week about the decision, this information is almost antidotal – it doesn't come across as self-serving.

ATTORNEY PROFILE PAGES – THE TRADITIONAL APPROACH VS. THE CLIENT-CENTERED APPROACH

The following chart describes the differences between the "traditional" presentation of attorney profiles and profiles using the client-centered approach:

	Traditional Approach	Client-Centered Approach
Form of Writing	Written in 3rd person; approach is to make the attorney appear as authoritative as possible	Written in first person; approach is for the attorney to communicate with clients that the attorney understands the nature of the legal matters and describes how the attorney typically serves clients
Education & Background	Highlighted, and focused on achievements of attorney	De-emphasized
Transactions and Litigation	Usually highlighted and heavily promoted with long great legal accomplishment lists	Incorporated into discussions about how attorney serves clients; separate list may be presented in linked click-on box
General approach	**Quantitative and information-focused**. The more attorneys, the more top law schools, the more awards and achievements they have, the better.	**Qualitative and message-focused.** Rather than long lists of articles authored, trials won, or transactions represented, each page is focused on what the attorney can do for clients
Call to Action on Page	Usually none other than providing contact information for the attorney	Attorney invites clients to call him or her, and often contact form is provided for clients to complete
Positioning of Attorney	"Pedestal" approach used; attorney positioned as great authority on the law	Service provider approach used; attorney positioned as a person who cares and has the legal expertise to help clients
Client perceptions of attorney positioning	Prospective clients may believe that the attorney is too "high-powered" and busy with more important matters than their matters. Clients may feel reluctant to call attorney.	By speaking in first person and actively inviting clients to call; attorney breaks down communication barriers. Message to prospective clients is "your matter is important to me."

NOTE - THE CLIENT-CENTERED WEBSITE DOES NOT OMIT INFORMATION ABOUT ATTORNEYS, THEIR CREDENTIALS, OR THEIR ACHIEVEMENTS; RATHER IT RE-SHAPES AND RE-FOCUSES SUCH INFORMATION ON HOW CLIENTS WILL BE SERVED BY THE EXPERIENCE AND EXPERTISE OF THE ATTORNEYS.

Let's examine how a "traditional" website and a client-centered website will look for The Corporate Firm, with the attorney profile of Joe Blow (the firm's managing partner and head of the firm's corporate section). When reading the profiles, try to do so as a prospective client. Are there any specific areas that stand out as being particularly appealing from the perspective of a potential client? Are there any aspects that spoke to you and made you feel like you would want to contact the firm? Finally, if your firm already has a website, take time to look at it now from the perspective of a client. Are there ways that your website might be improved to better resonate with prospective clients looking for your firm's services?

ATTORNEY PROFILE – JOE BLOW, ESQ. (TRADITIONAL ATTORNEY PROFILE)

Law School: Big University School of Law, 1980 (summa cum laude, Order of the Coif, and Managing Editor of Law Journal)

Undergraduate School: State University, 1977 (B.A. Political Science, Honors)

Mr. Blow is the Managing Partner for The Corporate Firm, and has served on the firm's management committee since 1993.

Joe Blow, Esq.
Joe.Blow@MyLawFirm.com
Phone: 555-555-555
FAX: 800-555-5555

Mr. Blow currently serves as the primary external counsel to Big Company 1, Corporate Giant 2, and MegaCorp 3, all of which are Fortunate 100 companies. Mr. Blow has helped over two dozen companies go public, and helped clients secure over $1 billion in private placement and public offering funding from debt and equity placements. Mr. Blow has also represented clients in numerous acquisitions, mergers, and divestitures, including representing Big Company 1 in its successful acquisition of Target 1, where he was instrumental in persuading the Department of Justice that the merger would not have a monopoly or anti-competitive effect on the Widget industry.

Mr. Blow has been named a Distinguished Attorney by The Prestigious Law Magazine for the past ten years. Mr. Blow has more than 30 years' experience of legal practice in the following areas: Corporate Law, Securities Law, Business Finance, Business Formations, and Real Estate Law.

The following is a list of notable transactions in which Mr. Blow served as lead counsel for corporate clients [list of 20 transactions provided].

Mr. Blow is a member of the firm's corporate, securities, business finance, and business formations practice groups.

Mr. Blow has spoken at numerous Bar Association conferences, and has served on many Bar Association committees. Mr. Blow is also a past president for the State Bar Association.

Mr. Blow is the author of the following articles: Securities Law and Private Placements after *Smith*, [list of 15 other significant articles that Mr. Blow authored].

Mr. Blow is a member of Great Town's Bar Association, the State Bar Association, Great Town's Business Council, and several civic clubs and associations where he has been a past officer.

ATTORNEY PROFILE – JOE BLOW, ESQ. (CLIENT-CENTERED ATTORNEY PROFILE)

For more than thirty years I've been advising businesses ranging from newly-formed companies to large publicly-held companies on a variety of business law matters. I enjoy practicing business law and helping clients – both large and small – succeed. Here's how I typically serve clients:

Joe Blow
Joe.Blow@MyLawFirm.com
Call Me: 555-555-555
FAX: 800-555-5555

Business Formation
- ➢ I advise clients about the best form of business entity to use, taxation treatment, and shareholder agreements. My focus is not only in helping clients understand business structure, tax, and employee benefits issues, but also to consider shareholder agreements in the event of one owner wanting to sell his or her interest in the company, and successorship issues in the event of the death or disability of owners.
- ➢ I set-up a cross-functional team of our attorneys to serve the needs of clients at no cost. The goal of our team is to learn about your business so that we can provide pro-active advice about changes in laws and regulations that may affect your business, and so that we are prepared to serve you at a moment's notice if a new matter arises.

Ongoing Corporate Representation

As companies grow, new legal needs often arise. As the firm's corporate practice group leader, I often represent clients in matters such as contracts, licensing, mergers, acquisitions, divestitures, equity and debt financing, public offerings, and private placements. I've had the pleasure of representing several Fortunate 100 clients and many privately-held clients in a variety of sophisticated transactions (including public and private debt and equity funding of over $1 billion); please click here to see a representative transaction list.

I've also authored more than a dozen published articles and given numerous talks on these matters at State Bar conventions and other presentations.

More About Me

I've been named a Distinguished Attorney by The Prestigious Law Magazine for the past ten years. I believe this honor is the result of attention to detail whether I'm representing a Fortunate 100 company in a mega-merger or a newly-formed company securing their first office lease. I strongly believe in civic responsibility, and have served as an officer for several of Great Town's civic organizations.

I graduated from Big University School of Law, 1980 (summa cum laude, Order of the Coif, and Managing Editor of Law Journal), and received my undergraduate degree from State University, 1977 (B.A. Political Science, Honors).

I would welcome the opportunity to talk to you more about how our firm can assist your business. Please call me at my direct line at 555-555-5555 or, if you prefer, fill out the contact form and let me know of a good time to call you.

WHAT ARE THE DIFFERENCES BETWEEN THE TRADITIONAL APPROACH AND THE CLIENT-CENTERED APPROACH FOR ATTORNEY PROFILES?

Here is a short list of the differences:

- The traditional approach is written in the third person, which is designed to place the attorney on a pedestal in the way that the accomplishments are presented. In the client-centered approach, the attorney speaks directly to prospective clients – "here's what I can do for you."
- The traditional approach reads as a list of "great legal accomplishments" for the attorney. The client-centered approach includes the same legal accomplishments, but ties them directly to how clients benefit from these items.
- The traditional approach simply lists some of the organizations to which the attorney belongs. The client-centered approach does more – it includes a personal statement about the value that these organizations serve. The Corporate Firm understands that civic responsibility is an important view held by many of its prospective clients; the firm therefore wishes to explicitly state that they share this view. The client-centered approach does not rely on prospective clients to infer that civic involvement is really important to the attorney – the attorney tells prospective clients this directly.

PRACTICE AREA PROFILES – _HOW_ ARE SERVICES DELIVERED?

Most law firm practice profiles consist of lists of various services that the firm provides. A list of corporate legal services, for instance, might consist of the following:

>   Business formation
>   Tax and partnerships
>   LLC's
>   Capital funding
>   Private Placements
>   Initial and Secondary Public Offerings
>   Shareholder Agreements

As discussed previously, practice area pages should be addressed around how the firm delivers services to clients, not simply a list of services that may be provided (which can be interpreted as it's up to the client to determine what legal services are required). Thus instead of simply stating "business formation", or listing types of business formations, the firm could state the following:

> We understand the legal issues associated with the formation of a new company. A determination must be made about the best legal entity form based upon tax and other considerations. Ownership interests and registration issues need to be undertaken. Successor and potential equity owner sales interests need to be thought through to avoid future conflicts in the event that an owner wishes to sell equity interests. Intellectual property and other assets might need to be legally transferred to the company. We can guide your company through these issues to make sure that your company is set up for success, not only now but also as your company grows.

By this description, prospective clients don't feel that it is up to them to determine what legal service(s) they need; they know that the firm's attorneys will speak to them about the best legal organization form for their company. Further, prospective clients have been provided value in that they understand that there are other matters that should be considered at the outset of the business formation. Describing these issues demonstrates that the firm is thinking in advance about the interests of the clients adds value to the clients.

By focusing all firm website content on how the firm serves clients, the firm will be much more effective in communicating a message that will resonate with clients.

CHAPTER 10 - WEBSITE DEVELOPMENT AND CONTENT MANAGEMENT SYSTEMS

Don't try this at home - Avoid any temptation you might have to develop your website on your own. It's not worth the extensive time that it takes to become proficient at website code, database construction and interaction, graphic arts, content management systems, and software platforms. Regardless of whether you wish to have a custom website developed or use a website template, have a content management system (CMS) incorporated into the website (either a custom CMS or a CMS platform such as Joomla). If database interaction is required (which will the case if the website utilizes a CMS), PHP and MySQL are the much-recommended solution over ASP/SQL (Microsoft products) and other similar solutions.

WHO SHOULD DEVELOP MY WEBSITE? PICKING THE RIGHT WEBSITE DEVELOPER.

SHOULD I BUILD MY WEBSITE MYSELF?

This question is the same as a non-lawyer asking whether it would be a good idea if he represented himself in a personal injury matter.

Your website is your personal 24/7 face to the world. It should be a significant part of your marketing program. Because it's available 24/7 for the world to see, and may often be the sole factor in determining whether a client calls you or someone else, your website should look as good and professional as possible – ***no exceptions***.

Professional website development can be complex, especially in terms of writing scripts to interact with databases. Equally challenging is having the artistic ability to design an aesthetically-pleasing layout to match a law firm's brand. Most attorneys lack a professional skill base in both of these areas. Becoming proficient in Dreamweaver, PHP, Adobe Photoshop, and MySQL databases takes a significant amount of time.

In contrast, for perhaps $1500-$5,000, you can have a professional website designer and developer build a custom website to match your firm's brand which includes a content management system. These costs are even lower if a website template is used.

Please just say "no" to developing your firm's website yourself.

OK, I Understand, But I Really Want to Learn Website Development

If you want to learn website development, hire a website developer and buy a book about website coding (such as a book on Dreamweaver). If your website will be using PHP and MySQL, you might also want to pick up books about these subjects.

> *If you're really interested in learning about (and perhaps even trying) website development, buy Adobe Dreamweaver software license. Dreamweaver creates much cleaner code and has much more functionality than Microsoft Front Page.*

Website Templates – to Use or Not to Use?

Website templates can be found from a variety of online vendors, and can be licensed for a relatively low fee (usually less than $100 if it's on a non-exclusive basis). The templates must be customized to add content about the firm, attorney profiles, contact information, practice area information, and any other content that the firm may wish to have included. Blogs can also be added if desired.

Templates have a variety of advantages, most importantly that the general look of the website is known in advance. Templates developed using style sheets that can be easily modified to change colors, font types, header appearance, and other website aspects. Templates typically can be finalized much quicker than starting a website from scratch, but, by the very nature of being a template, some of the "originality" that may be sought may not exist (however, changes in pictures, colors, fonts, etc., can be used to give the website an original look).

Aside from originality concerns, the primary disadvantages of template use can be the circumvention of the development of the **purpose of the website**, the **goals to be achieved** by the website, and **meaningful search engine optimization** to generate clients. Instead, templates are treated as "fill-in-the-blank" forms – substitution of the generic information for the information pertaining to the law firm.

Naturally, these disadvantages can be overcome.

WHERE CAN WEBSITE TEMPLATES BE FOUND, AND WHAT ASPECTS SHOULD I LOOK FOR IN A TEMPLATE DESIGN?

There are a number of website template providers that can be found on the Internet, including our publisher www.EsquireInteractive.com. They have numerous templates that can be used, including templates for non-law websites that can be easily modified for a law firm website.

I would strongly suggest either selecting a template that is built on a content management systems (CMS) such as Joomla, or making sure that your developer can take the template design and incorporate it into a Joomla or other CMS-based website.

Additionally, make sure that the latest coding releases have been used. For example, if the coding incorporates Joomla, make sure it runs on the latest version of Joomla. The current version of Joomla is 1.5. Joomla templates (and Joomla extensions) that are "native 1.5" were designed to run on Joomla 1.5, templates (and extensions) that are "legacy 1.5" were designed in an earlier version of Joomla and then subsequently modified for version 1.5. (NOTE – it's best to avoid templates and Joomla extensions that are not native 1.5, as legacy 1.5 templates and extensions may not run correctly.) To find see what version of Joomla is the latest, please visit www.Joomla.com.

Also, consider choosing a template that incorporates the "Web 2.0" design elements suggested previously. The layout should look clean, the navigation should be uncluttered and user-friendly, and the design should not look as if a bunch of boxes were put together.

Note that in most cases your developer should be able to modify the template to fit your needs, so it's not necessary that the template be exactly what you're looking for. Your developer should be able to advise of the cost of such modifications.

UNDERSTANDING THE DIFFERENCE BETWEEN THE DESIGN PROCESS AND DEVELOPMENT PROCESS – ENSURING THAT BOTH TYPES OF EXPERTISE ARE COVERED

The website development process requires two different types of expertise: design expertise and coding expertise.

Designers are much like architects; their job is to translate the ideas and website elements (such as navigation) into the look and feel of the website. Typically, designers use programs such as Adobe Photoshop to create the layout of the website for their client's approval. While this layout will look almost exactly like the web page when viewed, because it has not yet been converted into html, the "links" won't work.

During this phase changes can be made fairly quickly, as the design is not in code form. The design is usually created in a "layered" format. Layered formats mean that the image is created using layers, such that the background might be created first, then the borders second, a picture layer next, etc. Creating the image in layers allows the designer to easily edit and make changes to the image, colors, text, and other aspects.

The goal of the design stage is to create the final layout of the website (or at least the home page and the inner page layout). Once the layout is final, it's time for the developer.

The job of the developer is to build the website in accordance with the website design. It's the developer's job to do so using the best methods available so that (1) the website loads quickly in all major browsers, and (2) subsequent changes can be easily made. The developer receives the images from the designer and uses the image files to build the web pages, and links are built into the code to tie the pages together.

Professional developers use what are called Cascading Style Sheets (or CSS or "style sheets" for short). Style sheets are a separate set of instructions for web browsers that tell the web browsers how to display certain styles, elements, and pieces of information, such as title and sub-title tags. Thus instead of formatting section titles or various elements every time these are used on every page in a website, a style is created in the style sheet defining how the browser should display these items. Style sheets have two significant benefits – they eliminate excess code on web pages (which speeds up page loading), and if global changes are desired, a simple change in the style sheet changes the elements throughout the website.

WHAT YOUR SHOULD LOOK FOR IN A WEBSITE DEVELOPER

Here are a few aspects to consider:

1. Does the developer (or the developer's company) have the expertise to do both the design and development work? It's often the case that individuals are very good at one aspect or another; typically individuals are not great at both aspects.

2. Look at the developer's website from an aesthetics standpoint. Does it look good? Did it encourage you to contact them? Did they appear to standout from other developers?

3. Look at the developer's website from a technical perspective. Does it appear that the pages load fast? Are there broken links or other technical problems?

4. Do they seem to understand the subject matter? Do they have any experience with law firms?

5. Do they build content management systems or develop on Joomla or another major CMS platform?

6. Do they understand the role of search engine optimization in helping law firms reach prospective clients?

BE A GOOD CLIENT – TAKE AN ACTIVE ROLE IN THE DEVELOPMENT PROCESS

We've probably all had the experience of working with difficult clients. The ones that are continually slow at producing documents, won't review materials you've prepared in a timely manner, and make clear that they have more important things to do than help you.

Of course this isn't an ideal working relationship. Please keep in mind that as you need input from your clients in order to be successful, your website developer will also need timely input and approval from you at various stages in order to do his or her job well.

Most developers are conscientious and take great pride in doing a good job satisfying their clients. They also try to be careful about scheduling assignments so that they can give full attention to projects. If you don't respond timely, workflow may be impacted.

Here's what you need to know –

1. Building a website can be compared to building a house. It's best to think everything through carefully before breaking ground, not when the house is almost completed. Take the time to understand the website at the outset.

2. Developers will want you to "sign off" at various times in the development process, such as when the artwork for the home page is finalized. If significant changes are to be made after approval, realize that extra time (and costs) will be involved – the same as if the client wanted changes to a contract after it's been finalized.

3. Provide timely input. The developer should give you a clear idea about when your input will be needed. Further, good developers tend to carefully schedule work (especially when complicated projects are involved) so that the needs of all clients can be timely met. If you're not able to provide input when needed, understand that the development process may be extended for a period longer than just the delay time if other projects are placed ahead of your website in the development queue.

CONTENT MANAGEMENT SYSTEMS – WHAT ARE THEY, AND WHY THEY SHOULD BE INCLUDED IN LAW FIRM WEBSITES

A CONTENT MANAGEMENT SYSTEM (CMS) IS A SYSTEM THAT PROVIDES A WAY FOR A WEBSITE OWNER TO EASILY ADD, CHANGE, OR MODIFY SIGNIFICANT WEBSITE CONTENT WITH LITTLE OR NO WEBSITE CODING KNOWLEDGE REQUIRED.

Here is a partial list of modifications that can be done with a content management system:

- Add new top-level navigation tabs
- Add sub-level navigation tabs
- Change or add new content (such as to the "About Our Firm" or Attorney Profile pages)
- Add slide-show navigation
- Add and index new articles (such as articles about practice areas, or articles authored by firm attorneys)
- Add firm news and announcements, such as new firm attorneys
- Change text and pictures on pages, including the home page

Best of all, it takes very little time to learn how to manage a CMS, and no html knowledge or developer help is required. Therefore, a CMS is highly desirable.

There are two methods of integrating a Content Management System with a website: have a developer build a custom CMS around the specific needs of the website or use a CMS platform already developed (such as Joomla). Before discussing these options, it's first necessary to discuss dynamic vs. static web pages.

DYNAMIC VS. STATIC WEB PAGES

THE DIFFERENCE BETWEEN DYNAMIC AND STATIC WEB PAGES

Dynamic pages are web pages that require interaction with a database in order to display page content. Websites built that use a content management system require dynamic pages, as content (such as articles) are stored in databases and then are pulled into the pages when the pages are created.

Similarly, web pages that display results from a user-initiated search also require dynamic pages. For instance, suppose you're interested in finding a house in Phoenix with 4 bedrooms, a pool, and costing between $200,000 and $500,000. If you visit a home search website and select these criteria for a search query, a web page will be produced displaying a list of all houses in the website's database meeting your search criteria. This web page does not separately exist; rather it's built based around scripting code (such as PHP) that interacts with the database (where all of the house information is stored). Once the user initiates the search, the database is searched and the results that match the search are returned and built into a new page.

Static pages, on the other hand, never change unless the website coding for the page is directly modified. A page that has text for the firm's address might be a static page. As long as the firm is at the current location, the address doesn't need to be changed.

DYNAMIC VS. STATIC WEB PAGES – WHY SHOULD I CARE?

If your website will use dynamic pages (which likely will be the case, especially if you have a CMS), a decision also needs to be made about choosing a scripting program and database. The most popular choices here are PHP and MySQL (both of which are Open Source and don't require a paid license) or ASP and SQL (which are developed by Microsoft, and, with respect to SQL, requires a server license). More about these in a moment; now back to our discussion on content management systems.

CUSTOM CONTENT MANAGEMENT SYSTEMS

Custom content management systems are just as the name implies – they are customized around the needs of the client and the website. Part of a custom CMS might allow the website owner to add new attorney profile pages. To add a new attorney profile to the firm's website, an administrator would login to the CMS administrative panel for firm attorney profiles, which might look something like this:

> CMS Admin Panel – Firm Attorney Profiles
>
> Click on a link below to add a new firm attorney profile or to modify the profile of an existing attorney.
>
> Add new attorney profile   Edit existing attorney profile

Assuming the "add new attorney profile" link is clicked, the following page might look like this:

Attorney First Name	[ ]
Attorney Last Name	[ ]
Practice Areas	[ ]
Law School	[ ]
Law School Graduation Year	[ ]
Honors	[ ]
Organizations	[ ]
About Attorney	[ ]
Upload Attorney Picture	[Browse to Select]
Articles/Publications	[ ]

[Submit Profile]

On this page, an administrator simply fills in the boxes with the information about the attorney, and then uploads the picture of the attorney to be included on the firm's website.

When the information has been added and the "Submit Profile" button has been clicked, the firm's website is automatically updated with the new attorney's profile information. A new web page is created, the attorney is added in the firm's list of attorneys web page (in the correct alphabetical place), the attorney is added as a member of the appropriate practice groups, and the attorney will appear if a search is conducted on the firm's website using the attorney's name.

As you can imagine, having a CMS can save an incredible amount of time and developer costs. Without a CMS, not only would expensive developer help be required (assuming no one at the firm knows website coding), but the developer would also need to create a new page for the attorney and create the appropriate links and modify other pages to make the changes.

Using a CMS, similar sections can also be developed for practice areas, articles, the home page, and much more. Articles, for instance, can be added and can be "staged" to go live on a certain date in the future, if desired.

The cost to build a custom CMS really depends upon the level of information to be added and the degree of customization involved. For very simple websites, it may cost from a few thousand dollars to significantly more, it just depends upon the complexity of the customization desired.

NON-CUSTOM CONTENT MANAGEMENT SYSTEMS – OPEN SOURCE LICENSED SOFTWARE AND CONTENT MANAGEMENT SYSTEMS VS. PROPRIETARY LICENSED SOFTWARE AND CONTENT MANAGEMENT SYSTEMS

In addition to having a custom content management system, there are pre-built content management systems that can be used, and the website in essence is built on the CMS platform. The CMS platform uses a database to store information, and the platform consists of coding to access the database to find and return information and also to create new pages.

> ***The next several paragraphs describe a myriad of content management systems, platforms, database types, and scripting codes that must be used to interact with and display information from databases. My recommendation is that unless you're planning on having a custom CMS built, consider having your website developed on Joomla. To find more about Joomla, skip to the Joomla subsection below.***

There are many options and configurations for content management systems, platforms, database types, and scripting interaction to work with databases. For the sake of brevity, the following explanation is a generalization concerning the foregoing; the exceptions are not going to be discussed as doing so would require significantly more space and would not add anything productive.

There are <u>proprietary</u> licensed software content management systems (which generally charge a license fee) and <u>Open Source</u> content management systems (which generally do not charge a fee). Each content management system must use scripting software to interact with databases and to display content; two of the most popular scripting languages used for websites are ASP.NET, a Microsoft product, and PHP, which is one of the most popular Open Source scripting languages.

Instead of being included in static html pages, websites using content management systems store content in databases. There are a number of different types of databases; the two most popular of which are SQL (a Microsoft product which requires a Microsoft SQL server license and payment), and MySQL (which is Open Source, and doesn't require a license fee in most instances).

ASP.NET works with Microsoft SQL databases on a Microsoft operating system platform, and PHP works with MySQL databases on a Linux-type of server platform. Content Management Systems using Microsoft ASP.NET/SQL systems are usually developed by a for-profit companies (and thus require a paid license for the CMS), while Open Source PHP/MySQL systems often use an Open Source CMS which is free, such as Joomla.

As a result, the most popular choices are: (1) an Open Source scripting and database (such as PHP and MySQL, respectively) and an Open Source CMS (such as Joomla), or (2) a Microsoft-based system (ASP.NET and SQL) and likely a paid-license CMS.

For law firm websites, in my opinion, Open Source is the much-preferred option for the following reasons:

1. Either an open-source or paid CMS will work perfectly fine, and both will have much of the same core functionality.

2. The Microsoft solution will require additional license fees, especially in the dedicated server hosting environment.

a. Using a dedicated server, the operating system (assuming Microsoft 2008 Web Edition) will likely cost around $15-$30 per month. The database (assuming Microsoft MS SQL 2008 Web Edition) will likely cost another $40-$60 per month. Thus over the course of a year a Microsoft-based system will likely run an extra $660-$1,080 in addition to the basic hosting plan.

b. In a shared hosting environment, these costs will be much lower; perhaps $15 or so per month (or $180/year), as the costs for the Microsoft licenses can be shared across the server with other hosted websites.

3. A paid CMS license must be obtained. The cost of the CMS license will vary depending upon which company's CMS is used.

4. There is a huge amount of developer work taking place on PHP. Some of the major software applications, such as WordPress (discussed in Chapter 17), run only on PHP. There is good reason for the tremendous amount of developer work on PHP; developers in general support Open Source projects.

5. Some of the most popular content management systems, such as Joomla and Drupal, run only on PHP/MySQL. Joomla, for instance, has over 3,500 extensions that have been developed that can be integrated into a Joomla CMS. This same amount of third-party development is not occurring with respect to non-Open Source content management systems.

PHP AND MYSQL VS. ASP AND SQL – WHAT ARE THEY, AND WHICH OPTION IS BETTER?

I'm guessing that right now many of you are wondering "Which option really is better? Wouldn't I be better off with Microsoft? Where's my coffee?" (wait – that's my question).

There a number of articles comparing MySQL and SQL, with strong preferences for one or the other in terms of which one is "better", with no clear consensus. It may be that in large corporate environments with heavy computing needs for financial, inventory management, and other intensive applications, SQL may have some advantages over MySQL. In general, if you ask five developers for their opinion, you're going to get at least six different answers (not really sure why this happens – that's just how developers are).

A Note about Open Source

Open Source generally refers to the design, development, and distribution of software in which the source code is made available for free. The major shift in open source arose out of a conference in 1998 involving Netscape and others prominent in the software industry, which ultimately resulted in certain open source standards being established, which include making source code available and free licensing and use of the open source software.[14]

It appears that these efforts began for various reasons, including (1) a belief that software platforms could be better developed in a collaborative atmosphere (with, in some cases, dozens or more developers contributing to advance the software), (2) updates and fixes could be rolled out quickly, and (3) a "hacker" – type mentality that better software and platforms could be developed than existing software and platforms that required licensing fees (such as Microsoft systems). Many developers have a strong interest in contributing to Open Source projects, as these same developers often are also creating applications that can be run on Open Source systems (thus they have a strong incentive to ensure that the underlying systems function well).

JOOMLA

With respect to Open Source content management systems based upon PHP and MySQL, two of the most popular content management systems are Joomla (www.joomla.org) and Drupal. Joomla appears to be the much more popular of the two systems and is my personal favorite, so the remaining sections will discuss Joomla.

The Benefits of Joomla Attorney Websites

Joomla is an award-winning content management system (CMS). A CMS is a software management system or platform that allows users to easily add new website pages, links, and content. A significant advantage of the Joomla CMS is that it requires almost no website coding knowledge to administer after a website has been built.

With a website built on the Joomla platform, attorneys can easily make changes to their law firm's website, such as adding or updating attorney profiles or practice area pages, announcing firm news, changing pictures, and adding articles about recent changes in the law. Changes made in the Joomla CMS are made instantaneously to the law firm's website – there is no need to wait for a developer to make coding changes. Additionally, because

---

[14] http://en.wikipedia.org/wiki/Open_source

developer help is usually not required, a law firm can realize significant cost savings by reducing or eliminating developer fees.

THE JOOMLA OPEN SOURCE PLATFORM FOR LAW FIRMS

Unlike non-CMS platforms that require extensive customized coding to interact with databases, Joomla database scripts have already been created as part of the CMS. Thus when new articles or pictures are added, Joomla automatically creates links to the new content once a user has selected where the content should be placed. Joomla's flexibility also allows users to modify navigation, easily add slideshows, and incorporate multi-media content (such as movie files).

Joomla is Open Source, meaning that it's available to anyone free of charge under a general Open Source license. Because it is free, it's become the world's most popular content management system, with almost 13 million downloads.[15] Because of this popularity, web developers world-wide have developed over 3,500 applications (called **extensions**) that can be easily incorporated into a Joomla CMS.[16] These include newsletter, blogging, contact management, website banner management, news feed management, and many other applications.

CREATING WEBSITES ON JOOMLA VS. HTML (NON-CMS/DATABASE WEBSITES)

Creating websites on Joomla is not much different than creating a website in html. In either case, both start with creating an image (usually done in Adobe Photoshop or a similar program) for the website design. When the design has been finalized, the next step is to create the coding layout for each of the pages and to create the navigation for the website (and link the pages of the pages). With Joomla, there are design templates for layout, with html or non-Joomla websites, a grid is created to hold content for each of the pages.

Finally, content must be added. In a non-CMS website, content is either added directly to the coding in each of the pages or, if a database is used, directly to the databases that are created by the website developer. With Joomla, content is also added to the databases, but the content is added through the Content Management System, which can usually be done by an administrator who does not need to have website coding knowledge. Once the website is built, Joomla-based extensions can also be easily added, if desired.

---

[15] http://www.joomla.org/announcements/general-news/5248-vote-for-joomla.html
[16] Ibid.

CHAPTER 11 – SEARCH ENGINE OPTIMIZATION

Search Engine Optimization (SEO) is the process of making changes and adjustments to websites and web pages for the purpose of securing higher search engine rankings for desired search terms. Ideally, if a prospective client seeking a law firm enters a term in a search engine (such as Google), a law firm will want its website listed at the top of the first page of the search results. Because users typically don't go past the first few pages of the search engine results, it's extremely important that a law firm's website be included high in the search results displayed in order for the firm to be seen and considered by prospective clients.

SEARCH ENGINES, SEARCH ENGINE COMPANIES, AND SEARCH ENGINE RANKINGS – WHY IT'S IMPORTANT TO BE ON THE FIRST PAGE OF THE SEARCH ENGINE RESULTS

Search engine companies, such as Google, develop proprietary algorithms to (1) classify Internet web page content and (2) return a list of web pages in response to the search queries of users.

To do so, search engines send out what are known as "bots" to "spider" the billions of web pages that make up the Internet. The goal of the bots is to determine what each web page is about based on factors such as the meta tags for the page, the "readable" page content, and the incoming links to the page. This information is then stored on the search engine's computers. When a user enters a search query, the search engine, using its proprietary algorithms, searches this stored information and returns a list of websites and web pages based on the user's specific query.

The order of the list of websites/web pages is also based on the proprietary algorithms of the search engine company. This list of websites and web pages is referred to as the "organic" search engine rankings. It's critical for companies competing for clients and business on the Internet to receive high rankings, as a recent Iprospect/Jupiter Research study found that about **68% of the time users won't go past the first page of the search results, and about 92% of the time they don't go past the first three pages**.[17]

---

[17] Iprospect/Jupiter Research Study, April, 2008, http://www.iprospect.com/about/researchstudy_2008_blendedsearchresults.htm.

Importantly, this study also found that the percentage of searches in which the user doesn't go past the first page is increasing, from 48% in 2002, to 60% in 2004, to 62% in 2006, and to 68% in 2008.[18]

The major search engine companies, such as Google, do not accept money for organic ranking placement, as doing so would compromise the integrity of the search results. The search engines do, however, accept money for the paid advertising placements that are displayed on the search results pages (which is referred to as search engine marketing – see Chapter 15). Google generally doesn't make money when a user clicks on one of the links in the organic search engine rankings, but it does make billions every year from clicks on the paid ads.

Ideally, law firms would like to have their firm's website listed at the top of the search engine rankings whenever potential clients seek the services offered by their firm. Unlike the yellow pages, where users may flip through a number of pages looking for a firm and might even start in on a random page in the attorney advertising section, user interaction is very different on search engines. First, as noted above, most users don't go past the first page, and very few go past the first three pages of the search results section. Second, while there may be thousands of search results pages in response to a user's search query, it's not possible with most search engines for users to start their search in the middle of the listings. As a result, companies (including law firms) seeking clients and sales on the Internet have a huge incentive to be on the first page of the search results, as those companies capture an overwhelming majority of the clicks (and business).

IT'S IMPORTANT TO BE #1 FOR THE SEARCH TERMS USED BY PROSPECTIVE CLIENTS

Search engines return results based on a specific user search query, and based on the proprietary algorithms of the search engine company. With respect to search engine rankings, it's important to understand several key points:

1. The **same** query conducted on different search engines will produce a different list of web pages. A search for "phoenix dui attorney" on Google will have different results than the same search performed on Bing.

---

[18] Ibid.

2. The specific **words and order of the words** used in the search query will produce different search results. A search for "phoenix dui attorney" will produce different results than a search for "dui lawyer in phoenix".

3. **It's very rare that the same web page will rank highly for two unrelated terms,** primarily because in order to achieve high rankings, a web page must be focused (or optimized) not only on one topic, but on only one or two key terms. For instance, it's unlikely that the same page of a law firm's website will rank highly for both "dui attorney" and "divorce lawyer".

4. **Law firm website pages should be optimized around terms that prospective clients actually use when searching for legal representation.** The terms used by prospective clients usually relate to their problems or legal needs. Prospective clients, therefore, are much more likely to use "phoenix dui lawyer" as a search term than "best lawyers in phoenix". As a result, it's important that a law firm's web pages be optimized around the terms actually used by prospective clients, instead of around some other nice (but seldom used) term of being the "best" or "top" law firm. Further, depending upon your clients, it might be more likely that a term such as "wills lawyer" will be used rather than "estate planning attorney".

WHAT WORDS DO PROSPECTIVE CLIENTS USE? USING WORDTRACKER

Wordtracker (www.wordtracker.com) gathers information from sources using metasearch technology based on searches performed on the top search engines, including Google, Bing, Yahoo!, and Ask.com. The search terms can then be entered in Wordtracker to get an approximation about how many times specific search terms are used. Wordtracker also provides tools that allow users to see how many other websites "compete" for selected search terms, and that help website owners find other useful search terms that may be optimized.

Wordtracker offer a free week trial; paid subscriptions are approximately $59/month or $329/year.

NOTE - In addition to Wordtracker, Google and other search engines have tools that can be used in connection with a search engine marketing (or pay-per-click marketing) program that provide information about the frequency of search terms used. These tools are part of the keyword creation process. See Chapter 15 for Search Engine Marketing, as well as the appendices to the book.

THE BASICS OF SEARCH ENGINE OPTIMIZATION (SEO)

The following sections present a very basic overview of search engine optimization. There are complicated search engine programs and techniques used by search engine companies that go beyond the scope of this book. Receiving high search engine rankings requires implementing the basic techniques discussed below, and other factors, such as receiving many quality contextual incoming links to a law firm's website. Because search engines generally favor websites that have been around longer than brand new websites, it also takes time to move up significantly in search engine rankings. Competition for search engine terms also plays a critical role; the more websites that compete for the same search terms, the more difficult it is to be ranked at the top.

With the foregoing in mind, and as noted previously, search engine optimization, or SEO, is the process of making changes and adjustments to websites and web pages for the purpose of securing higher search engine rankings for desired search terms. These changes include both "on-site" optimization (changes that a website owner can make to his or her website) and "off-site" optimization (changes made to other websites, such as links to the first website, over which the first website owner has little or no control). On-site optimization includes architecture changes, navigation changes, changes to meta tags, content changes, and more. Off-site optimization includes various strategies such as link building that will increase the relevancy of a firm's website for search engine purposes.

It's important to use the optimization opportunities available so that your firm's website scores well in the factors used for search engine rankings. Proper optimization leads to higher search engine rankings and more traffic to your firm's website from potential clients seeking the services offered by your firm.

> *Search engines don't consider factors like experience, the expertise of a law firm's attorneys, or any "best firm" or similar rankings. Instead, the search engine rankings process on Google and other major search engines is completely automated. As a result, the website of a newly-minted attorney can rank significantly higher than the website of a law firm with dozens of attorneys having decades of experience.*

> *While much is known about the <u>general factors</u> concerning high search engine optimization ranks, because search engines closely guard their search engine algorithms, the exact factors and weighting are not known.*

THE GENERAL FACTORS USED BY SEARCH ENGINES IN RANKINGS

The general areas of importance in search engine rankings are the Title, the Description, and (to a much lesser extent) the Keyword meta tags, the "readable" on-page content, and the incoming links to each page. Each of these areas is discussed below.

THE TITLE TAG

The title tag contains the name (or title) of a web page, and is displayed in the top of a browser window (for Internet Explorer, it's shown in the blue bar at the top of each web page). The title and other meta tags and other web page coding for a web page can be easily seen; if Microsoft Internet Explorer is being used, right click on the page, scroll down and left click on the "view source" link, and the result will be the coding for that page (including the coding for the meta tags). The title tag is the first indication to search engine bots as to the content of a web page.

TITLE TAG SIZE AND PLACEMENT OF KEY WORDS

Ideally, the title tag should be approximately 45 to 65 characters in length, and should not repeat any words more than twice. (In the early days of the Internet it was popular to use the same word repeatedly to get higher rankings. This practice now has the opposite effect, as the excessive use of the same words is considered spam and leads to lower rankings.)

Here are some ideas to keep in mind when creating title tags:

1. <u>Front-load the important words that prospective clients are likely to use when performing a search.</u> See the example on the next page.

2. <u>Use words that prospective clients are likely to use in searches.</u> Prospective clients may be more likely to use the word "wills" than "estate planning", and are much less likely to use words such as "litigator".

3. <u>Minimize the use of common, non-descriptive words, like "the", "and" etc.</u> While a few of these words will almost certainly be required, keep them to a minimum in order to best use your allocation of space to more important words.

4. <u>Be Specific in the Web Pages Optimized.</u> It's much better for search engine optimization purposes to have each practice area be on a separate web page and then optimize each page around the specific practice area than to put all of a firm's practice areas on the same page (in which it would be difficult to achieve high rankings for any one of the firm's practice areas). Even better, sub-specialties of practice areas (like "traffic accident lawyer" and "slip and fall lawyer") should be put on separate pages which can then be optimized for search engine purposes.

5. <u>Remember</u> - the Title Tag should be a summary of the content of the page to which it is associated. If you're creating a title for a page about car accident injury cases, the main text of the page shouldn't be around personal injury cases in general with only a small mention of car accident injury cases. Similarly, don't create a title with words that aren't actually shown in the visible page content (NOTE – words included in images *cannot* be read by bots; while they can read the alt tags (words in the coding used to describe the picture), alt tags are not as powerful as on-page content).

Now for an example. If your firm practices divorce law in Chicago, a good title (and good subject to build a web page around) might be "Chicago divorce lawyers". The title might look like this:

"Chicago divorce lawyers; lawyers in Chicago for divorce."

COMMON TITLE TAG MISTAKES – WHAT NOT TO DO

Now that you know more about how to create effective title tags, let's go over some common mistakes concerning title tags. These mistakes can be summarized as follows:

1. <u>Not including title tags, or not including any information in the title tags.</u> When title tags are not included or left empty, Internet Explorer shows the title as "Microsoft Internet Explorer" in the blue title bar.

2. <u>Using words that are meaningless for search engine optimization purposes.</u> For search engine purposes, the title should describe what the page is about. As a result, titles such as "Welcome to XYZ Law Firm's Website", or "XYZ firm is

located at 1234 Main Street" do not serve any purpose for search engine optimization (unless, in the latter case, this is part of a title for a web page concerning the firm's location).

3. <u>Using the same title for every page of a firm's website.</u> An example of this mistake is having the title of "XYZ Law Firm practices personal injury law in California" on every page of the firm's website. This will not be helpful for search engine optimization purposes.

4. <u>Using Title Tags that are not consistent with page content.</u> The job of search engine "bots" is to spider web pages and determine the content of the pages for indexing purposes. However, when the title tag is inconsistent with the content on the page, the result is confusion and low search engine rankings.

THE DESCRIPTION TAG

The description tag is the second meta tag read by search engine bots. An example of a description tag is the following:

<meta name="description" content="Chicago divorce lawyers. Our experienced Chicago divorce lawyers offer free consultations for clients seeking to end their marriage. Call us today and let us help you get what you deserve, and learn about the marriage dissolution process in Chicago from experienced divorce attorneys."/>

The Description tag consists of words in quotes following the word "content".

<u>The Description tag serves a dual purpose</u> – it provides information about page content, and it can be a form of advertising as the first part of it (about 130 characters) will be displayed in the search engine results (along with the web page url). Therefore, description tags should also be written as a call to action, with the goal of getting a prospective client to click on the link displayed in the search engine results and go to the firm's website.

The description tag should be up to 250 characters in length. The notes about front-loading key words, not excessively using keywords, and using search terms that prospective clients are likely to use also apply to preparing the description tag. The Description tag should also be consistent with the Title tag and the on-page Page Content.

Like Title tags, care should be used not to repeat key words more than two or three times, as shown in the above example.

On-Page or Visible Text

On-page or visible text refers to the text on web pages that can be read by search engine bots. Search engine bots cannot read text embodied in images, or text that is part of animated video. (Note – search engines can read "alt tags", which are descriptions developers can add to web code to describe an image, and which can be read out loud to those who are sight impaired. However, because it's up to the developer to provide a proper image description – not intentionally referring to a picture of a tree as being an apple, for instance, and because the alt tag (like the keyword tag) became the subject of stuffing, it appears that the alt tag has little, if any, current relevance for SEO purposes. Nonetheless, the alt tag should still be used for ADA purposes.)

The same "spam" rules that apply to header and description tags also apply to on-page content. In the early days of the Internet, in addition to "keyword stuffing" in the meta tags, website owners would also repeat the same word on a web page hundreds of times, which led to high search engine rankings. Again, there is a variety of opinions in the search engine world about the density of key words included in the on-page content; my personal recommendation would be about 3-5%.

There are no rules about how much text can be on a web page. The general consensus is that there should be at least 250-400 words of on-page text, but there is not any consensus about what might constitute "too much" content. I would suspect that at some point having too much content would prove negative in search engine rankings, but this point is probably well beyond what any of us would otherwise want to put on a page.

KEYWORDS – HOW LONG WILL THEY LAST?

The keyword tag allows website owners to include a list of keywords that describe or relate to web page content. Originally keyword tags were designed to aid search engines in determining page content.

Like other meta tags, keywords soon became abused with keyword stuffing and spam (using the same or similar words repeatedly) in order to gain higher search engine rankings. In part because keywords do not have to appear in a page's visible content, Google has stopped giving any SEO value to keywords, and it's unclear whether other search engine companies will follow the lead of Google. Currently some of the search engines still give SEO value to keywords; therefore, it's a good idea to continue to include keywords in website code.

Keywords for the Chicago divorce attorney example might consist of: Chicago divorce attorney, Chicago divorce lawyer, divorce law firm, marriage attorney, divorce lawyer in Chicago, etc.

HIGH SEARCH ENGINE RANKINGS PART 1 – WEB PAGE CONSISTENCY

In order to receive high rankings the web page must have internal consistency among the title, description, and keyword tags and the on-page content. In other words, if a firm desires high search engine rankings for the term "Chicago divorce lawyer", these words should appear in the title, description, and keyword tags, the headline(s) in the main body of the page, and in the on-page content under the headlines. The terms should not be over-used or under-used in any of these places; otherwise search engine rankings will be lower.

Further, as mentioned above, it's not feasible to optimize a page for more than a couple of search terms at most. While the on-page content available may be virtually unlimited, the room in the title tags and description are not; and when a decision is made to "front-load" a specific term, there is no longer the availability to "front-load" a second term.

We'll call the main term the primary search term, in the example above the primary term would be "Chicago divorce lawyer". With this search term a possibility is to also optimize the same page for the term "divorce firm in Chicago". This will be referred to as secondary optimization. A few notes about secondary optimization:

Secondary optimization should be thought of as just that – the optimization of the secondary term will likely not achieve as high of rankings as the primary term.

If the "secondary" term is deemed to be an important term for search engine optimization purposes (such that it is likely to be used frequently by prospective clients), consideration should be given to creating a new page that would be optimized for this term.

While the secondary optimization term should be related to the primary optimization term, care should be given not to over-use words that may be part of both the primary and secondary optimization terms (such as the term "divorce" in the above example).

HIGH SEARCH ENGINE RANKINGS PART 2 – LINK POWER

Incoming Links

If another website provides a link to your firm's website, such link (from the perspective of your website) is referred to as an "incoming link". Your website then can be thought of as the "linked site". Incoming links are a crucial part of search engine rankings, as they are seen as confirmation of the validity of content on the linked site.

In the early days of the Internet, the more links to a site, the higher the search engine rankings would be for the linked site (and more specifically, for the main terms used on the linked site). As a result, website owners quickly developed strategies around link building, while Google and other search engines figured out ways to tweak their search engine algorithms to undo much of these efforts.

The initial strategies consisted of reciprocal linking strategies ("you link to my site, and I'll link to your site"), followed by what are known as "link farms". Link farms are not places where farmers grow links; rather they are an advanced form of reciprocal link building whereby one website owner would agree to place links of all the other websites from the link farm on his or her website, and such other websites would also agree to place links of such owner on their websites.

Search engines subsequently modified their algorithms so that both reciprocal linking and link farms have no search engine value. There has been speculation that participating in a link farm will actually have negative search engine value, as search engines may try to penalize owners for engaging in what the search engines believe to be unethical search engine optimization.

Anchor Text

Not all links are created equal. **In general, a link from a high-traffic, "authoritative", contextually-related website will have much more value for SEO purposes than a link from a low-traffic, less-important, non subject-related website**. For instance, a link in a front page article on the website of popular law journal to your law firm's website will have much more weight than a link from the website of your local hardware store.

> ⚡ *For SEO purposes it's the <u>link power</u> that matters the most, not the number of links.*

The text included in the link itself (called **anchor text**) also influences search engine rankings. For instance, a link in an article stating "for a list of top-notch <u>Chicago divorce attorneys</u> ...", would have more weight than "<u>click here</u> for a list of top-notch divorce attorneys in Chicago" for the term "Chicago divorce attorneys". The reasoning that is that the website owner in the first case is telling readers that the website being linked to is an authoritative website on top divorce lawyers in Chicago. In the second case, the search engines can determine that the website being linked to probably has something to do with divorce attorneys in Chicago, but it's not entirely clear.

LINK POWER AND OPRAH

Perhaps no one in the United States has more influence than Oprah Winfrey. Oprah can instantly make a product an overnight sensation by including it on her "favorites" list, or make an unknown book a best-seller by recommending it as a "must-read" to her audience. (Side note to Oprah – You're the best! Any chance of mentioning this book on your show?)

Oprah's influence didn't come by accident – people gave it to her, by watching her show, by reading books that she recommends, and by buying her favorite things. In addition to making books and company products popular, she's also made a number of people popular, such as Dr. Phil and Dr. Oz. These people in turn now wield influence, and have the ability to make products and other people popular, although to a lesser extent than Oprah.

Link power for SEO purposes is similar to real world influence power. A website over time may have built up tremendous "Oprah-like" influence by virtue that (1) it receives high traffic, and (2) many other "authoritative" websites link to it. As a website builds up more influence, the websites to which it links (or secondary websites) also benefit from the increased influence and become more "authoritative", similar to the people and products promoted by Oprah. These secondary websites in turn receive higher search engine rankings and more traffic, which in turn makes them more influential and authoritative for SEO purposes.

The second aspect of link power concerns subject matter influence. Websites, like people, are considered to have a certain amount of authority with respect to a specific subject matter. As a result, a link from a top legal website to a law firm's website about a specific area (such as personal injury law) will be much more beneficial to the law firm for SEO purposes than a link from a top home repair company website, even though both websites may be deemed to be equally authoritative. Thus to increase a law firm's search engine rankings for the services it provides, the law firm would want to (1) create search engine optimized pages around the services that it provides, and (2) have incoming links from sites that would be considered both authoritative and contextually related by the search engines with respect to such services.

It should be noted that the search engines generally rank web pages and not websites as a whole. Thus often an incoming link is to a web page other than the home page, in which case it is the specific page that is linked that receives the high rankings (as opposed to the website as a whole). Ideally a law firm would want other authoritative websites on divorce matters linking to its web pages about divorce, and authoritative websites on estate planning linking to the firm's estate planning pages.

By the way, Oprah's website is www.Oprah.com. Please let me know if you're able to get a link from her website.

WHAT DO SEARCH ENGINES VALUE?

No, it's not honesty, trust, or long romantic walks on the beach.

For any search term, search engines want to return a rank-ordered list of the "best" websites matching the search query. What constitutes "best" has changed over time as search engines have changed (and continue to change) their algorithms. Thus a website that is considered today to be the "best" for a particular search term may be several pages back in the search results tomorrow if the algorithms are changed.

In the early days of the Internet, much of the content on the Internet concerned scholastic papers and research. Determining the authority for a particular web page (which often consisted of part of an article spread over several pages), search engines usually looked at the amount of content, the meta tags (especially title), and the links to the article, mostly from a scholarly viewpoint in determining what was "best". Also, there often was a high correlation between the amount of text in a particular article and how highly the article was ranked for the subject matter.

Now, it appears that the "best" website for SEO purposes is not the one that is the most authoritative from a scholarly standpoint, but rather from a popularity perspective. For instance if the term "travel" is entered in Google, the top websites listed have nothing to do with scholarly work on travel or the travel industry, but instead are made up of the top websites used for making travel reservations.

DESIGNING A WEBSITE FOR HIGH SEARCH ENGINE OPTIMIZATION – GETTING IT RIGHT FROM THE BEGINNING

Often, after having a website built, a law firm discovers the importance of search engine optimization, and wishes to have its website "optimized" for search engine purposes. While this can be done, it is much easier and less costly to prepare a search engine optimized website during the development process than after-the-fact.

Therefore, as part of the website design process, a firm should identify key search terms for which high search engine rankings are desired, and a comprehensive competitive marketing analysis should be undertaken to see what other firms are achieving high rankings for those search terms. Often, the websites receiving high rankings for terms tend to have significant content on the search terms, and also many incoming links from other influential and contextually relevant websites.

Once a competitive analysis is done, it is possible to prepare a plan around how to optimize a website around key search terms. Such reports, and the search engine optimization companies that prepare these reports, are the subject of the next chapter.

CHAPTER BONUS – GOOGLE BOMBS

A *Google bomb* (or "link bomb") is Internet slang for a certain kind of attempt to raise the ranking of a given web page in the Google search results, often with humorous or political intentions.[19] One of the first major uses of a Google bomb was to link the phrase "miserable failure" to the official White House website and page of President George W. Bush, so that if a user searched on Google for the term "miserable failure", a link to the White House website would be appear at the top of the search rankings.

Google has since implemented algorithms designed to stop this practice.

---

[19] http://en.wikipedia.org/wiki/Google_bomb

CHAPTER 12 - SEARCH ENGINE OPTIMIZATION COMPANIES AND SEARCH ENGINE OPTIMIZATION PLANS

There are many search engine optimization companies, most of which use professional standards and techniques, and others that use "black hat" techniques that may result in a website being banned from search engines such as Google. This chapter discusses specific aspects to consider when hiring a search engine optimization company, and also the elements of an effective Search Engine Optimization Plan.

There's a huge SEO industry on the Internet. The industry ranges from very professional companies good at conducting competitive analysis reports and developing specific plans about how to improve the search engine rankings of websites to those who won't tell you (and may not know themselves) what they are doing. There are also a very few who engage in what are referred to as "black-hat" techniques, which consist of intentionally deceptive techniques that can result in high search engine rankings initially, but can also result in a website being banned from search engine consideration when these techniques are uncovered by the search engine companies (such as Google).

THE GOALS OF SEARCH ENGINE OPTIMIZATION

Search engine optimization companies have become somewhat maligned over the past few years, often by website owners who have not bothered to optimize their own websites (and who may be disappointed with the rankings of their website). These website owners often don't understand search engine optimization or believe that it shouldn't be necessary (Google should just rank their website highly for some unspecified reason).

The goal of search engine optimization companies <u>is not</u> to engage in forms of trickery that will bring immediate first page rankings for website owners. Instead, it's to engage in a very careful and detailed analysis of a firm's business and clients and the firm's competition, and to provide useful recommendations as to changes that can be made to a firm's website to achieve higher rankings. Often such recommendations will be in the nature of adding more content (and pages) to a firm's website, and to significantly change content and meta tags on existing pages of the website.

This goal of search engine optimization is not inconsistent with the goals of search engines – to find and index website content for the purpose of displaying search results to users seeking specific content. Thus if the content and meta tags of a web page can be revised to make it more clear to the search engines that the web page is about a specific term, both the firm and search engine users stand to benefit from the changes.

If you're considering using a search engine company, here are some questions to ask:

1. <u>Does the company understand law firm business and clients?</u> In order to effectively reach prospective clients, an SEO company has to understand what prospective clients are seeking when they search the Internet. If they don't understand the practice of law and the legal needs of your clients, they can't do an effective job.

2. <u>Will the company share with you exactly what they are doing and how it will help the search engine rankings of your law firm's website?</u> Many search engine companies have ongoing campaigns and charge a significant amount for their services. Is it worth it? It depends on exactly what they are doing. If they won't tell you what they are doing or why they are doing it, go to another company.

3. <u>Does the company have a success story that they can share with you?</u>

4. <u>Does the company promise #1 search engine rankings?</u> Companies that guarantee number 1 rankings usually should be avoided. Even Google cautions against using such companies (see http://www.google.com/support/webmasters/bin/answer.py?answer=35291). Google's basis is that because search engines are automated, companies cannot (and should not) guarantee #1 results.

5. <u>Does the company guaranty quick results?</u> While it may be possible to move quickly from #300 to #100 in the search results, it typically takes a number of months to move to one of the first three pages, and even longer to move to the first page. The actual time to see significant increases in search engine rankings will vary greatly depending upon the competition for key search terms. In instances where there is significant competition, it may take many months to a year or more to see significant improvements.

6. <u>Does the company claim that Google, Bing or Yahoo! give their clients favorable treatment?</u> If they do, they should be avoided. None of these search engines give favorable treatment to any search engine optimization company.

7. <u>Do they claim to get your firm listed in thousands of search engines?</u> There aren't thousands of searches engines in the United States – there are only a few dozen at most. The "thousands" of search engines include websites like CNN.com whose searches are powered by Google, as well as other website owners that have included Google search boxes.

THE ELEMENTS OF AN EFFECTIVE SEARCH ENGINE OPTIMIZATION PLAN

While search engine companies may vary in terms of exactly what they will do for clients, the following are elements that should be included in a professional search engine optimization plan.

A BASELINE ANALYSIS REPORT

The goal of a baseline analysis report is to determine where a law firm's website ranks on Google, Bing, and Yahoo! vis-à-vis other law firm competitors. As a necessary step, the SEO expert should consult with the firm to understand (1) what legal services the firm provides, (2) what search terms are likely to be used by prospective clients, and (3) the geographic area in which the firm competes. Based on this understanding, the search engine company identifies with the firm a list of search terms that prospective clients might use to search for the firm's services. Software like Wordtracker can also be used to identify search term opportunities.

Based on the search term list, the SEO company can find out where the firm's website ranks across the major search engines (Google, Bing, and Yahoo!) for each of these search terms. Usually search engine companies use software that run these searches very quickly. The software generates a list of the top ten websites on each of the search engines for each of the key words, as well as showing where the firm ranks.

Additionally, the Baseline Report should include the title, description, and keyword meta tags, the on-page content, and the incoming links for the top ten websites for each key word across each of the major search engines.

RECOMMENDATIONS REPORT

Based upon the Baseline Report, the SEO company can prepare a Recommendations Report, which will provide recommendations to the firm client as to what changes should be done to secure higher search engine rankings. The Recommendations Report can be quite detailed, and often consists of recommendations in terms of (i) revising existing content and page meta tags to make them more search engine friendly, (ii) providing much more content in certain areas to secure higher rankings, and (iii) seeking incoming links and other strategies to get more websites to link to the law firm's website.

SEARCH ENGINE OPTIMIZATION PLAN

The SEO company should go through the Recommendations Report in detail with the law firm, and a concrete plan for improving search engine rankings can then be prepared. The Search Optimization Plan should be detailed in terms of what will be done by when, so that the law firm clearly understands the scope of work to be undertaken by the search engine optimization company.

MEASUREMENT REPORTS

Once the SEO Plan is being implemented, the SEO company should provide the law firm with reports (usually on a monthly basis) that detail (i) what has been undertaken by the SEO company during the preceding month, (ii) where the law firm ranks on each of the major search engines with respect to each of the keywords, and (iii) further recommendations on improving search engine rankings.

SEARCH ENGINE OPTIMIZATION TIMETABLE FOR IMPROVEMENTS

As noted above, effective search engine optimization usually takes a number of months. The first part of the search engine optimization process may take a month or so with respect to developing the baseline and recommendations reports, and designing the changes that are to be made to the website itself.

Even after these changes are implemented, Google will not immediately give a website high rankings with respect to the search terms that are optimized. Instead, Google's algorithms seem to incorporate a "real world" scenario where new content is added to a website, and then time passes between the addition of the new content and other websites finding out about and linking to the new content (as opposed to a website receiving many links to new content immediately after the new content is added). Thus firms that optimize their websites should not expect immediate, over-night results. And, as previously noted, the actual rankings will be dependent upon many other factors, including competition in the form of other websites (and firms) for similar search terms.

SEARCH ENGINE ETHICS

Most reputable search engine optimization companies have adopted a code of ethics, which usually encompasses many of the items discussed above (particularly, no promises as to #1 rankings, and a commitment not to engage in black hat techniques). It's important that the SEO company not engage in any black hat techniques, as doing so can have a particularly painful consequence – the firm's website could be removed from being indexed by one or more of the search engines. If a website is removed, it will no longer appear in the search engine rankings in response to a search query from a user.

The next part of the book discusses how to increase the presence of your website on the Internet.

PART V – INTERNET MARKETING AND NETWORKING

All law firms should consider Internet marketing, as it can be one of the most powerful and cost-effective forms of marketing. The following chapters discuss ways that law firms can increase their Internet presence for the purpose of seeking new clients.

CHAPTER 13 - LAUNCHING YOUR WEBSITE – NOW THAT YOUR SITE IS LIVE, WHAT SHOULD BE DONE NEXT?

After your website is live, submit your website's url to the major search engines – Google, Bing, Ask.com, and Yahoo! – so that these search engines will begin crawling your website and indexing page content. There are also a number of free directories that can be used to help search engine rankings. If you have a blog, start writing and contacting other blog owners.

Now that your website is live, you'll want to submit your website address to the major search engines so that their bots will begin to spider your website and index the content of your pages. Page indexing is necessary so that when a prospective client searches Google and the other major search engines for the services offered by your firm, your website can be found.

IS KEVIN FEDERLINE A SEARCH ENGINE GURU, AND IF SO, WHY DID BRITNEY LEAVE HIM?

Kevin Federline, the sometime rapper and former husband of Britney Spears, has a search engine website - http://searchwithkevin.swagbucks.com/. Should we believe that Kevin's tough guy/rapper persona was merely a cover-up for his underlying nerdiness as a search engine code-developing intellectual? Will "Search with Kevin" soon topple Google as the place where the majority of searches will be conducted?

Sadly, the answer to all of these questions is no. Although he has a search engine website, Kevin really isn't a search guru. Instead, all of the searches on his site are powered by Google/Ask.com. According to an Experian® Hitwise® survey, as of October 3, 2009, Google accounts for about 71% of all U.S. searches, with Yahoo! Search, Bing and Ask.com accounting for approximately 16%, 9%, and 2.5% percent, respectively. The remaining 52 search engines in the Hitwise Search Engine Analysis Tool accounted for 1.04 percent of U.S. searches.[20]

What you should know is that there are many companies who claim that they will submit your website to "thousands" of search engines, usually only for $50 or so. In reality, there

---

[20] Experian[sm] Hitwise, *Google Receives 71 Percent of Searches in September 2009, October 6, 2009*, http://www.hitwise.com/us/press-center/press-releases/google-searches-sept-09/

are only a few dozen "search engines" at the most for US-based searches, after Google, Bing, Yahoo!, and Ask.com searches are excluded, all of the remaining search engines combined account for a very small percentage of the searches conducted in the US).[21]

In addition to the major search engines, there are other search engines that require the submission of a fair amount of contact information about your firm, people, etc., and require valid e-mail addresses as part of the submission process (which later can be used for e-mail marketing purposes). Because these search engines combined account for only a very small percentage of all US searches, and because the particular users tend not to be representative of the general population (typically skewed more toward the tech-savvy crowd), my suggestion is to not spend the time submitting your website's url to these search engines. Eventually, through other website links, even these search engines will find your website, and you won't have had to spend the time or provide contact information or receive spam as part of the process.

> *There is a belief held by some in the search engine industry that it's better to have search engines such as Google "discover" your website through a link, rather than go through the submission process. I don't believe that it matters one way or another, and therefore always do a site submission as a soon as a website is live, or immediately after a significant website re-development.*

HOW TO GET YOUR SITE INDEXED BY THE SEARCH ENGINES – THE SITE SUBMISSION PROCESS

Once your website is live, you'll next want to submit your site to the major search engines so that your web pages can be indexed (so that your website can appear in the search engine results). Fortunately, the major search engines make the process fairly simple.

GOOGLE SITE SUBMISSION

Go to http://www.google.com/addurl/. On this page, type in your website's domain name, the letters shown in the scrambled letter box and click the submit button. It takes about ten seconds to complete.

---

[21] Ibid.

Google usually indexes new websites quickly after url submission, typically within a few days. It may be much longer than that before your website begins to be displayed in the search engine results pages as a result of what is known as the Google Sandbox, which is discussed below.

YAHOO! SITE SUBMISSION

Before submitting your website URL to Yahoo! for indexing, you must first have a Yahoo! ID (If you do not already have a Yahoo! ID visit https://edit.yahoo.com/registration?.src=fp&.intl=us&.done=http://m.www.yahoo.com/.) To submit your URL for indexing on Yahoo! go to http://search.yahoo.com/info/submit.html and click "**Submit Your Site for Free**". On the next page click "**Submit a Website or Webpage**" and enter your URL and click "**Submit URL**".

ASK.COM SITE SUBMISSION

To submit your website for indexing on Ask.com you must have a prepared site map added to your website for the search bots to crawl. The site map needs to be added with the "auto-discovery directive to robots.txt". For more information on how to correctly add your site map visit http://about.ask.com/en/docs/about/webmasters.shtml.

BING SITE SUBMISSION

Submitting your website URL to Bing.com is easy. First go to http://www.bing.com/docs/submit.aspx. Here you will be asked to type in the characters you see on the page and submit your URL; once added click "**Submit URL**".

WHAT IS THE GOOGLE SANDBOX, AND HOW DO I GET OUT?

The Google sandbox refers to the time delay between when Google first indexes a website and the time that the website begins to be shown in the organic search engine results. While not directly confirmed by Google, there appears to be solid evidence that Google imposes a "penalty" on new websites in the rankings process that typically lasts about 6 months (but can vary from less than a month to more than eight months). During this time, a website will receive lower rankings than it otherwise should receive solely by virtue of it being a new website. The only way to quickly exit the Google sandbox appears to be by receiving incoming links, especially incoming links from other influential websites.[22]

---

[22] Webconfs.com, http://www.webconfs.com/google-sandbox-article-11.PHP

IMPROVING YOUR WEBSITE RANKINGS – WHERE TO LIST YOUR WEBSITE.

The following are some additional places to submit your website for free.

GOOGLE MAPS

Google Maps provides free listings to law firms and other business owners. Listings often appear on the first page of the search results when a user types in a search term looking for a law firm in your area. Google Maps listings include the name of your law firm, url to your website, and phone number. Your firm is also highlighted on a map showing its location.

To add a listing for your firm to Google Maps, go to the Google Local Business Center at http://www.google.com/localbusinesscenter and sign in using your Google Account information. (To get a free Google Account please visit https://www.google.com/accounts/Login.) The Google Local Business Center provides local businesses with free listings, the ability to include coupons or special offers on your listing for free, free updates to your listing, and account information letting you see where your clients are coming from and the search terms they used to find your listing.

YAHOO! LOCAL

Advertise your law firm on local search results with Yahoo! Local. Yahoo! Local is similar to Google Maps in that it displays a map with local area law firms when a user submits a search for a law firm in their area. Yahoo! Local listings include name of the law firm, phone number, address, and website url. To sign up for Yahoo! Local, visit http://listings.local.yahoo.com/csubmit/index.PHP, and complete the information about your law firm for the free local business listing.

CITY SEARCH

City Search provides local information for websites such as Hotels.com, Expedia, Hotwire, and MSN. To sign up for a free Citysearch account, go to www.citysearch.com and click on the "**Sign Up**" link in the upper right hand corner.

A Sign In/Sign Up page will pop-up where a new Citysearch account can be created. Fill in the information on the right side of the page (email, name, member name, acceptance of terms) and click "**SIGN UP**".

A pop-up will appear telling you that an email has been sent to your account providing instructions on how to confirm your account. Click the **link** in the e-mail.

On the next page you will create a Password and click "**SUBMIT**".

The next page you will be taken to is your profile page. Here you can upload a photo and edit your profile information, see reviews you have posted, and view any lists or items you have saved while visiting the site.

YELP

Yelp (www.Yelp.com) is a website designed around local user recommendations. Yelp is not only a good place for law firms to list their business, but also for satisfied clients to add a recommendation (see Chapter 18 for more information on Yelp client recommendations).

To add your firm to the Yelp listings, visit http://www.yelp.com/business and view the video tutorial about adding your firm to the listings. To get started with your business listing, click on the red "Get Started" button and follow the prompts. You'll first be asked to enter your business information to see if your firm is already in the Yelp database; if it isn't, you'll need to complete a very short profile and click a confirmation link that will be sent to your e-mail. Then, after your submission is approved, you'll be sent instructions on how to "claim" your business listing.

LOCAL.COM

Law firms can add a free business listing to Local.com at http://advertise.local.com/. The sign-up process is similar to that of Yelp.com such that you'll be asked to first enter your business to see if it's already in the database, and then create a listing if it's not.

After finalizing your business listing, you'll be asked whether you want to upgrade your listing for an approximate $50/month. (see http://advertise.local.com/business/UpSell.aspx#livechat for a list of the features included with a paid listing.)

CHAPTER 14 - LAW FIRM MARKETING METRICS – HOW SHOULD OUR MARKETING SPEND BE ALLOCATED?

Like other businesses, law firms have a limited amount of money that can be spent on marketing. To maximize the effectiveness of a firm's marketing budget, it's necessary to concentrate spending in the areas that offer the biggest bang for the buck. There are simple ways to measure campaign effectiveness with both Internet and offline marketing campaigns. By measuring the actual effectiveness of different forms of media, it's possible to focus more advertising spend on the campaigns that are successful and to minimize or eliminate spend in areas that are not as successful.

HOW DO OUR CLIENTS FIND US?

Retailer John Wanamaker once famously said "I know that half of my advertising money is wasted, I just don't know which half." Fortunately, there are more tools (and advertising opportunities) available today than there were a century ago when Mr. Wanamaker was making millions in department stores.

Regardless of whether a specific marketing/advertising budget exists, all law firms are limited in the amount of funds that can be spent to generate new clients. This chapter discusses many of the new marketing and advertising Internet opportunities available, and provides information about how to measure both online and offline advertising campaigns. First, the client acquisition cost is discussed.

CALCULATING AND UNDERSTANDING YOUR CLIENT ACQUISITION COST AND AVERAGE CLIENT VALUE

On average, how much does it cost your firm to acquire a new client? While this seems like a simple question, few firms have any idea of the answer.

Your law firm's client acquisition cost ("CAC") may be determined by calculating your firm's total marketing spend over a particular time period (such as a year) divided by the number of new clients brought in during that period. Ideally, the marketing spend should include almost every type of "hard" or "soft" marketing and advertising expense – your firm's website, business cards, client development lunches, phone book ads, the value of business development time spent with potential new clients, and little league team sponsorship. Don't, however, include new clients resulting from the referral of current clients. Let's assume your total marketing spend for last year was $50,000, and your firm had 50 new clients. Your CAC would be $1,000.

Now that your CAC is known, how does this number compare to the <u>value</u> of a new client? In other words, if all firm revenue less all firm expenses (except partner draws) are divided by the number of clients served over the course of a year, how much income is generated by the average client?

Let's assume that a small firm realized $750,000 in revenue over the course of a year, and serviced 50 clients. Rent, secretarial, paralegal, marketing, and other costs amounted to $250,000. The firm would have net income of $500,000 to be split among the partners, and the average client value ("ACV") would be $10,000 ($500,000/50 clients). Thus in this example, it costs $1,000 in advertising (between hard and soft costs) to gain a new client, and each new client contributes $5,000 to overhead costs ($250,000/50), and $10,000 for the firm's partners.

Assuming that the firm's partners are working at capacity and don't wish to hire additional attorneys, and that other firm costs are fixed, the firm wishes to see if it can better allocate marketing spend to reduce its CAC. In order to do so, it must take a comprehensive look at its marketing program so that marketing and advertising costs can be reduced.

THE COMPONENTS OF AN EFFECTIVE MARKETING PROGRAM

Implementing an effective marketing program requires: (1) determining the marketing opportunities available to reach prospective clients, (2) selecting several marketing opportunities to use and implementing marketing campaigns, (3) measuring the results of each opportunity, and (4) re-allocating marketing spend to the lowest-cost and most effective marketing opportunities.

Most law firms engage in only item (2) above – choosing where to spend marketing dollars. Fortunately, with the Internet and other technology advances, there are more opportunities than ever for firms to advertise, and also to measure the effectiveness of advertising spend. The next sections discuss each of the four marketing components above; first, however, a short discussion covering some of the fallacies concerning marketing effectiveness is presented.

WHERE DO PROSPECTIVE CLIENTS LOOK FOR YOU FIRM'S SERVICES?

The question "Where do prospective clients look for your firm's services?" is not the same as the question as "Where do your clients find out about your firm?" Prospective clients for your firm may be searching Google for legal services; however if your firm's website isn't listed near the top of the search results, they likely won't find your firm's website from a Google search.

There's a common perception among attorneys and law firms – we don't need to worry about Internet marketing because we get all of our clients from [phone book, billboard, TV, etc.] advertising. When asked about how much Internet marketing the firm does, the typical response is "we have a website, so anyone can find us."

Two issues that may arise in this scenario are (1) the firm may not realize when prospective clients are using other forms of advertising, and (2) the perception that having a website constitutes Internet marketing.

IS OUR PRIMARY FORM OF ADVERTISING THE BEST FORM OF ADVERTISING?

Let's first consider where a law firm advertises by assuming that a firm does 100% of its advertising in phone books. It's likely, therefore, that most of its clients (let's assume 100%) result from phone book advertising. The firm might conclude that phone book advertising is tremendously important. But what happens when prospective clients turn to other sources (such as the Internet) to find an attorney?

If the firm continues using phone book advertising as its sole advertising venue, it likely won't realize the shift among prospective clients to the use of other sources to find an attorney. Instead, the high percentage of "phone book" clients for the firm will remain the same this year as in previous years (100% of new clients will still come from phone book advertising); but the number of new clients will decrease, as potential clients previously using phone books now use the Internet or other sources to find and hire attorneys.

The firm may mistakenly believe that the downturn in the number of new clients is a result of a bad economy, more competition, or other factors. It may also conclude that Internet marketing is not all that effective, because its website is not leading to new clients, without realizing that its website is not really an effective marketing tool because of low search engine rankings.

IS OUR FIRM'S WEBSITE A FORM OF INTERNET MARKETING?

If a firm has a website, it may mistakenly conclude that it is engaging in Internet marketing. *__If a firm's website is not listed in the first couple of search results pages for search terms relative to the legal services being provided by the firm, it is not engaged in Internet marketing, it only has an Internet presence.__* Recall the study mentioned in the previous chapter that found that about 68% of the time users searching on Google and other search engines don't go past the first page of the search results, and 92% of the time users don't go past the first three pages. If the firm's website is not being listed on the first couple of pages of the search results for the search terms used by prospective clients, the firm's website isn't an effective tool for reaching prospective clients that don't already know about the firm.

THE TIMES; THEY ARE A-CHANGING

The lesson for law firms should be that the world has changed dramatically as the result of technology and the Internet, and that our marketing efforts must also change in response.

To illustrate this concept, one of my first Internet companies – www.RVListingsOnline.com – sells RV listings to both dealers and individuals wishing to sell their RV's. For those not familiar with RVing, upper end RV's are expensive, with many now selling for over $500,000, and some even selling for more than $1 million. RV buyers are thus willing to search throughout the country to find the right RV, and dealers can earn a tremendous profit on an RV sale (at least in a good economy).

One day, one of our company's representatives approached an RV dealer in the St. Louis area to see whether he would like to have his RV inventory shown on our website. The price quoted was reasonable – only a few hundred dollars to feature his entire RV inventory for an entire year. If he sold just one RV over the course of the year he would more than recoup his cost.

While the owner's wife immediately was in favor of our listing service, the owner was not pleased. In fact he was very angry at the Internet, and how it had hurt his business. Specifically, he was mad that people from St. Louis were driving all the way to Ohio to buy RV's, and once back in St. Louis, the buyers expected him to fix their RV's whenever something went wrong. His RV sales, where he used to make most of his money, were almost non-existent. He couldn't understand why more sales weren't being generated, as he had continued to advertise in the local paper just as he had been doing for the past twenty-plus years. All he knew was that the locals were driving a long way to buy an RV from someone else. Presumably the percentage of his RV sales resulting from newspaper still remained high; he just wasn't selling many RV's anymore.

Of course a logical response to this dealer might have been that if he had done the same thing these other RV dealers were doing – understand that RV sales had become increasingly national in scope, and use the Internet to market his inventory – buyers from Ohio might drive to his store in St. Louis to buy RV's. Instead, this owner chose to be mad at the Internet, and not to have his inventory listed with us or any other similar companies.

THE TYPES OF MARKETING OPPORTUNITIES AVAILABLE TO LAW FIRMS TO REACH PROSPECTIVE CLIENTS

Before discussing how to measure the effectiveness of marketing campaigns, it's first necessary to **identify** and **try out** several forms of marketing. Most of us are familiar with the "traditional" forms available to law firms: phone book, billboard, television, and newspaper advertising, little league sponsorship, etc. In addition, there are now many Internet advertising possibilities available, which include law firm websites, search engine optimization, law firm directory inclusion, search engine (or pay-per-click) marketing, website-targeted marketing, blogs, and social network marketing.

These types of Internet marketing are discussed more thoroughly in other chapters of this book. What does need to be noted in this Chapter is that *each of the foregoing is a separate type of Internet marketing available to law firms*, and, as such, should be (i) considered for use by a law firm, and (ii) if used, should be measured for effectiveness to the extent possible. For instance, there will be a cost to engage in a comprehensive search engine optimization (SEO) program, which should be measured against the cost to be included in legal directories. A law firm should measure both types of programs to determine which is more effective in generating clients.

Once a law firm has identified the marketing opportunities available, the next step is to allocate money to be spent based for each of the marketing opportunities, and to determine how to measure the effectiveness of each marketing opportunity.

MEASURING THE EFFECTIVENESS OF MARKETING OPPORTUNITIES

Most law firms fail to measure the effectiveness of marketing campaigns, especially paid advertising. ***One of the primary goals of this chapter is to urge firms to measure, to the extent possible, all forms of paid advertising and marketing.***

PHONE NUMBER AND E-MAIL ACCOUNT MEASUREMENT FOR NON-INTERNET CAMPAIGNS

Let's first talk about non-Internet advertising. For any long-term advertising (more than nine months) involving a significant amount of money, firms should consider using a separate e-mail and phone number to judge advertising effectiveness. As an example, for phone book advertising, get a new local number from a company offering local numbers and use this number <u>only</u> in the firm's phone book advertising for the next year. A new phone line isn't necessary; when the number is dialed, the call will automatically be transferred to your main number.

These types of numbers are relatively cheap; an additional number usually costs about $10/month, with a significant number of minutes for free, and thereafter a low cost/minute. Remember – the per minute cost will only be charged by those calling your firm as a result of the phone book or other campaign. There are a number of companies that provide these types of numbers; do an Internet search for the term "phone numbers" and a number of companies will be displayed.

Each month you'll receive a phone bill for the local number provider. In addition to the phone bill, the calls received from some phone number providers can also be integrated into website statistics programs, such as Google Analytics (discussed below). These programs work by sending a simultaneous "ping" (or contact) to a specially-created web page used to keep track of calls. Thus calls can be tracked in the same interface panel as online visits from Internet marketing campaigns.

Similarly, along with the new phone book number, a new e-mail account can be created for inquiries from phone book advertisements. The e-mail account might be called contactanattorney@XYZlaw.com, or whatever e-mail name you would like to use. With this e-mail account you'll be able to see exactly how many electronic inquiries the firm received based on the phone book advertisement.

After six months or so, review the number of inquiries received (and hopefully the new clients generated) from the phone book advertising. If possible, you would like to calculate the CAC and then determine if it is higher or lower than the CAC from other marketing or advertising. If you're unable to track exactly which clients came from this source, you'll at least know the <u>number</u> of contacts.

Similar methodologies can also be used for other advertisements, such as billboards, television advertisements, or other non-Internet marketing campaigns. To find out more information about how phone number tracking methodologies, please visit www.hostednumbers.com, and see the tutorials at http://www.hostednumbers.com/HowItWorks/#ReportingAnalytics.

MEASURING INTERNET CAMPAIGNS AND MARKETING

E-mail account measurement can be easily done for both non-Internet and Internet marketing. For example, if a firm is listed in a legal directory, both the telephone and e-mail marketing should be used to measure exactly how many inquiries were received. In addition, a firm can use two other forms to measure clicks from Internet marketing – having a domain re-direct url and using website statistics programs.

In the first instance, say a firm wishes to find out how many clicks to its website it receives from being included in a specific law firm directory. One way in which clicks can be measured is to create a re-direct url. With the re-direct url, a potential client clicks on the law firm's link in the directory, and then is then taken to a page such as www.XYZlawfirm.com/directoryAlisting.php, for a split second, and then is immediately re-directed to another page (either the home page or some other landing page determined by the firm). The firm's website statistics (which are discussed below), would show that there was 1 visit to the www.XYZlawfirm.com/directoryAlisting.php page; thus the firm would know that one person arrived at their website from law firm directory A. Similar links could be created for other law firm directories or other targeted placement (such as site targeted ads, which are discussed in greater detail in Chapter 15). Note that the user would not actually see anything on the intermediate re-direct page; to the user it would look like they went directly from the directory page to the home page of the law firm's website.

If the firm pays to be listed in law firm directory A for a year, at the end of the year the firm can go back and analyze the number of e-mails and the number of visits that resulted directly from being included in law firm directory A, as well as phone book and other advertising campaigns. When this information is known, decisions can be made for the next year with respect to marketing spend allocation so that more money is spent in the advertising opportunities that are generating the most clients.

WEBALIZER AND GOOGLE ANALYTICS

As noted above, creating a re-direct web page allows law firms to see how many clicks are generated from specific campaign. This section describes how this information may be seen.

Many hosting companies offer a software program known as Webalizer, which is a website traffic statistics program that provides a wide range of information concerning a website's Internet traffic, such as the search terms used to find a firm's website, the number of pages viewed during a given time period (a day or a month, for example), and the number of visits during a given time period. The Webalizer (as it's officially known) is a fast, free web server log file analysis program that can be downloaded at http://www.mrunix.net/webalizer/. These statistics can be extremely useful, as you'll have a huge amount of information and statistics to help better understand where your website traffic comes from.

There are different ways that a law firm client can see Webalizer statistics; if you already have a website ask your hosting provider whether you already have Webalizer associated with your website, and if so, how you can login to see these statistics. Webalizer provides general statistics at the top level (usually shown by month), and users can drill-down to view more detailed statistics for specific days, hours, web pages and much more.

The following screen shots show the traffic for a "live" website; the images after that are the "drill-down" information about traffic patterns, daily and hourly statistics, and other detailed information.

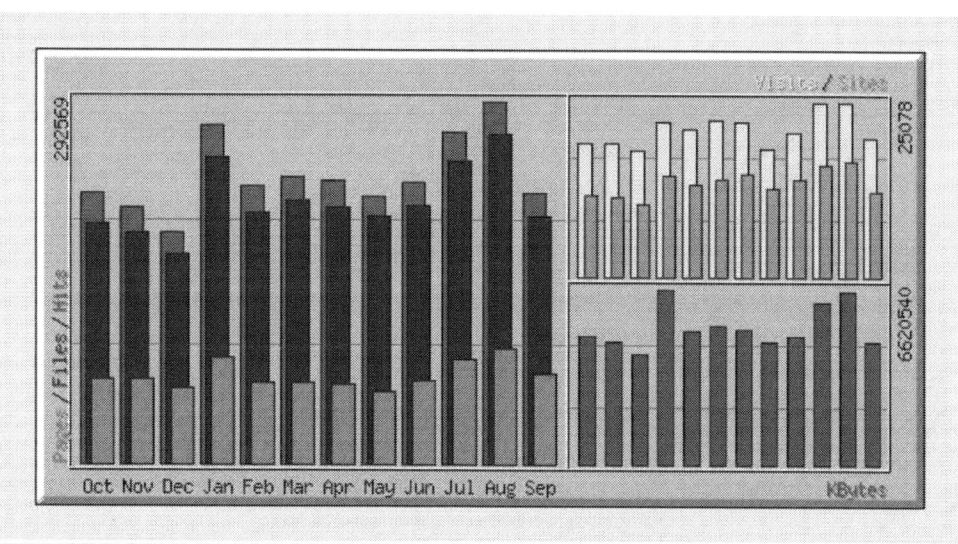

Summary by Month

Month	Daily Avg Hits	Daily Avg Files	Daily Avg Pages	Daily Avg Visits	Sites	Monthly Totals KBytes	Monthly Totals Visits	Monthly Totals Pages	Monthly Totals Files	Monthly Totals Hits
Sep 2009	7508	6904	2493	683	12099	4635201	19813	72320	200239	217737
Aug 2009	9437	8574	2995	806	16394	6538058	24989	92874	265808	292569
Jul 2009	8610	7900	2708	808	15993	6147519	25078	83953	244917	266940
Jun 2009	7578	6924	2235	687	13930	4844370	20638	67062	207722	227366
May 2009	6972	6418	1903	590	12779	4657452	18311	59020	198986	216137
Apr 2009	7595	6898	2133	737	14651	5106799	22125	63998	206969	227871
Mar 2009	7468	6852	2134	722	13926	5217177	22401	66165	212419	231525
Feb 2009	7985	7253	2357	757	13211	5000336	21223	66002	203097	223587
Jan 2009	8795	7981	2763	716	14484	6620540	22218	85666	247418	272664
Dec 2008	6043	5452	1982	583	10347	4175429	18083	61454	169013	187357
Nov 2008	6913	6209	2278	633	11275	4635015	18999	68346	186271	207406
Oct 2008	7033	6242	2228	615	11622	4827652	19067	69083	193504	218023
Totals						62405548	252945	855943	2536363	2789182

The chart above provides website statistics that might be comparable to the web traffic for a small law firm. Note however, that actual statistics could vary dramatically based on search engine rankings and whether the firm is conducting any search engine (or pay-per-click) marketing or any other types of advertising campaigns.

As discussed in Chapter 5, you'll notice that the number of hits is significantly more than the number of visits. In September, for example, the website received a total of 20,516 visits, which resulted in 225,750 hits (about 11 hits for every visit). Each visit resulted in about 3 page views; thus each page took a little over three hits on average to display.

What's important to understand is that many online advertising companies present their website traffic in terms of the number of hits, not the number of visits, and non-Internet savvy advertisers mistakenly believe that a hit is equivalent to a visit (which would lead to the misperception that there is significantly more website traffic). If you're contemplating online advertising, make sure that you find out about **the number of visits** per month that the website receives, not the number of hits.

The preceding chart provides more information about how users arrive at the website (some of the information specific to the company has been intentionally blocked out). The first chart shows the top 30 referrers for that website for the month, and the chart below shows the search strings that users enter in Google and other search engines to find the website. **This information is crucial for law firms, as finding out the referrers provides feedback for firms that are paying to be included in directories, and the search terms offer insight into the actual search terms being used by prospective clients to find the firm's website.** Referrer information is also critical to analyze whether any other Internet-based marketing programs are effective, such as banner placement or other types of marketing on third-party websites.

The graph above shows additional information regarding the website's statistics on a daily basis and hourly basis. If a marketing campaign was initiated during the month, such as a local newspaper ad, the firm's website traffic could be analyzed to see if website traffic increased in response to the ad.

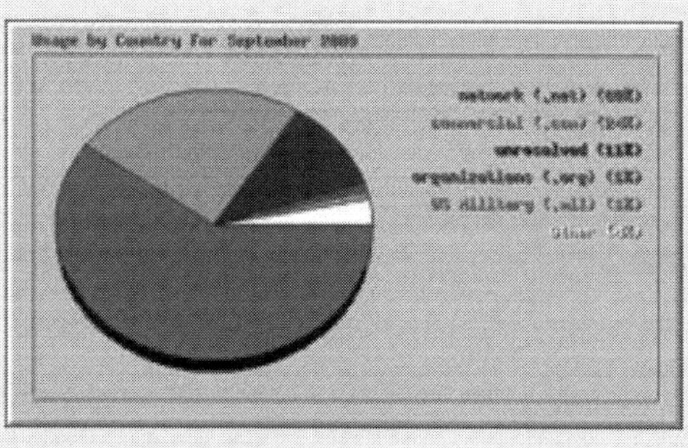

The information set forth in the preceding chart provides information about the location of users accessing the website, and what browser and operating system configurations are being used. This information is usually not critical for law firms; it's much more important for e-commerce companies that are concerned about potential cross-browser and other platform issues.

In addition to the information above, Webalizer also provides detailed information about error messages and other technical information, which can be helpful to ensure that there are not any broken links or other issues.

GOOGLE ANALYTICS

In addition to Webalizer, Google Analytics, which is free, can be incorporated into a firm's website. Google Analytics provides a great deal of statistics concerning where website traffic is generated, as well as information about visitor conversion. "Conversion" indicates when a website user has taken a specific action; for e-commerce websites a "conversion" might occur when a website visitor purchases a product. Because law firms don't sell products on their websites, a conversion for a law firm can mean another action taken, such as a user filling out and sending a "contact us" form.

Google Analytics is fairly easy to use. A website owner first needs to sign up for a free Google Analytics account at http://www.google.com/analytics/. After signing up, website owners (or their developers) need to place a small piece of code on the conversion page (which may be the "thank you for contacting us" page displayed after a user has completed and submitted the "contact us" form). When a user clicks on one of the law firm's Pay-Per-Click ads and follows through to the conversion page, a "conversion" will be said to have occurred. This is another way of measuring advertising success.

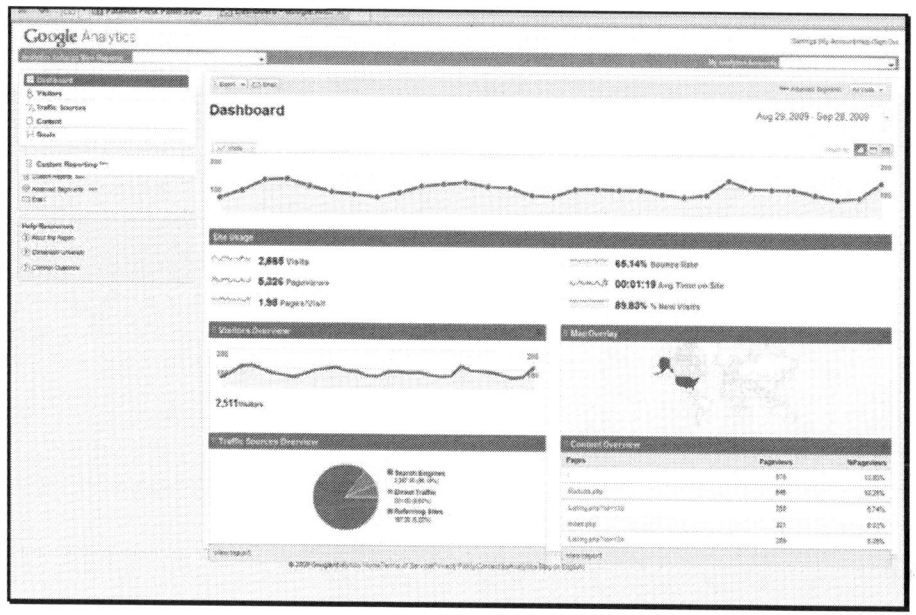

Google Analytics

OTHER STATISTICS PROGRAMS

In addition to the website traffic statistics programs noted above, there are a number of much more sophisticated website statistics programs available, which typically start out at around $1,000 or so per year and range upwards into tens of thousands of dollars per year (often the cost is based on the amount of website traffic). The sophisticated programs are aimed at high-end e-commerce companies, where it's critical to know how users are arriving at the site, what their traffic patterns are while on the site, and where they are dropping out of the sales funnel (or where they are leaving the website before making a purchase). For most law firms this information is not necessary.

MEASURING THE EFFECTIVENESS OF DIRECTORY AND ONLINE PROGRAM INCLUSION

There are a number of directories that law firms have historically participated in, as well as many new directories and companies that promise to bring clients to law firms. How can these directories be measured? Does it make sense to pay hundreds (or thousands) of dollars to be included in these directories? Could marketing dollars be more effectively spent on other forms of advertising? Do these directories deliver new clients?

First, before paying significant money to be included in any directory or online advertising program aimed at providing new clients, law firms should consider whether their prospective clients are likely to use or even know about the directory or program, or whether the directory or program is more commonly used within the legal community (perhaps as a means for attorneys to find out information about other attorneys). Ask the company *what type of marketing and advertising programs* they implement to reach prospective clients.

Recall the first Internet misperception mentioned in Chapter 1 – if you build it, they will come. A company may have a great-looking directory website, but if they're not getting prospective clients for your firm's services to their website, it's not going to make financial sense to be listed in their directory. It typically takes substantial marketing and search engine optimization efforts to reach prospective clients.

Second, law firms should find out how many leads the law firm directory is likely to deliver. Again, it may be the case that "leads" delivered (users finding your site from the directory site) may not be potential clients, but rather opposing counsel seeking more information about you or your firm. Ask to see how many clicks an average firm listed in the directory or program receives.

Third, as discussed above, many directories and websites advertise their website traffic using the term "hits". Now that you know the difference between hits and visits, you know to make sure that the traffic for visits (and not hits) is supplied.

Fourth, ask how many searches are conducted on the website per month, especially if it can be broken down into searches concerning the areas of law that your firm practices. For instance, if there is an area on the website for potential clients to search for a law firm, ask how many times a search has been conducted by filling in the box and clicking the "search" button. The company or directory should have access to this information.

Fifth, ask whether the directory will provide you with statistics specific to your account. With many directories a law firm can see statistics such as the number of times that their ad is shown, and the number of times that their listing is clicked on by prospective clients.

Finally, if your firm participates in an online directory program and if you have a website statistics program such as Webalizer, look to see where your website visitors are coming from for the past few months. The website from which the clients have come from is called the "referrer". Webalizer (and many other statistics programs) will show the top referrers for a given time period, and also (for keyword searches done in Google and other search engines), the search terms typed in by the users. This information is vital to understanding how users are arriving at your website and to judging the effectiveness of your marketing programs.

RE-ALLOCATING MARKETING SPEND

Revisiting the quote from Mr. Wanamaker included at the beginning of this chapter, it's important to determine what marketing spend is effective and what marketing spend is ineffective. If it costs $5 to generate a prospective client in one area and $500 to generate a prospective client using another form of marketing (which very easily can be the case), a firm would obviously want to invest more marketing dollars in the less expensive form of marketing and fewer dollars in the more expensive form of marketing.

After six months or so, start calculating your CAC from each of the forms of advertising in which your firm is engaged. In some instances the numbers may not be exact as you may not know for sure what advertising form(s) led to the new client; in these instances you'll have to guess (or perhaps include a portion of the new client result in more than one category).

Ideally, once your Client Acquisition Cost has been calculated, and once you can see the number of users visiting your website as a result of inclusion in directories, organic search engine optimization (SEO), Pay-Per-Click advertising (or search engine marketing), you'll have more information about the cost of getting prospective clients from each of these methods. While SEO can take time up-front, the benefits of effective SEO are likely to be long-lasting. PPC costs, conversely, will be on a direct cost basis – you'll know for any time period exactly how much you've spent and how many clicks to your firm's website were generated. Directory advertising will be a function of how much money you've paid to be included for a certain time period divided by the number of website visitors (hopefully, prospective clients) generated from the directory. Once you know the cost for all these methods, it's possible to determine which advertising method is the least.

The lesson from this chapter is to **know how much it costs on average to generate clients using various forms of marketing, and then re-allocate marketing spend to the most cost-effective methods of generating clients.**

The next chapter discusses one of the most cost effective methods of connecting with clients actively seeking your firm's services.

CHAPTER 15 – SEARCH ENGINE MARKETING (OR PAY-PER-CLICK ADVERTISING) ON GOOGLE, BING, AND YAHOO!

Search Engine Marketing, sometimes also referred to as "sponsored search" advertising, pay-per-click (PPC) advertising or cost-per-click (CPC) advertising, can be one of the most cost-effective and easiest ways for a law firm to advertise. Ad campaigns can be created quickly and often can begin running the same day they are created. With PPC advertising, costs can be extremely low (sometimes less than ten cents per click), daily budgets can be set, and campaigns can be easily modified.

Search engine marketing consists of paid ad placements that are displayed with the search engine results generated in response to a user's search query. Most of us who have used one of the three major search engines – Google, Bing, and Yahoo! – are familiar with these ads, as they are displayed at the top and/or to the right of the "organic" (or non-paid) search results. The ads displayed (we'll refer to them as PPC ads) are triggered off keywords bid on by advertisers. This chapter discusses PPC advertising aspects common to the search engine marketing companies discussed above, and also on some specific areas that are more applicable only to Google (especially because Google currently powers approximately 71% of all US searches).[23]

OVERVIEW OF SEARCH ENGINE MARKETING – GOOGLE PPC EXAMPLE

Suppose you practice divorce law in Chicago, and you want to have an ad for your firm displayed whenever a user conducts a search on Google for "Chicago divorce lawyer". First you'll need to create an AdWords account with Google, which is Google's search engine marketing program. Thereafter, you'll need to (1) create a campaign (such as "Divorce Law"), (2) create an Ad Group (such as "Chicago Divorce"), (3) create a list of keywords (such as "Chicago divorce lawyer") to trigger the display of your ads in response to a user's search, (4) set a bid amount, such as $.50, which would be the maximum amount that you would be charged when a user clicks on your ad (and is re-directed to your website), and (5) create the ad text to be displayed in response a user's Google search using the ad keywords you specified (i.e. "Chicago divorce lawyer"). The ad displayed can have

---

[23] Experian[sm] Hitwise, *Google Receives 71 Percent of Searches in September 2009*, October 6, 2009, http://www.hitwise.com/us/press-center/press-releases/google-searches-sept-09/

up to 25 characters in the top line, and 35 characters in the next two lines, and might look something like this:

> Chicago Divorce Lawyer
> Free consult. For the Settlement
> You Deserve. 15 yrs. Experience.
> www.ourfirmwillgeteverythingforyoufromyourspouse.com

When a user clicks on your ad, they'll be taken to your website (to your home page or any other page you specify).

Based upon the competition for the keyword term "Chicago divorce lawyer", Google determines which ads will be shown and the placement of ads on the search results page. These decisions are made by several factors, the most important of which are the **click price bid** by the advertiser and the advertiser's past **click-though rate** for ads. The more you're willing to pay for a click and the higher percentage of clicks that your ads generate, the better page placement you'll receive (and the lower your cost per click charge will be).

How Much Will You Be Charged Per Click?

You will never be charged more for a click than your bid price. The actual amount charged by Google is made up of several factors: the next highest bid amount following your bid which is then adjusted by the Ad Rank of the ad showing beneath you by your Quality Score, then round up to the nearest cent. Because Google wants to maximize revenues, it's willing to charge advertisers that receive high click through rates a lower cost in order to encourage advertising. Remember – Google makes money when a search results ad is clicked, not when one of the organic (or free) results is clicked; therefore, Google has a strong motivation to reward companies that can advertise effectively so that a higher percentage of searches will result in a paid ad being clicked.

Bidding on the Google Search Network usually requires a minimum bid of five cents per click, although higher minimum bids may be required in many instances in order to have ads displayed. Ads on the Google Content Network (the ads that are commonly shown in boxes on many websites with the "Ads by Google" text in the box), are less expensive, and might start at only a couple of cents per click.

THE MINIMUM AD BID DOES NOT MEAN THAT YOUR ADS WILL BE DISPLAYED

In many instances where there is significant competition (such as national class-action lawsuits for mesothelioma) bids may be significantly higher (sometimes $20 or more per click). In an average-size city where there are perhaps a dozen or so firms competing in areas like criminal defense and similar matters, the cost per click may be around a quarter. The cost really comes down to how many other law firms are bidding on similar keywords, which in turn is dependent upon whether keyword bidding will be primarily from local attorneys or attorneys throughout the US, as well as the anticipated profit per client. Law firms naturally will be willing to pay more per click for keywords relating to matters that have a high profit margin.

One benefit of PPC ads is that spending can be controlled by setting daily limits. For instance, if a firm doesn't want to spend more than $10.00 per day on a specific campaign, this amount can be entered as the daily budget, and if this limit is reached in any day, the firm's ads are no longer displayed until the following day.

THE ANALYTICS DASHBOARD/ADMINISTRATION PANEL

As discussed in greater detail below, after registering for a search engine marketing account on Google, Bing, or Yahoo!, multiple campaigns and sub-campaigns can be created around a variety of different practice areas and client-targeted ads. Campaigns often use a variety of techniques (such as geo-targeting) to maximize the effectiveness of the campaign and to minimize marketing spend. As a result, campaigns typically involve dozens or even hundreds of keywords used to trigger various ads.

All of the search engine companies have a dashboard/administration panel that provides detailed analytics for each campaign and sub-campaign through statistics such as the number of impressions for each ad and keyword, the number of clicks received, the click-through rate, average ad placement ranking, average cost of a click, and total spending for each campaign and keyword. Based on this information, campaigns and sub-campaigns can be modified by changing or adding keywords, new ads can be created, multiple ads can be tested to determine which ads perform better, and prices and budgets can be adjusted.

Additionally, it's possible to track conversions across different keywords, campaigns, and sub-campaigns. A "conversion" occurs whenever a user clicks on a PPC ad, is taken to the advertiser's website, and then proceeds through the website to a certain page (called the conversion page). For e-commerce companies, the conversion page is usually a page that follows the purchase of an item; for non- e-commerce websites it might be a "thank you for your inquiry" page that is shown following the completion and submission of a "contact us" form.

Thus in the example above, if a user enters the term "Chicago divorce lawyer" in Google and eventually completes a firm's "contact us" form, a conversion will be said to have occurred for the keywords "Chicago divorce lawyer".

THE BENEFITS TO LAW FIRMS OF PAY-PER-CLICK ADVERTISING

Because of the usually low cost and because no cost is charged if an ad is not clicked, PPC advertising has become extremely popular with advertisers, and extremely profitable for companies like Google that earn billions of dollars each year in advertising revenues. Here are some of the reasons for the popularity among advertisers:

- Campaigns can be set up very quickly (from an hour to perhaps a couple of days or more, depending upon the complexity of the campaigns).

- Ads can begin to be shown very quickly; often on the same day they are created.

- Advertisers only pay when users click on the ad and are re-directed to the advertiser's website. Advertisers don't have to pay if their ads are shown but are not clicked.

- Costs per click can be extremely low; sometimes less than ten cents per click.

- Ads can be targeted to users in a specific geographic area.

- Ads can be started, paused, and restarted at any time.

- Except for a very small up-front charge (ranging from no charge to about $50), there is no required spend.

- In many cases, advertisers can choose a time of day and even specific days of the week for their ads to be shown.

- Advertisers can set maximum daily spending limits up front, and can easily adjust these limits.

- Search engine companies provide advertisers with a tremendous amount of easy-to-understand information about advertising campaigns, such as impressions (number of times an ad is shown), number of clicks, conversions (such as users that complete a "contact us" form), average ad placement, average cost per click, total cost of clicks, and much more.

- Advertisers can create multiple ads for a single client service, and can then see which ads perform the best and stop using the under-performing ads.

- Fairly elaborate campaigns can be created using dozens or hundreds of keywords, and can be further refined to better target users and to reduce advertising costs.

- They slice, dice, clean windows and mow the lawn. (OK, perhaps they're not quite this good…yet.)

PAY-PER-CLICK ADVERTISING ON GOOGLE, BING, AND YAHOO!

The appendices to this book go through the steps of creating PPC campaigns on each of Google, Bing, and Yahoo! While there are some differences between how PPC campaigns are created and managed on each of these search engines, the primary elements of PPC advertising on each of these search engines are the same: Create a campaign structure, create sub-campaigns, develop keywords for each sub-campaign, set budgets, and manage campaigns. These elements are briefly described next, but for more information on creating and developing an account, please see the more detailed information in the appendices.

PAY-PER-CLICK CAMPAIGN CREATION – DETERMINING A CONSISTENT STRUCTURE TO BE USED

After creating an account with one of the search engine companies, the next step is to create a structure for your firm's ads. The essence of the structure is that if multiple campaigns are to be created you don't want the same keywords to be used in more than one campaign.

Designing a campaign is similar to an outline. First you'll want to make a decision on how to organize the campaigns, and then break down the main campaigns into sub-campaigns.

For instance, a personal injury firm might want to create its campaigns around either the type of injury sustained (head, arm, lung, etc.) **or** how the injury occurred (medical malpractice, traffic accident, construction, etc.). **Whichever structure makes the most sense is fine, what is to be avoided is mixing two (or more) different campaign structures that could potentially have ads that would be applicable to both categories or ads that might not be applicable to either category**. This could occur, for instance, by creating one campaign around the type of injury sustained and a second campaign around how the injury occurred, which would leave uncertainty around which category to place an ad for head injuries sustained as a result of a traffic accident (as it would be applicable to both campaigns). (A more detailed explanation of campaign structure and how they can become difficult to manage if a consistent structure is not used is discussed in **Appendix 3**.)

DETERMINING THE KEYWORDS TO BE USED

Here's one area where you can go a little wild. Feel free to use as many keywords as you think might be appropriate. Then substitute words ("attorney" for "lawyer"), use common abbreviations (maybe "atty", or CA for "California"), and switch the order of the words ("California divorce lawyer" and "divorce lawyer in California").

The only caveats here are that (1) don't use keywords that are unlikely to result in potential clients because they are not specific enough unless some other tool is used to limit where the words are shown, or (2) use the same keywords in multiple campaigns (thus have the same keywords triggering ads for different campaigns). In the former case, it's not wise to use the term "divorce attorney" (which would be national in scope) unless you're using geo-targeting to restrict the ads so that they are shown only to those searching in Chicago; otherwise you might receive (and be charged for) thousands of clicks from those in other states who would not be potential clients for your firm. (More about geo-targeting is discussed in the Appendices.) For the second item, you would not want to create one campaign around "Chicago Law Firm" and a second campaign around "Chicago divorce lawyer" and included the keywords "Chicago lawyer" in both campaigns. In this case, if someone types in the search term "Chicago lawyer", it's unclear which ad would be shown – the general ad for Chicago Law Firm or the ad for Chicago Divorce Lawyer? *The lesson – don't use the same keywords in more than one campaign.*

CREATING MUTIPLE ADS FOR THE SAME CAMPAIGN ON GOOGLE

Within a campaign, you may want to test different advertising messages to see which message is the most effective in generating clicks. Suppose with your divorce practice in

Chicago, you're not sure which type of ad will perform the best – the one previously described, or another one that highlights your educational accomplishments as a Harvard Law graduate, and that you see clients on Saturdays. In addition to the previous ad, you could create a second ad, as follows:

> Chicago Divorce Lawyer
> Harvard Law School Grad.
> Open on Saturdays for Clients.
> www.ourfirmwillgeteverythingforyourfromyourspouse.com

Additional ads could also be created. Google will begin alternating this ad with the first one above (and any other ads created), and over time will automatically begin showing the ad(s) receiving the higher percentage of click-throughs. You can also disable or delete the under-performing ads yourself.

You might find that the first ad is receiving a click-through rate of 5% (which would be very good), while the click-through rate of the second ad is only .5%. Based on this knowledge, you might want to discontinue having the second ad shown. Of course, you'll want to let both ads run for a long enough period to make the determination that one ad really is performing better than the other ad.

LIMITING THE GEOGRAPHIC SCOPE OF WHERE YOUR ADS WILL BE SHOWN

If your law practice is limited to a certain geographic location your ads can be targeted so that they are shown only to users searching from the geographic areas you specify. By using geographic targeting, your ads won't be shown to users outside the geographic area of your practice who aren't likely to become clients, and thus you won't potentially have to pay for clicks from such persons.

On Google, this limitation is called "geo-targeting." When a Google campaign is created, the advertiser can use geo-targeting to limit the geographic area to states, cities or even zip codes. See **Appendix 3** for more information on how to use geo-targeting in Google. Other companies have similar geographic targeting limitations; see the Appendices for more information.

BEYOND SEARCH ENGINE MARKETING – HOW TO GET YOUR ADS DISPLAYED ON SPECIFIC WEBSITES AND COST PER THOUSAND IMPRESSIONS (CPM) BILLING

Google has a program called "AdSense" by which website owners can choose to have Google place ads on their websites. Once a website owner creates an AdSense account with Google, the website owner does not have to take any further action – Google's automated programs place "contextually relevant" ads on the websites, and the website owners are paid by Google (either based upon how many times the ad is clicked or how many times the ad is displayed (also called impressions)).

On the flip side, through Google's AdWords program, advertisers can target their ads to be displayed on specific websites that participate in Google's AdSense program. During the campaign creation, advertisers can specify the types of websites where they want their ads to be displayed (an estate planning attorney may wish to have their ads targeted to websites focusing on retirement, for example), and they can also check to see whether specific websites that might be of interest participate in Google's AdSense program. Thus a law firm can bid to have its ads placed on specific websites chosen by the firm.

Additionally, Google now provides advertisers with a choice as to how they wish to pay for ads displayed on other websites. Advertisers can elect to bid on either on a CPC (cost-per-click) basis or CPM basis (cost per thousand impressions, which might be $2.00, for example, which would be charged irrespective of the number of clicks received). It's then up to the advertiser to determine which basis will be more cost-effective.

Another great element of this program is that advertisers are not limited to having only text ads placed on the targeted websites. With many participating websites, ads can be full banner ads (which often can be animated), and in some circumstances, video ads can even be shown. The types of ads and the size requirements vary, so when the campaigns are created, you'll have to check with each website to see what types of advertising are allowed.

If you wish to have a banner ad shown that would take the place of four text ads, you'll likely have to bid a higher amount than would be required for a regular text ad, as a banner ad takes up more room than a text ad. While determining the ad amount may sound complicated, in actual practice it's quite simple – determine the amount that you're willing to pay, make your bid, and then wait to see if your ads are being shown. If they aren't shown, you'll need to increase your bid.

With respect to website targeting, some websites allow advertisers to target specific pages of the website, while other websites don't offer this flexibility. If page targeting is allowed, advertisers can search through the website and target their ads to be shown on specific pages that might be the most relevant to their practice, such as a page with an article about estate planning, for instance, for an estate planning attorney.

THE GOOGLE SEARCH NETWORK AND THE GOOGLE CONTENT NETWORK

The Google Network is made up of two networks – the Google Search Network and the Google Content Network. **The Google Search Network** includes Google and other websites where a user enters a search term and results are displayed along with ads. Thus if a user is searching on Amazon.com (which is included in the Google Search Network) for a book about divorce, the search results will show books about divorce as well as ads having to do with divorce, which may include a law firm's divorce ad. When a campaign is created, advertisers can choose whether they wish to have their ads shown only on Google or the other partners included in the Google Search Network, which includes Google Maps, Google Product Search, Google Groups, and entities such as Virgin Media, Amazon.com, and other websites and companies.

As mentioned above, **the Google Content Network** includes websites that participate in Google's AdSense program, as well as other websites that may have contractual relationships with Google. Participating websites in the Google Content Network have ads placed on their websites by Google that are determined by Google to be "contextually relevant" to the web page content. As an example, Google notes that in a blog about baking brownies it might place an ad about brownie recipes.[24]

Participants in the Google Content Network include websites such as About.com, Lycos, NYTimes.com, InfoSpace, Reed Business, howstuffworks.com, business.com, foodnetwork.com, HGTV.com, as well as hundreds of thousands of websites and blogs ranging from some of the largest websites on the Internet to small "mom and pop" websites and blogs. The Google Content Network is the world's # 1 ad network.[25]

---

[24] See http://adwords.google.com/support/aw/bin/answer.py?hl=en&answer=57723.
[25] See http://www.google.com/adwords/contentnetwork/#utm_source=gcn&utm_medium=redirect&utm_campaign=gcn_redirect

When creating a campaign, law firms can also elect to participate in the Google Content Network, or to opt-out completely of the Google Content Network. If a firm wishes to participate in the Google Content Network, the firm has three choices: (1) to have ads placed across the Content Network on contextually related websites and web pages as determined by Google, (2) to have ads placed across the Content Network on contextually related websites and web pages as determined by Google EXCEPT for websites specifically excluded by the law firm, or (3) to ONLY place the laws firm's ads on websites in the Content Network that are specified by the law firm. Option 1 is the default option; options 2 and 3 must be specified by the law firm. The details for excluding websites or targeting specific websites are described in Appendix 3.

Law firms can also make different default click bids for clicks arising from the Google Search Network than the Google Content Network. Because ads in the Google Content Network are not directly triggered off of a user's search (and instead are placed on web pages that Google deems to be "contextually relevant" to the text on a page), there may be a lower chance that the person viewing the page (and the ads on the page) is looking for a law firm. Instead, such person may simply be visiting the web page of a friend on MySpace, which might happen to contain text about divorce. Because the reason for a person being on a page that may have a divorce ad is less clear than a person actively conducting a search for a divorce attorney, click bids on the Google Content Network are usually lower than click bids on the Google Search Network.

Additionally, within the Google Content Network, law firms targeting ads to specific websites can make click bids for each specified website. Thus if a law firm believes that a specific website is a particularly good fit, it may bid a higher amount for having its ads displayed on such website.

It should also be noted that as there are literally billions of web pages served with Google ads (especially on websites such as MySpace that alone generates millions of pages of ads), it's possible that a law firm's ads could very quickly be shown a huge number of pages very quickly. For this reason I offer two pieces of advice: (1) **set daily limits** so that you inadvertently don't spend more than you've budgeted, and (2) **monitor your account closely**, especially in the beginning. The first month after launching a campaign the statistics should be reviewed every day. Gradually as patterns appear and campaigns are modified less frequent monitoring is required.

For information on how to create an ad campaign on Google visit: http://www.adwords.google.com/select/Login. To learn how to create an ad campaign on

Yahoo!, visit: http://www.smallbusiness.yahoo.com/searchenginemarketing. To learn how to create an ad campaign on MSN, visit: https://www.microsoft.com.)

IMPORTING CAMPAIGNS TO BING AND YAHOO! FROM GOOGLE

Because Google powers the largest percentage of searches in the US, often advertisers start with Google for search engine marketing campaigns, and then roll-out campaigns to Yahoo!, Bing, and other search companies. Campaigns can become complex very quickly, and a law firm with many practice areas might soon have dozens of different campaigns around many practice areas that might be made up with hundreds of keywords. Fortunately, Yahoo! and Bing offer ways of importing campaigns from Google that may make the campaign process somewhat easier for these search engines. Here are the steps for importing campaigns; however many users might find it easier to re-create the campaigns in these search engines, especially if the campaigns themselves are not overly complicated.

YAHOO!

Your Yahoo! account may or may not support the Import Campaign feature. If it does not, you can still import your Google campaigns to Yahoo! by using the bulk function to download your campaign. For a complete list of directions on how to download your campaign information from Google to upload on Yahoo! visit http://help.yahoo.com/l/us/yahoo/ysm/sps/screenref/2102563_bulk_dl.html. If your Yahoo! account supports the Import Campaign feature you will first click the "**Campaigns**" tab on your Yahoo! dashboard, then click the "**Import**" tab located under the Campaigns tab.

Once the Import Campaign page opens select either the XML link or the CSV link to download a new bulk template file to your computer. To add the campaign information to your template, see the directions for **Creating and Importing a New Bulksheet** by visiting http://help.yahoo.com/l/us/yahoo/ysm/sps/screenref/16507.html?terms=import+ppc+campaign+from+google.

BING

To import your Google PPC campaign to Bing you must first start by gathering all of your data into a Google AdWords report. For the data requirements for the report, visit https://help.live.com/help.aspx?project=adcenter_live_std&market=en-us&querytype=keyword&query=&tmt=&domain=adcenter.microsoft.com&format=b1 and click "**Data requirements for import**".

Once the campaign information has been added to the Google AdWords report save it to an Excel spreadsheet. Then, edit the spread sheet to make sure that it matches the adCenter template. For a complete list of directions on how to create the report and save the file visit https://help.live.com/help.aspx?project=adcenter_live_std&market=en-us&querytype=keyword&query=&tmt=&domain=adcenter.microsoft.com&format=b1.

Once you have created the campaign file click the "**Campaigns**" tab on your Bing dashboard, and then click "**More**" and "**Import campaigns**". Next, in the Select a language and market drop-down list, select the language your ads are written in and the market where you want your ads to be shown. Then select the time zone you want to use for the campaign. Click "**Import file**". In the Choose file dialog box select your file and click "**Open**" to import your campaign to the table.

To make your imported campaign live you must submit your imported ad groups. To do this, select your imported campaign, and at the top of the Campaign Selected page set your budget for the campaign by clicking on "**Change Settings**" and entering a value in the Campaign budget box and click "**Save**". Once a budget has been set click "**Submit**". For more information on importing your Google campaign to Bing visit https://help.live.com/help.aspx?project=adcenter_live_std&market=en-us&querytype=keyword&query=&tmt=&domain=adcenter.microsoft.com&format=b1.

MORE INFORMATION ABOUT SEARCH ENGINE MARKETING

Google, Bing, and Yahoo! each have more information on their search marketing programs, including tutorials, available on their websites. For more information about search engine marketing, please see the following web pages:

For Google: https://adwords.google.com/support/aw/?hl=en_US

For Bing: https://help.live.com/help.aspx?project=adcenter_live_std&market=en-us&querytype=keyword&query=&tmt=&domain=adcenter.microsoft.com&format=b1

For Yahoo!: http://help.yahoo.com/l/us/yahoo/ysm/sps/

CHAPTER 16 – PROMOTING YOUR FIRM AND FUTURE SERVICES THROUGH E-NEWSLETTERS

Firm e-newsletters are a great way to stay connected with current and former clients, and to reach new clients. There are a variety of software and third party solutions that can be used to collect and manage e-mail addresses and comply with mandated opt-out procedures. In order to collect an e-newsletter distribution list, ask clients for permission to be added to your e-newsletter distribution list, and, on your website, offer to send prospective clients something of value so that they will subscribe to your newsletter (such as a top ten list to comply with employment laws, or a white paper that would be of value). Because the formatting for e-newsletters only needs to be done once, it's easy to create and send out e-newsletters.

WHAT ARE ELECTRONIC NEWSLETTERS?

Electronic newsletters (or "e-newsletters") are short newsletters delivered to the e-mail accounts of subscribers. They can (and should) also be included on a law firm's website.

If done correctly, e-newsletters are a great source of maintaining contact with current and former clients in a fairly unobtrusive way. More importantly, they can be a tremendous source of new client generation, especially from former clients who may have hired the firm for only one matter.

THE REASONS FIRMS AVOID E-NEWSLETTERS

The main reasons law firms avoid e-newsletters is because they are perceived as taking too much time to prepare and that they are of limited marketing value. The time to prepare misperception stems from the belief that detailed content is required, complicated formatting is involved, and a significant coordination effort is required among those that may be writing content. All of these beliefs are incorrect.

Unlike written newsletters – which are generally several pages long, and which require additional print costs – e-newsletters should be short. An effective e-newsletter should not contain more than five articles, each of which should be brief, perhaps a few paragraphs at the most. If more space is required, the article should be summarized in the e-newsletter and a link should be included to the firm's website where the complete article can be read.

Once the general layout of the e-newsletter is created (like the e-newsletter header and footer), new e-newsletters can be created quickly. With third party e-newsletter solutions, a user logs into their account, clicks to create a new e-newsletter, and enters content into the area provided. Links from the content to the firm's website can then be entered, and stored images can be added, if desired. When the e-newsletter is ready, it can be sent to the distribution list immediately, or it can be scheduled for delivery at a later date.

Distribution lists can be created using existing client contact information, and the list can be supplemented with e-newsletter sign-ups from the firm's website. If a subscriber wants to opt-out and no longer receive the firm's e-newsletters, they can do so by clicking a link automatically placed in all e-newsletters. The opt-out process is automated; once a subscriber clicks on the link to opt-out, the firm does not need to take any additional action to remove the subscriber from the distribution list.

E-NEWSLETTER VALUE TO CLIENTS AND CALL TO ACTION

Effective newsletters have three components. First, they serve to add value to the recipients. Let subscribers know about new changes in the law that might affect their business, or an upcoming presentation to be given by your firm. You might even include a small trivia item at the end of the e-newsletter or some other item that would be of interest. The value to subscribers doesn't need to be significant; it does need to be enough so that they will continue to read the e-newsletter and not opt-out.

Second, as noted above, the articles should be very short. Ideally you want clients to be able to read your article in the "preview" window of Microsoft Outlook with minimal scrolling. The whole e-newsletter should take under a minute to read - that's about all the time that subscribers will allow (consider how much time you might devote to reading an e-newsletter). If an article requires more space, provide a summary with a link to your website for the full article. If e-newsletters are too long, instead of being considered as a value-added resource, they will be viewed as another lengthy e-mail that must be read, in which case the opt-out link will be quickly utilized.

Third, the newsletter should serve as a call to action, if possible. Summarize new regulations that might impact clients. Hit the important points, note that there are other more complicated issues with the new regulations, and suggest that they call you.

Perhaps your firm wishes to announce a seminar on human resource legal issues and updates. If this is the case, provide a link where clients can register. Don't, for instance, simply say "call us if you would like to attend." Remember - as with any call to action, once you have the person's attention, it's important that they be able to take the desired action *now;* don't rely on them taking the action later. Recipients that read your newsletter at 10 pm know that they're not going to be able to reach a live person by phone to register for the conference; don't assume that they will have the same enthusiasm (or even remember) to call your firm the next day.

For attorneys that practice in areas other than corporate law, even if one of your e-newsletter subscribers is unlikely to need your services again, consider that they may be your best (and least expensive) form of advertising. Let them know about new attorneys or practice areas at your firm, your sponsorship of the local baseball team – basically anything to stay in contact with them to keep your firm "top of mind". Good e-newsletters keep you connected with clients long after you're finished providing legal services; hopefully they will recommend you to one of their friends or family members if your services are required.

TWO THINGS KENNEY CHESNEY WON'T DO

If you've read Chapter 7, you know the two things Kenney Chesney won't do. In addition, you also know the importance of creating headlines that will grab a user's attention. Create article titles and summaries that are likely to interest subscribers and make them want to click the links to the full articles on your firm's site. Of course you'll want to provide valuable information, but there's always a way to do so (especially with the title) in a non-boring way.

E-NEWSLETTERS AND LEGAL OBLIGATIONS

In all e-newsletters, a clear link must be included which gives the subscriber the opportunity to "opt-out" of future e-mails. Most of the popular e-newsletter programs have automated opt-out features whereby a subscriber can simply opt-out by clicking a link, and thus no action needs to be taken by the firm to update the list.

While not legally required, some e-newsletters go a step further by using what is referred to as "double opt-in". Double opt-in means that subscribers indicate twice that they wish to receive a firm's e-newsletter – first, by signing up on a website, and second, by clicking on a "confirmation" link that is sent to the subscriber's e-mail. Double opt-in procedures have met with some resistance as they nearly always result in lower subscription rates, as initial subscribers may reconsider whether they want to receive a newsletter and not confirm their subscription.

Of course, appropriate disclaimers should be conspicuously included advising that the information provided in the newsletter doesn't constitute legal advice. Some jurisdictions may also require specific other language to be included – find out if this is the case where you practice, and include any required text.

E-NEWSLETTER FEEDBACK – ADVANTAGES OVER PRINTED NEWSLETTERS

A significant benefit of e-newsletters is that in addition to knowing the number of subscribers to whom the newsletter is sent, with most programs you'll also be able to track information such as how many times the newsletter was opened, how many times each of the links contained in the e-newsletter was clicked (such as a link to an article on the firm's website), and how many times the e-newsletter was forwarded. These statistics also show "undelivered" or "bounce-back" e-mail, which might result if a user provides an incorrect e-mail address, or may no longer be at the original e-mail address used. As a result, unlike printed newsletters in which there is no way of knowing what articles are read, link clicks from e-newsletter articles provide great feedback regarding the information that subscribers find to be of interest.

DROPPING OFF SUBSCRIBERS – WHERE ARE YOU TAKING THEM, AND WHAT DO YOU WANT THEM TO DO AFTER YOU'VE DROPPED THEM OFF?

Suppose you send an e-newsletter that has summaries of several articles, with links to your firm's website where the full article may be read. When a subscriber clicks on the link to one of the articles, where will you take them, and what do you want them to do after they've read the article?

To be effective, develop an action plan for the "drop-off" article page, and incorporate the action plan into the article page itself. The action plan might consist of the following:

1. <u>A Call to Action for More Information</u>. "Are you wondering whether bankruptcy is the best solution for your company? Call me or fill out the attached form and let me know of a good time to call you." If there is such a call to action, it should come from a *specific attorney, preferably with a picture of the attorney.* Don't simply have a general "call our firm to get more information" message – this type of message doesn't resonate well with most website visitors.

2. <u>Cross-Promotion.</u> Cross-promotion can be used to promote almost anything concerning your firm, such as an upcoming seminar or other articles on your website. Let readers know about other areas of the law practiced by your firm, and why these areas may be of interest to them. Use headlines that will encourage readers to click on links to these other articles.

3. <u>Previous e-newsletters.</u> Include links to past e-newsletters and/or popular articles on your firm's website (you'll now know which articles are popular based on the e-mail statistics programs).

Almost any action plan will be much more effective than only including the article. Remember – the more time that users spend on your firm's website, the more likely that such users will develop positive feelings for your firm and the firm's attorneys (and the more likely it is that such users will become firm clients).

HOW TO GET STARTED WITH AN E-NEWSLETTER

The basic elements that you'll want to have with any newsletter system are (i) the ability to sign-up for the newsletter on your firm's website, (ii) the ability to easily create and send newsletters to subscribers, (iii) the ability to track the statistics previously mentioned (number of times opened, forwarded, links clicked, etc.), and (iv) the ability for subscribers to opt-out of future newsletters.

There are a couple of different options with e-newsletters – to license an e-newsletter system (whereby the newsletter is sent through your server), or to use a third party e-newsletter system (whereby the newsletter is created and sent through the third-party's server). In the former case, if your firm's website uses Joomla (see Chapter 10), there are e-newsletter modules developed by independent developers that can be integrated directly into Joomla. There are other Joomla-integrated newsletter programs being developed and released – check Joomla extensions to see a list. In addition, there are other non-Joomla e-newsletter programs that can also be used with your existing website.

The second (and perhaps more popular) option is to use a hosted third party e-newsletter system, such as Constant Contact (www.ConstantContact.com).[26] Third party hosted e-newsletter solution providers typically charge based upon the number of e-newsletters sent and/or the number of recipients for each e-newsletter. Many of these companies offer free trials, and almost all of them have template options for easy e-newsletter creation, as well as robust statistics for e-newsletter distribution.

E-NEWSLETTERS AND SPAM FILTERS

One problem associated with transmitting e-newsletters is spam filters which can block newsletters from being delivered to recipients. This is another reason for the importance of website statistics – so that the firm will know if there are problems with e-mails being delivered.

In general, Internet Services Providers (ISP's) try to block large e-mail spam distributions through various spam filters. The filters are fairly complex and often use a system of "scoring" to determine the possibility that the e-mails are spam, such that a mass e-mail distribution originating from Nigeria might have a high score, while the same distribution originating from a US server might have a much lower score.

A firm sending out e-mails using a licensed program and its own server should therefore check the statistics for e-newsletters sent out to ensure that the e-mails are being delivered to recipients. Just because a normal e-mail reaches a client does not mean that the e-newsletters will similarly reach same recipient.

Most of the major third-party hosted e-newsletter companies have taken steps to become "white-listed" with the major ISP's such as AOL. Consequently, there is a much lower chance that e-newsletters will be bounced if they are sent out by one of the major e-newsletter distribution providers than if they are sent out by a non – "white-listed" server.

---

[26] Our publisher Esquire Interactive is a Business Partner of Constant Contact.

There are some steps that law firms can take to minimize being caught by spam filters (and potentially blacklisting from occurring). These include:

1. Using appropriate subject lines. Don't capitalize all of the words, or use words such as "free".
2. Don't include attachments.
3. Minimize the use of pictures.
4. Include opt-provisions.
5. Don't over-use pictures.

BLACKLISTING

A blacklist is a database of Internet IP addresses and servers which are known senders (or suspected senders) of spam. There are multiple "black lists" that exist, and major Internet Service Providers ("ISP's") can have their own list, rely on the lists of third parties, or do both. Different ISP's therefore have their own lists of protocols for determining blacklists; getting on a blacklist is likely as easy as sending one mass e-mailing in which recipients report the e-mail as "spam" to the ISP.

ISP's can also use spam software and other e-mail tools to identify spam based on certain "scoring" criteria. Thus if an e-mail receives scores over a certain number, then the IP address and/or server from which the e-mail campaign was initiated might be blacklisted.

What you should know is that once an ISP has designated an e-newsletter as being spam, the ISP will prevent it from being sent to any of its users. No notification is sent by the ISP to the sender; rather it's up to the sender to determine that a problem is occurring. Future e-mails from the same server would likely experience the same delivery problem for that ISP.

If e-newsletters are sent from a firm server (either in-house or at a hosting facility), the statistics for the e-newsletters should be monitored to see the number of "bounced" (or undelivered) e-mails. While there will usually be some undeliverable e-mails (such as users cancelling e-mail accounts, moving to a different job and no longer using the same e-mail account, etc.), if there is a significant drop-off in the percentage of e-mails being opened, this may be a sign that blacklisting may have occurred with one or more ISP's. In such instance, the firm might need to look over the e-mail addresses of the undelivered e-mails to see if they are all from the same ISP (if the majority of the undelivered e-mails are AOL accounts, for instance, then there may be a blacklist problem with AOL for the firm's e-newsletters). Note that blacklisting will not result in the all of the e-mails being rejected.

Fortunately, many of the major ISP's (such as Yahoo!, AOL, and Google) offer bulk e-mail senders an opportunity to become "white-listed" by registering with them.[27] Becoming white-listed usually consists of supplying certain information about the company to the ISP, and the ISP in turn evaluates the information and chooses whether to allow the company's e-mail to be delivered to its subscribers without being blocked by any spam programs.

---

[27] For Yahoo!, the bulk e-mail "white-list" application can be viewed at http://help.yahoo.com/l/us/yahoo/mail/postmaster/bulkv2.html. For Google, please see http://mail.google.com/support/bin/answer.py?hl=en&answer=81126 (this isn't actually an application but guidelines for bulkmail senders). For AOL, please see http://postmaster.info.aol.com/whitelist/

CHAPTER 17 – BLOGGING

Blogging is one of the most effective methods of communicating with prospective clients and one of the least-used marketing opportunities. Effective blogs are created around a purpose, which may be to demonstrate expertise, show understanding, and create a dialogue with prospective clients and others. Because so few attorneys blog, those that blog effectively will have a major advantage over other "non-blogging" attorneys in terms of having their message resonate with clients.

BLOGGING OVERVIEW AND FAQ'S

What are Blogs?

Blogs are short for "web logs", and have been around since the end of the 1990's. Blogs are designed like a mini-website where the blog owner can easily make postings about interests, add pictures, and create a blog roll (a list of other blogs or websites liked by the blog owner). Blogs quickly became popular because they allowed owners to establish an Internet presence without having to create a full website, learn web code, or worry about hosting costs.

Why Should I Blog – Who Would be Interested in What I'm Doing Every Day?

First, let's talk about what a blog is not. A blog is not the place to share what you had for lunch or what you did yesterday.

The Blog Purpose

An effective blog should have one or more purposes, such as demonstrating legal knowledge in a particular area and showing a personal side so that potential clients can feel like they will want you to represent them.

It's important to remember that many clients, particularly clients having lower incomes and those that seek certain types of legal services, may have little or no personal contact with attorneys. These clients may not care about whether you graduated from a top law school, or how many scholarly articles you've written. What they really want is an attorney who they can identify with and relate to. Someone who genuinely cares about their problems.

It may be that the "human" side of a blog is the determining factor in having the client call you instead of another firm. *Ultimately, clients hire attorneys, not resumes*. Thus the goal is to show your "non-legal" side to clients.

WHAT SHOULD I BLOG ABOUT?

In addition to being an attorney, there's a good chance you're also a human being, maybe even one with hobbies and interests. Share them with others. If you like to fish, talk about a recent fishing adventure to a favorite spot, or what type of fishing you like to do. Same thing if you like to bike or watch old movies – talk about what you like, don't like, and invite others to agree or disagree. Remember - blog postings don't have to be (and shouldn't be) long.

> ***Of course if you blog about fishing you'll want to have a disclaimer saying that no fishing advice should be implied and that changes in fish habits may have occurred that might render the fishing hole less desirable.***

By sharing just one interest, you'll set yourself apart from 99.9% of other law websites. In the increasingly competitive world of law firm marketing, taking a simple step such as this will make you stand out from your competitors, and give you an advantage over other law firms.

THE ELEMENTS OF A GOOD BLOG

In addition to identifying the purpose(s) for your blog, there are a number of other elements for good blogs:

> ➢ Pick specific areas to blog about; such as your practice area.

> ➢ Have a goal in mind for your blog. For a practice area blog, the goal could be to demonstrate your knowledge about that practice area.

> ➢ As noted above, make at least part of your blog about non legal-related items that you care about or are involved in. Don't underestimate the marketing value of non-legal postings. If you're an avid fisherman, talk about favorite fishing places, upcoming trips, or other fishing-related matters.

- Keep your blog postings short, and write in a personal, non-legal style.

- Don't use legal citations unless your blog is geared *specifically* to other lawyers.

- If you read other blogs on topics you frequently write about (such as fishing), refer to and link to those blogs. Example – "Like John Smith [link to John's blog], I also had a successful fishing trip for marlins in the Florida Keys in March, despite adverse weather conditions."

- Use tagging for your blogs (discussed below). For instance blogs could be tagged "DUI updates", "great fishing spots", etc. Tagging enables blog readers to quickly access all of your postings on a particular subject.

- Don't be boring. Blog postings should not be about your daily events, but rather centered on specific topics.

- Allow comments to be made, but use a spam filter to prevent automated blog entries (typically one requiring users to type in a partially hidden code). If you don't have a spam filter, you'll likely receive hundreds of attempts every month to add spam "comments" to your blog.[28]

How Often Should I Blog?

There is no set time interval; what is important is to create new blog postings on somewhat of a set schedule – perhaps one or two every week. In the beginning, you may wish to make a number of postings within a short time frame so that your blog doesn't appear barren. After a number of postings, especially if you're using categories to organize your postings, your blog page will soon look (and be) active.

Blog Categories versus Blog Tags – What is the Difference, and How Should Each Be Used?

Blog tags are much like keywords about a blog posting, and are generally displayed at the end or just after the end of each blog positing. For example, in a blog posting about breathalyzers used in DUI cases, tags for "breathalyzer", "DUI", and "alcohol testing" could be used.

---

[28] See www.Akismet.com for a WordPress spam filter.

Blog Categories, on the other hand, function more as a way to group multiple postings under a single topic. In the example above, a category could be created called "Our DUI Defense Practice", which would encompass a number of postings, while the category "Fishing Expeditions" would encompass other postings (leaving open the possibility that a posting might be applicable to both categories).

A creative way to use blog tags are what is called a tag cloud. A "tag cloud" shows tag words in different sizes in proportion to the number of times that the tag word is used. Thus if the tag "DUI" is used in more blog postings than any other tag word, "DUI" would be shown in larger and/or bolder font than other less-frequently used tag words. In addition to showing a comparison of tag words based on the number of times used in postings, a user can click on one of the tags and immediately see a list of all blog postings in which the tag has been used.

CAN CATEGORIES AND TAGS BE ADDED AFTER A POSTING IS PUBLISHED?

Yes. The edit button can be used to make changes to blog postings, including changes by adding tags and categories.

CREATING A BLOG TITLE

Ideally the blog title should be catchy, and serve as a call to read. Thus the title *Marriage, Marlins and More!* is probably more interesting than *Joe's Blog*. Don't, however, let the lack of a clever name prevent you from starting a blog. The name of your blog can be changed at any time, so when that burst of creativity happens, change the title.

CREATING MY FIRST POSTING – HOW DO I DO IT RIGHT?

To borrow from Nike – just do it. Follow the suggestions above, keep your first posting simple, and no one gets hurt.

For fellow fishing enthusiasts, a first post might be about a favorite fishing spot. A legal blog posting might be about new case law or statutory changes being considered. Look at others blogging about fishing or the law for examples. You'll soon realize how easy a blog posting is to write.

A blog is NOT a legal treatise or law review article. Thus unless your blog is specifically directed to lawyers, fight the urge to compare and contrast legal decisions, and don't use legal citations.

Before writing your first posting, take a few minutes to think about the general categories that you are likely to write about. For your divorce practice, you might have a general "Divorce" category, along with sub-categories such as Spousal Support, Filing Requirements, and Custody Matters. For fishing postings, you might have sub-categories for Best Fishing Places, Fishing Equipment, and General Discussions. You can always add new categories and sub-categories, and can re-arrange categories and sub-categories, but it will be helpful if you can start with a general structure.

For your first posting, if you're using WordPress, click the "**new post**" link/button in the admin panel. On the next page you'll see areas to be filled in for the name of the posting, the category, and the content of the posting. If you're using another blogging program, you should see similar links or buttons in the admin panel.

After completing your entry you can review it, save it, or publish it. Note that saving a posting *is not* the same as publishing it. "*Saving*" allows the writer to return to the posting later to complete it, "*Publishing*" is used to have the posting placed in the writer's blog where it can be viewed by others. Publishing a posting can be done instantaneously by clicking the "publish" link/button, or a future date can be set for publication. This delay feature is useful, as you may want to write several blog postings on one day and have them published over the course of a week or two.

HOLD THE PRESSES – CAN I CHANGE A POSTING AFTER IT'S BEEN PUBLISHED?

The short answer is Yes – you can change a posting any time you wish.

Conventional blog etiquette suggests that you include language at the bottom of a revised posting advising that the posting has been revised, and a short explanation of what was revised. There are some in the blogosphere that advocate that the original post be red-lined to show changes from the original version. The concern is that if another person links to and comments on a posting on your blog, the person's comments may not make sense if you subsequently revise the posting without adding an explanation or otherwise showing the revisions.[29]

---

[29] Blogging for Dummies, Brad Hill, 2006, Wiley Publishing Inc, pp. 268-270.

BLOG HOSTING

WHAT BLOG PLATFORM SHOULD I USE?

A blog platform consists of the underlying coding that allows a blog to be created and easily managed (such as to add new postings, categories, comments, etc.). Four of the most popular blogging platforms are WordPress, Type Pad, Movable Type, and Blogger.com (Blogger is owned by Google). WordPress is my personal choice as it can be hosted on the author's own website, it offers many customization and plugin options, it's compatible with PHP, it can be integrated into websites that utilize the Joomla Content Management System (see Chapter 10), and can even be managed using an Iphone application. It also offers a complete XML export of all posts and comments in the event that the author subsequently wishes to switch to another blog platform. Best of all, it's free.

For these reasons, other blogging platforms will not be discussed; but note that there is no right or wrong blogging platform – options other than WordPress are perfectly fine. In general, most of the top blog platforms have the same features.[30]

WHERE SHOULD MY BLOG BE HOSTED – ON THE FIRM'S WEBSITE OR SOMEWHERE ELSE?

While WordPress offers the option of hosting your blog for free on their website, it's far better to host your blog on your firm's website for ease-of-access for your website visitors and to improve your website for search engine optimization purposes. First - you don't want your firm's website users going back and forth between the firm's website and wherever your blog is hosted. If they leave your firm's website (even to go to your blog), they may be unlikely to return to your firm's website. Keep visitors on your website for the whole process.

Second – for SEO purposes, it's much more beneficial to have links from other websites or blogs to your firm's website (and thus increase your firm's website in search engine optimization rankings). If these links instead go to the website where your blog is hosted, your website won't benefit by potentially higher SEO rankings.

---

[30] If you want to know which platform a blog uses, using Internet Explorer, right click in the blog itself, then scroll-down and left-click on "view source". You'll then be able to see the coding for the blog, and at the top of the page it will identify the blog platform being used. In most cases, it's possible to get exactly the same look using any of the major blog platforms, such that if you like a particular blog built on Type Pad, the same layout and look could be developed on WordPress.

> *NOTE – if you plan on having a WordPress blog hosted on your own website, you'll need to work through http://WordPress.org, not http://WordPress.com (the latter being strictly for blogs hosted with WordPress). The remaining discussion assumes that you will use a WordPress blog hosted on your firm's website.*

WHO USES WORDPRESS?

Literally millions of blogs have been developed on WordPress. Prominent WordPress blogs include blogs for companies such as Best Buy, The Magazine from The Wall Street Journal, GE Reports, and Xerox, as well as the likes of Ben & Jerry, Sir Richard Branson, The Lance Armstrong Foundation, and Freakonomics.[31] With respect to the Technorati Top 100 most popular blogs (announced in January, 2009), a total of 27 self-hosted blogs used WordPress, with the second most popular self-hosted blog result being Movable Type (with 12 blogs).[32]

A NOTE ABOUT OPEN SOURCE, PHP, AND MYSQL

WordPress is an Open Source project. Open Source projects typically mean two things: one, that there are many people working on the development and refinement of the code to make it better (in the case of WordPress, hundreds of people all over the world), and two, that anyone is free to use it without having to pay a license fee. With popular Open Source projects such as WordPress there is often a third benefit – developers creating plugins and modules that can be easily added to your blog. In the case of WordPress there are several thousand applications that have been developed, most of which are free or low cost.

WordPress is built on PHP and MySQL, and licensed under the GPL (General Public License). MySQL has become the world's most-used open source database, and is used by companies such as Yahoo! and Twitter.[33] PHP is a scripting language typically used in conjunction with MySQL databases to create dynamic website pages.

---

[31] See http://wordpress.org/showcase/tag/fortune-500/
[32] See The Blog Platforms of Choice among the Top 100 blogs, http://royal.pingdom.com/2009/01/15/the-blog-platforms-of-choice-among-the-top-100-blogs/, referencing Technorati top 100 most popular blogs.
[33] http://www.mysql.com/why-mysql/

INSTALLING WORDPRESS

To install WordPress, go to http://wordpress.org/download/ to download the latest version of WordPress. On that same page is a link to detailed installation instructions, so the installation process won't be repeated here.

CHOOSING AND CUSTOMIZING YOUR WORDPRESS THEME

WordPress.org (http://Wordpress.org/extend/themes) has approximately 900 free themes available. With hundreds of themes to choose from, it's easy to be overwhelmed. Fortunately, most of the WordPress themes can be changed fairly easily through Cascading Style Sheets (or CSS – See Chapter 17), so you're not stuck with using that pink color in the theme that you otherwise really like.

How, then, should a good theme, be chosen?

In general, you'll want to choose a theme with the following:

- Designed to support that latest Word Press Release (see http://WordPress.org – the latest stable release is indicated in the "Download" box that is usually near the upper right-hand corner of the page)
- Includes multiple widget-ready placement
- Is compatible with the latest releases of Internet Explorer

Also, take a look at the star ratings and comments for themes. Generally you'll want to avoid using a theme if there are a lot of users who have experienced problems. There are also a lot of companies that create and license WordPress themes, and which can also create a custom WordPress theme for your blog. In general, even if one of the free WordPress themes is chosen, it can be easily modified by your developer to match your firm's website.

> *WordPress blogs require PHP version 4.3 or later, MySQL version 4.0 or greater, and the mod_rewrite Apache module. If your hosting provider is using a non-Microsoft server environment, WordPress should function fine. In general, the default hosting option assumes a non-Microsoft server environment. For more information about PHP and MySQL vs. ASP and SQL, please see Chapter 10).*

UNDERSTANDING THE WORDPRESS CONTROL PANEL

Blog Options

WordPress allows a number of options and settings. The following describes some the of the settings that you'll likely want to implement.

Number of Postings on One Web Page

This setting limits the number of your postings that will be displayed on one web page. If the number of postings is not limited, the web page will keep growing longer every time a posting is made until it (quickly) becomes unbearably long. Limit postings to 5 or less per page.

To set the limit on the number of postings, you will need to go to the "**Settings**" tab in your WordPress blog and click "**Reading**". On this page you can set the maximum number of blogs you want to appear on the page at one time.

Access to Your Blog

WordPress (and other blog platforms) give the author the ability to restrict who can access the author's blog through various types of passwords and acceptance configurations. As you want to encourage users to read your blog, you won't want to set any of these security options. By default WordPress allows access to everyone, so no settings will need to be changed here.

Other Blog Settings

Once your blog is set-up, the best way to learn about blog settings is to click on the different settings and links in the blog administration panel. You'll quickly see the various options that are available, and can customize your blog accordingly.

HELLO, IS THERE ANYBODY OUT THERE? - PROMOTING YOUR BLOG

Don't assume that because you have a blog on your website, users will be able to find it. Follow the promotion rule mentioned earlier – if you have important content on your website that you want users to see, prominently promote the content on your home page and other pages of your firm's website.

Ideally, your website will incorporate a Content Management System (or CMS – see Chapter 10) whereby you can easily copy a portion of your most recent blog posting (such as the title and perhaps the first few lines) and add it to your home page, with a link to the blog itself. If your website doesn't have a CMS, at least create an attractive link to your blog that will entice users to click on the link and be taken directly to your blog (such as an image with the blog title "Marriage, Marlins, and More Discussed Here!" – for a divorce attorney/avid fisherman). Be creative – in this example, there's a plethora of postings that could be done about knowing when to cut bait, there's more fish in the ocean, etc.

Your postings don't have to be particularly humorous, especially if that's not your style. Remember – the goal of non-legal postings is to convey to others that you're a real person, not just a resume.

SYNDICATING YOUR BLOG THROUGH RSS FEEDS

Blog syndication is the process of making your blog available to others. Typically syndication is done through RSS which stands for Really Simple Syndication. Blogs that have RSS typically have either the image Show to the right of this paragraph, or by a "Entries (RSS)" or similar link on the blog.

RSS turns your postings into a format called XML which can be sent out to blog subscribers by way of an XML feed. The XML feed can be added under a "favorites" tab (the "feeds" tab) in Internet Explorer where it can be easily accessed, or postings from the XML feed can be delivered directly to a Microsoft Outlook inbox using an RSS reader program such as Newsgator. For those to who utilize personal pages such as iGoogle, the XML feeds can be configured to be shown directly on the personal accounts page.

To receive your blog feed, readers will need to click the RSS symbol or link located on your blog. Once the symbol is clicked they will be taken to a page showing them what your blog feed will look like in either their "Favorites Center" or their inbox. They will also be asked if they want to subscribe to your feed by clicking on "Subscribe to this feed". Once they have subscribed to your blog, they will start receiving your blog feeds.

WordPress makes blog syndication easy, as RSS feed capability is already built into the blog. With other blog platforms, the blog owner sometimes needs to take several steps to enable syndication.[34]

SUBMITTING YOUR BLOG TO BLOG SEARCH ENGINES

There are a number of search engines designed specifically to scan and index blog content, and to return a list of blogs in response to a user's search query. Here is a list of a few of the more popular blog search engines, and instructions for submitting your blog.

TECHNORATI (WWW.TECHNORATI.COM): Technorati is sort of the original Google for blog searches in that it was created specifically for crawling and indexing blogs. Unlike Google, which only requires a simple typed-in address for a blog, Technorati employs a different process whereby authors must first register at Technorati and then claim their blog.

To claim your blog you must first become a member of Technorati by clicking the "**Join**" tab in the upper right hand corner of the home page. On the next page, fill in the information for your name, e-mail address, desired password, and click "**Join**". Please note, not all claimed blogs will be automatically added to the Blog Directory. For full details on what can be done to help ensure that your blog will be added to the Blog Directory, visit http://technorati.com/blog-claiming-faq/.

Next, an email will be sent asking you to verify your membership. Click the link provided in the e-mail to finish the registration process. Now you can claim your blog.

To claim your blog, access your Technorati profile page by clicking on your **user name** in the upper right hand corner of any page of Technorati (assuming that you're logged in). Scroll to the bottom of the page to "**Start a blog claim**" under "**My claimed blogs**" (which is at the very bottom of the page). Add your blog url here and click "**Claim**".

On the next page add the title to your blog, the url for your blog, and the RSS feed. (If you're using WordPress, click the RSS link on your blog, and then copy the url address for the next page). Next, add a description of your blog (1000 character limit), select up to 4 categories you would like your blog to be identified by, and include up to 18 site tags for your blog (site tags are keywords about your blog). Make sure that all information added is

---

[34] TypePad, for instance, makes syndication an easy option for bloggers with just a few clicks in the Syndication Setup Page (see http://tpsupport.mtcs.sixapart.com/tp/us-tp1/how_do_i_syndicate_my_weblog.html for more detailed information).

correct before finishing the process by clicking "**Proceed to the next step**" where you will be taken to a page thanking you for your blog submission.

GOOGLE BLOG SEARCH: Go to http://blogsearch.google.com/ping?hl=en, and type in the url of your blog feed.

ICEROCKET: Another popular blog search engine is IceRocket, which also powers the blog searches on Blog Search Engine (www.blogsearchengine.com). To submit your blog to the IceRocket search engine, go to www.icerocket.com and add the url for your blog.

BLOGARAMA: To submit your blog to Blogarama you must first register for a free account at http://www.blogarama.com/. Complete the form and click "**Submit**".

PING-O-MATIC: Once you have submitted your blog to the major blog search engines help increase your search engine visibility by submitting each new blog posting to Ping-O-Matic. Go to www.pingomatic.com, add your blog name and url, select the blog search engine services you want to ping, and click "**Send Pings**".

USING A SEPARATE FREE E-MAIL ACCOUNT FOR BLOG SUBMISSION

A number of blog search engines require the person submitting the blog to provide an e-mail account. As with other potentially spam opportunities, you may wish to use a free e-mail account other than your primary e-mail account (such as Gmail) to prevent possible spam from occurring.

SHOULD I LET SEARCH ENGINES PING ME, AND DOES IT HURT MUCH?

A "ping" or "pinging" has several meanings. One is the process of sending a message to an Internet server from a computer to see if the server is functioning. A second (described below) is the process of notifying blog search engines that you have made a new posting on your blog. A third – used by those much cooler than me – is as a substitute for the word "call"; such as "I'll ping you after work."

Pinging is important for the same reason that having search engines crawl your website is important. You want to notify blog search engines about your content so that the content can be indexed and shown to users in response to a search query related to your new content. Pinging differs in one respect as with pinging you *request* a blog search engine company, such as Technorati, to "crawl" your blog.

WHAT'S A "TRACKBACK", AND WHAT TYPE OF ANIMAL ARE WE HUNTING?

Wikipedia defines a trackback as follows:

> A trackback is an acknowledgment. This acknowledgment is sent via a network signal (a "ping") from the originating site to the receiving site. The receptor often publishes a link back to the originator indicating its worthiness. Trackback requires both sites to be trackback-enabled in order to establish this communication. Trackback does not require the originating site to be physically linked to the receiving site.
>
> Trackbacks are used primarily to facilitate communication between blogs; if a blogger writes a new entry commenting on, or referring to, an entry found at another blog, and both blogging tools support the Trackback protocol, then the commenting blogger can notify the other blog with a "Trackback ping"; the receiving blog will typically display summaries of, and links to, all the commenting entries below the original entry. This allows for conversations spanning several blogs that readers can easily follow.[35] (Links in original text not included here.)

Trackbacks are thus an important part of blogging, as if you reference another person's blog posting, you'll want to ensure that the other person is informed that their posting has been referenced. Assuming that the other person has enabled trackbacks, this process allows the other person to be notified automatically. Hopefully the other person will continue the conversation (and perhaps even add your blog to his or her blog roll), but at least you will have gained some publicity from your blog posting.

Similarly, with trackbacks you will be notified if another blogger references one of your blog postings, and then you can see (and possibly comment on) the posting made by the other blogger.

WIDGETS FOR BLOGS

A widget is a small box of information produced from coding that can be added to blogs, social networking pages, personal home pages (such as a Yahoo! home page), or a person's desktop screen. Common widgets are those for news, weather, stock quotes, clocks, calendars, Facebook friends, and more. A Facebook Share widget, for example, can be

---

[35] http://en.wikipedia.org/wiki/Trackback

added to a blog and thereby used to drive more traffic to a firm's Facebook business page. A Flickr widget can also be added to a blog to display images of a law firm and its attorneys.

There are a huge number of widgets available on the Internet that can be added to blogs. Many of these widgets are free; other widgets are free but may include advertising, (unless a user wants to pay (usually a couple of dollars) to have the advertising removed.

For some interesting and useful widgets to add to your blog, visit Widget Box (www.widgetbox.com) or WordPress (www.wordpress.org), or do a search for "WordPress widgets".

BLOGGING ABOUT YOUR PRACTICE AREA(S)

There a number of practice area items that can be written about; the following are some examples:

> ➢ Recent court decisions – summarize the decision in a couple of non-legal sentences, avoid talking about legal precedent, and state specifically what the decision means to current and prospective clients.
>
> ➢ Industry changes – if you're a construction attorney, talk about the downturn (or upturn) in building
>
> ➢ New firm practice areas, especially how these practice areas will help clients
>
> ➢ New firm attorneys

As discussed earlier, blogs should have a goal. Here, your goal may be to demonstrate the expertise of your firm in a number of different areas.

COMMENTS – TO ALLOW, OR NOT TO ALLOW – THAT IS THE QUESTION

Blogs are generally considered to be an interactive form of communication, so allowing comments to be posted is generally expected. After all, you do want users to encourage user comments on other great fishing places, right?

If comments are to be allowed, you'll want to do three things:

1. Include an anti-computer generated spam detection methodology option to prevent automated computer-generated comments, such as the popular "hidden-letter" boxes which require typing in the scrambled letters/numbers shown in the box that are not readable by computer programs.

2. Make sure that the option to approve all comments is selected (so that you decide which comments will be published).

3. Get a spam blocker to block all those prescription pharmacy ads. For WordPress, see Akismet (www.Akismet.com), which was developed by the same person who developed much of WordPress. The cost for this add-on is about $5/month.

Without spam blockers, once spammers find your blog, you'll start getting hundreds of spam "comments" every month that say something like:

"Great posting. I agree completely. Keep up the good work."

This will be followed by a number of links of the usual spam-type generated on the Internet and sent to e-mail addresses about prescription pharmacy products, adult websites, etc.

What these spammers are hoping for is that you'll be so pleased that someone has read and posted a reply to your blog that you'll accept the comment (and thus the links to their ads will be added to your blog, which will help them with SEO purposes and provide just a tiny bit of possible validity). When you start receiving these spam comments, simply delete them, and then order Akismet spam blocker (since you won't have done this yet, otherwise you likely wouldn't be getting this spam blocker if you're receiving these types of comments).

ATTRIBUTION AND OTHER BLOGGING ETIQUETTE[36]

Bloggers are very big on attribution. If you read something by another blogger and it even helps stimulate a thought in your brain that subsequently becomes part of one of your postings, you should provide a link to the blog of the other person. Here's an example:

---

[36] Blogging for Dummies, Brad Hill, 2006, Wiley Publishing Inc, pp. 268-274.

> After reading John Smith's blog about <u>fishing in the Florida Keys</u>, I was reminded of a fishing trip that I took there ten years ago and had a similar experience.

Here are a few other blog etiquette tips to follow:

- ➤ Don't make comments on other blogs to specifically promote your firm or anything else. You can, of course, provide a link to your blog and/or website, but your comment should be genuine comment to further the discussion.

- ➤ Don't try to move the conversation to your blog. Many blog owners work hard at developing followers, so trying to move the conversation to your blog will be viewed very negatively in the blogosphere.

Fortunately, assuming that you respect these rules, other bloggers will provide attribution to you, and not try to steal your thunder.

Will Blogging Help With Search Engine Optimization and Website Rankings?

Yes. Search engines love content, and, as a general rule, the more content on your website, the better. In particular, search engines love *fresh* content; in other words, content that is new to your website. More about the relevance of search engine optimization (SEO) is included in Chapter 11.

Other Ways to Get People to Your Blog and to Make Comments

Since you like fishing so much, how about finding other blogs about fishing and commenting on the postings made by the blog author? If you find a great fishing blog, add the link to your blog roll. A blog roll is a list of other websites and blogs liked by an author and included on an author's blog.

Having your blog listed on another person's blog roll is a compliment. It also doesn't cost you anything to promote someone else's blog.

The phrase "what comes around, goes around" is true in the blogosphere. Write a positive comment on someone's blog and there is a good chance that they will do the same on your blog, and perhaps also list your blog on their blog roll.

ADDING RSS TO YOUR FACEBOOK BUSINESS PAGE

Another easy way to get more traffic to your blog and to get people posting is to add the RSS for your blog to your Facebook business page. For more on this see Chapter 18.

POST LINKS ON TWITTER & FACEBOOK

Each time you add a new blog post, add a "Tweet" on Twitter and a link on Facebook. At this time it doesn't appear that a new blog posting can be shown automatically on Twitter, but it is possible to use RSS to Facebook so that postings can be displayed on a Facebook page. See Chapter 18 and the appendices for more information.

HOW BLOG COMMENTS HELP YOUR IMAGE FOR PROSPECTIVE CLIENTS

Receiving positive comments on your blog is a great sign that people like you (or at least your blog). In comparison to client recommendations on your website about your services (which you've obviously added), blog comments are seen as unsolicited, and thus have more credibility.

Your responses to blog comments also provide a unique window for prospective clients, as your responses can show directly how you interact with others. Use courteous, thoughtful responses to blog comments and prospective clients will assume that they will be treated in a similar, respectful manner. Seeing actual written interaction is much more valuable than simply informing users that your firm "Treats all clients with personal attention and respect."

BLOGGING AND THE POTENTIAL FOR LAWSUITS

One fear among attorneys with respect to blogs is that they will inadvertently be sued for providing legal advice or otherwise run afoul with some ethical rule as a result of their blog. For the most part, this fear is unfounded. Before commenting further, please be advised that this section is not intended to provide any legal advice whatsoever, including, but not limited to, advice that may be relevant to the ethical rules in your jurisdiction(s) of practice.

Now, after clearly stating this disclaimer, you'll want to include a similar disclaimer on your website, and perhaps an additional, separate disclaimer on your blog.

Will you inadvertently "slip-up" and provide legal advice to prospective clients? If someone asks you a legal question about a specific circumstance, are you going to respond with legal advice on your blog? Of course not.

Instead, you'll first make clear that because of legal ethics rules governing the practice of law, as well as other case-specific facts that would need to be known, you're unable to respond to specific legal questions. When discussing new case law developments, you'll also provide (or refer to) a disclaimer that makes clear that your blog cannot be relied upon for legal advice for any purpose. The disclaimer (which should include any required disclaimer language required in the jurisdictions where you practice) will also be included at the bottom of all of your website pages, including your blog pages.

Despite the numerous disclaimers, is it still possible to be sued? Of course – as attorneys we know that any type of lawsuit is possible and that we're always subject to potential lawsuits every time we may speak at a cocktail party or publish an article. The only way to avoid any lawsuit would be to abandon the practice of law.

Fortunately, the number of lawsuits against attorneys for legal advice not arising under either a traditional attorney-client relationship or direct verbal advice (such as when an attorney might serve on a board of directors) appears to be small. Further, as attorneys, we are well capable of assessing the risk of a potential lawsuit if we take reasonable precautions to advise against the attorney-client relationship, and balance such risks against the potentially significant client-generation benefits that blogging might have.

On balance, I believe the benefits of blogging far outweigh any potential risks.

CHAPTER 18 – FACEBOOK, TWITTER, LINKEDIN, AND OTHER INTERNET SOCIAL PROMOTION AND NETWORKING OPPORTUNITIES

There are many new Internet social networking opportunities to ethically promote yourself and your law firm, many of which can also be fun. If you've never tried social networking before, consider the opportunities available before dismissing the opportunities outright.

SOCIAL NETWORKING ON THE INTERNET – THE BIG PICTURE

There are a number of social networking opportunities on the Internet, including blogging, Facebook, Twitter, LinkedIn, and Plaxo. Chapter 17 on blogging and the sections below provide an introduction to these opportunities. The big picture question you may have is "what do these opportunities mean for me, and how can I use these opportunities to promote my law firm?" The following diagram offers an overview of the social networking process – namely, how you can use the Internet to expand your circle of influence beyond where you live and practice. The remainder of this chapter describes how some of these networking opportunities can be used for client generation purposes.

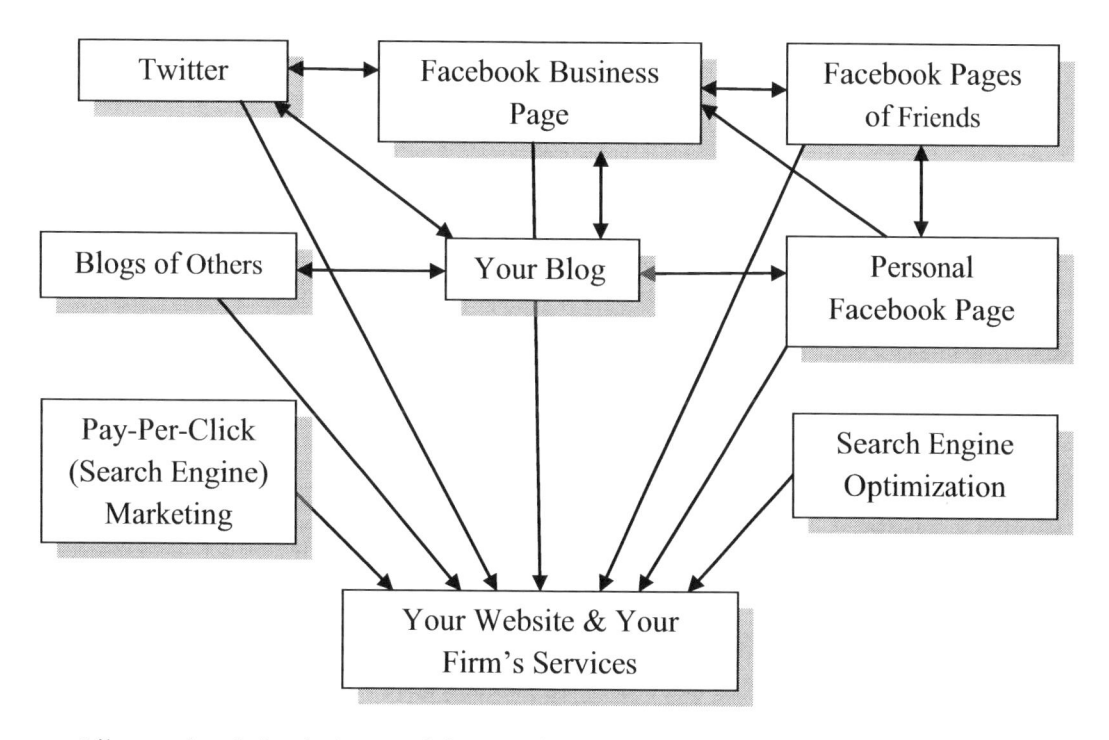

```
   Twitter  ⇄  Facebook Business Page  ⇄  Facebook Pages of Friends

   Blogs of Others  →  Your Blog  ⇄  Personal Facebook Page

   Pay-Per-Click (Search Engine) Marketing      Search Engine Optimization

                    Your Website & Your Firm's Services
```

Like good website design, social networking should be focused on <u>one or more specific goals</u> to be achieved. For an attorney, the primary goal is usually to drive traffic to the attorney's blog and/or website. Secondary goals are often to increase the Internet presence of the attorney's website for search engine optimization (SEO) purposes, to connect with potential clients by showing that the attorney is a "real person" beyond the law office, and to further deliver the attorney's message and the law firm's value proposition in a way that resonates with potential clients.

The diagram above provides a simple schematic of how social networking can be used to increase an Internet presence. It's important to note that the double arrows indicate *interactivity, not one-way interaction.* For instance, if you want to increase the exposure of your blog, don't assume that other bloggers will simply start writing about your blog on their blog. Instead, find other bloggers who have similar interests (both legal and non-legal interests) and post comments on their blog about postings that they have made. Ideally, you would like other bloggers to reference (and promote the ideas contained in) your blog.

Also, like any form of networking, Internet networking takes time, and it's best done at least with a vague plan in place. The following are some suggestions as to how to be successful in Internet networking, but as I'm sure you'll quickly notice, they're really not all that different than face-to-face networking opportunities.

1. <u>Develop a Plan.</u> Take time and sketch out some ideas about what type of people you would like to meet, what you want others to know about you, and what specific areas you are interested in and like to talk about (such as hobbies or an area of law).

2. <u>Get Involved in Areas that Interest You.</u> Most of us have been involved in networking, and probably have participated in clubs, civic organizations, and charitable events. We can tell fairly quickly which individuals are participating because they genuinely care about being involved, and which individuals are there only because they view it as a marketing opportunity. The same holds true on the Internet.

3. <u>Take the First Step in Initiating Contact.</u> Just as it might feel awkward initiating a conversation at a cocktail party where you don't know anyone, the same holds true on the Internet. Try starting with a group of fun-loving people who are always interested in meeting someone new – other attorneys. Create a profile on Facebook, and see if your former law school classmates are also part of Facebook, and if they are, send them a note and, as dorky as it may sound, a friend request. Find other attorney blogs, and add to the conversation on their blogs. You'll find that in general, people on Internet websites are quite friendly, especially if you pay them a genuine comment on a blog article they've written. They're also likely to visit your blog as well.

4. <u>Write About an Area of Interest, and Find Others With Similar Interests.</u> The best way to go about this is to write about an aspect of the law or your practice area you find interesting. Share your thoughts and experiences on the subject, and don't be afraid to add references to other blogs or writers that write on the same topic.

5. <u>Internet Marketing Takes Time.</u> Like the real world, it's unlikely that you're going to go to a social function or make a blog posting and have new clients waiting for you the next day. Just keep with it. It takes time to develop a readership base to your blog.

As you can see, there's not that much difference between Internet Networking and "real world" networking.

Next is an overview of several Internet networking possibilities. Please keep in mind that these are just a few of the many opportunities available, so don't feel that these are your only options.

FACEBOOK – WILL YOU BE MY FRIEND?

Facebook has become the most popular social networking website on the planet, with over 300,000,000 active users.[37] Facebook was developed in early 2004 by a Harvard University student for the purpose of helping students get to know one another. Very quickly The Facebook (as it was first known) expanded to other campuses, and received significant capital infusion and management expertise from the likes of one of the Paypal co-founders, and also multi-million dollar financings from venture capital firms. [38]

WHY HAS FACEBOOK BECOME SO POPULAR?

Facebook does an outstanding job in getting people connected. Once a user registers and adds a small amount of background information to his or her profile (such as where they went to high school and the year they graduated), Facebook begins suggesting "friends" that the user might know. In order to become "connected" with a person, a user simply clicks on the "send friend request" link. A short message can be added if desired ("remember when we came from behind to beat West High for the conference championship?), which is also delivered with the friend request. Unless the recipient has a very strong reason not to accept your friend request, friend requests are nearly always accepted. This is the case even if you knew the person only casually in high school, for instance. It's not important that you weren't best friends, so don't assume that being a close friend is a prerequisite on Facebook – it's not. (Also remember – the other person is probably also interested in adding friends to his or her Facebook page).

Congratulations, you now have a friend!

Many adults have embraced Facebook because not only is it a great way to better connect with current friends, family, and acquaintances, but also to connect with long-lost friends and acquaintances. If you use Facebook much, you may become better friends with people you only knew on a casual basis many years ago.

---

[37] http://www.Facebook.com/advertising/?src=pf
[38] Wikipedia, www.wikipedia.com, *Facebook*.

FACEBOOK – INITIAL IMPRESSIONS AND GETTING STARTED

As a warning, when you create an account on Facebook you'll find that three of the top navigation items – the Home and Profile tabs on the top left hand side of the page, and the one with your name on the top right hand side – appear to be almost identical. These and other navigation aspects are the most confusing parts of Facebook. Here's how these pages differ from each other, and my understanding of the rationale:

Home (left hand side) – The Home Page tab is located on the top left of the navigation bar. The Home Page is where you will find the latest news from your friends and pages for which you've become a fan. Your home page is only viewable by you.

Profile (left hand side) – Your Profile page is the public page that others (your friends) can see, and tells others about you. Here you will see threads of conversations you have had with your friends, and you can post "status updates" (including thoughts, sayings, just about anything you want to share with your friends), and links to videos and websites on your Wall. You can also include Info about your life (such as schools attended, birthday, home town, things you enjoy), and post Photos to albums. You can also access your Profile page by clicking on [Your Name] on the right hand side of the navigation bar.

Your Named Page (right hand side) – This page provides another way to access your Profile page.

Facebook also has several other confusing aspects. For instance, it takes some experience in trying to find out how to connect with friends, become a fan of your favorite team, and discover the difference between a group, fan page, and user profile. It also can be a bit frustrating as clicking on the "back" arrow on a browser to return to previous page does not always work.

RECOMMENDATIONS FOR FACEBOOK

Don't be afraid to get involved, create a profile page and join groups (especially groups like high school, college, and law school class groups). Also, don't be afraid to sign up for good causes, and to become a "fan" of groups you believe in (these can be sports, causes, or just about anything).

KEEPING CONNECTED – HOW TO ENCOURAGE OTHERS TO WRITE ON YOUR WALL

Your Wall (your Profile page) is your public face on Facebook. Your friends can write on your wall, especially to make a comment to something you may have posted. Facebook offers a place to make update postings similar to Twitter, although postings are not subject to the 140 character Twitter limitation. This box is at the top of your Profile page with the question "What's on your mind?" Fill in a short thought or message, and your posting is sent to all of your friends who can then go to your Wall to add a comment about your posting.

To generate postings to your wall (after first making Facebook friends), make a simple posting for your Wall – "I'm going to the Bears game this weekend, I hope that [fill in the name of current Bears quarterback of the week] can do a better job than [fill in the name of Bears quarterback for last week]." If you have friends who are Bears fans, or who hate the Bears, you're likely to get a number of diverse comments, which might include support, optimism, pessimism, empathy, or simply "they should get Favre."

In the world of Search Engine Optimization there is a term called "link bait", which means posting commentary or information on a person's website or blog that's likely to get linked to by other websites or blogs. Let's refer to these types of comments on Facebook as "posting bait", which, in addition to sharing thoughts, activities, etc., of the posting person, are designed to elicit thoughts, opinions, comments (or, in the case of a Bears quarterback posting, outright mockery or derision), from others.

Likewise, on your Profile page, you'll see comments from others about what they're doing or what's going on in their lives. Make comments, even if it's just clicking the "like – thumbs up" link. The more you get involved on Facebook, the more potential publicity for your business page, blog, and website.

I'M NO LONGER YOUR [FRIEND, FAN, GROUP MEMBER]

Don't be afraid to become the friend of someone on Facebook, or to become a fan or group member. If you really want to, you can always "de-friend" them later (or cease to be a fan or group member). Chances are that if the person (or group or business) has a hundred or more friends, it will probably be difficult for them to even figure out who left.

ADDING YOUR BLOG POSTINGS TO FACEBOOK

Adding the RSS feed from your blog to your Facebook business page is another way to add more content to your Facebook business page and to promote your blog and website.

To your blog postings through an RSS feed to your Facebook business page, go to http://apps.facebook.com/rss-connect/help.PHP?ref=hd. On this page you'll see the question "**How do I add the Social RSS application**?" followed by the answer "**To add social RSS to your profile click here…**" Click this link.

At the top of the next page, on the horizontal navigation bar, click "**Facebook pages**". The next page will ask whether you are "an administrator of a Facebook Page?" Click "**Add to Page**".

On the next page, select the name of your Facebook Page in the drop-down menu, and click the blue "**Add Social RSS**" box. On the next page, scroll down to the bottom half of the page with the four tabbed boxes. Here you *must* add the url for your RSS Feed (this is the url/complete website address for the home page of your blog), a 5 character Tag to identify it, and a Title that will appear at the top of your feed (which could be the same title as used to name your blog). You will also be able to set the display options, add a link to your website, and other options that are not required to activate the feed. Once this has been added click "**Update**".

Once your feed has been updated click OK. To see your feed on Facebook page click the + tab on the navigation bar above your wall and click "**RSS/Blog**". Your RSS feed will be displayed under this tab. To move this tab to left side of your page click the **"Boxes"** tab on the navigation bar, click on the **pencil icon** in the upper right hand corner of your RSS feed, and click "**Move to Wall Tab**".

LINKING YOUR FACEBOOK UPDATES TO TWITTER "TWEETS"

If you're on both Facebook and Twitter, you can have new messages on Facebook automatically posted as tweets on your Twitter account. The process of setting up this configuration is explained in **Appendix 6**. Note that if your posting on Facebook is longer than 140 characters, Twitter will truncate the posting by only including the first 140 characters; however, the Twitter posting will be displayed as a link so that a subscriber to your tweets can click on the posting and be taken to your Facebook page to read the full posting.

Currently, Twitter – to – Facebook postings are not possible.

TWITTER – SHOULD I TWEET?

Twitter offers users the ability to make short posts (140 characters or less), called "tweets", which can be viewed on cell phones, computer pages, or through other media. Because of the character limitation, tweets must be short. To be effective, they must be to the point. Abbreviations and shorthand are therefore perfectly acceptable.

It's easy to see how Twitter might be popular on a large college campus, where students can keep in touch with each other as to where they currently are, where they're going later in the day, what's going on over the weekend, etc. In my opinion, it's more difficult to see how Twitter can be used directly by attorneys to generate clients. It may be that the primary benefit is to promote the attorney's blog more than the "tweets" themselves, and thus Twitter may be viewed as another aspect of Internet networking, rather than an outright tool to connect with prospective clients.

THE TWITTER SIGN-UP PROCESS

The process for creating a Twitter account is set for in **Appendix 6**. Sign-up is free.

GETTING FOLLOWERS OF YOUR TWEETS

To be effective in any form of networking, you must connect with others. The same holds true on the Internet. If you want to build up a network of fans to follow your tweets and to expand your presence on the Internet, the best and quickest way is to subscribe to the tweets of others. While it's possible to start randomly subscribing to the tweets of everyone, it's more effective to look for others that share similar interests to your interests (law, fishing, or perhaps *Dancing with the Stars*). Unofficial Twitter protocol suggests that you at least consider becoming a follower of anyone who becomes a follower of your tweets; therefore, when you sign up to become a follower of the tweets of others, they will likely become a follower of your tweets.

Once your Twitter account has been created, place the Twitter logo on your website and your blog page, if you have a blog, and link the logo to your Twitter page. When you've made a new posting to your blog, a tweet can be made to notify others about the subject of the posting.[39] The tweet should be done in a way to encourage recipients to go to your blog and read your posting (recall the previous discussion about AOL headlines). A tweet of "see my new blog posting about the Jones case" isn't likely to get as many viewers as "the Jones case – has the court eliminated the Johnson rights doctrine?" will likely be much more effective.

MYSPACE

While MySpace still has a significant audience, I personally would not recommend creating a MySpace page. I believe that Facebook offers a much better networking opportunity, and, given the limited time that attorneys have, I would suggest concentrating on Facebook.

LINKEDIN

LinkedIn (http://www.linkedin.com) is an online community where professionals can create and foster business relationships, ask and share advice, and seek employment.[40]

To get started you'll need to create an account by providing your name, email address, and preferred password. Once the account has been created, information can be added to your profile such as current and past employment, schools attended, personal interests, groups and associations, honors and awards received, and contact information.

A network of others on LinkedIn will then be created for you based on this information which might include, for example, people that went to school with you. These relationships are known as your 1st Degree Connections. Friends and colleagues of your 1st Degree Connections are referred to as your 2nd Degree Connections, and friends and colleagues of your 2nd Degree Connections are your 3rd Degree Connections. 1st, 2nd, and 3rd degree

---

[39] Note that you can place a Twitter widget on your WordPress blog that will automatically display your Twitter "tweets" on your blog. See http://wordpress.org/extend/plugins/twitter-widget-pro/

[40] www.LinkedIn.com

connections are collectively included in the "My Connections" area in your LinkedIn Account and Settings. Eventually you too will be connected to Kevin Bacon.[41]

As a LinkedIn member you can join groups to connect with other members who share the same interests (perhaps others practicing the same areas of law your practice), professional goals (such as law firm marketing), and/or and experiences. Once you've joined a group, all members of that group become part of your network as 1st Degree Connections.

A Personal Account on LinkedIn is free and allows only direct contact through LinkedIn with your 1st Degree Connections. All individuals in your 2nd and 3rd Degree Connections can only be contacted through mutual friends that are your 1st Degree Connections.

By upgrading to a Premium Account (Business Account - $24.95/month, Business Plus - $49.95/month, and Pro - $499.95/month) you can personally contact any member of LinkedIn on your own using the LinkedIn InMail system. (To compare all accounts available on LinkedIn and confirm current pricing, please visit http://www.linkedin.com/static?key=business_info_more&trk=acct_set_compare). I don't have a suggested recommendation as to whether it's worth upgrading to a paid account, as the benefits are likely to be a function as to how actively LinkedIn would be used.

PLAXO

Plaxo (http://www.plaxo.com/) is an electronic address book that helps users connect with family, friends, and business associates. As a Plaxo member you have a profile page to let others know what you are doing (similar to that of most social networks). Based on the information added to your profile page and the contacts in your electronic address book, Plaxo recommends connections between you and other Plaxo members.

Plaxo is a free service that allows you to send unlimited messages to your contacts and connections. If you prefer to do more, Plaxo provides upgrades on three different levels for a monthly fee: Basic - $19.95/month, Plus - $44.95/month, and Power - $249.95/month. With the premium services you are able to contact members you are not connected with. To

---

[41] See http://en.wikipedia.org/wiki/Six_Degrees_of_Kevin_Bacon. The original concept came from actor Kevin Bacon who claimed that he had worked with everyone in Hollywood; either directly, or through another person (which would be one degree of separation). Subsequently a game was developed around how closely someone was connected to Kevin Bacon, with the theory that everyone could be connected to Kevin Bacon in six degrees of separation or less.

compare all accounts available on Plaxo visit
http://www.plaxo.com/PlaxoPro/purchase?r=f&url=http%3A%2F%2Fwww.plaxo.com%2Fevents&src=footer.

I suggest starting out with the free Plaxo account to stay current with any changes made to the contacts found in your electronic address book.

YELP

Yelp (http://www.yelp.com) is a website for users to share experiences and post reviews about services or products they've received from local professionals and businesses. Yelp has information about most cities in the US, and membership is free.

Law Firms can create a business account on Yelp to share information about services, hours of operation, location, etc. Yelp can also be used to promote firm attorneys and practice areas, and share a firm's value proposition with prospective clients.

If a firm has a client that was pleased with the services received, the client could post a recommendation on Yelp, which could then be seen by other prospective clients. Similarly a dissatisfied client could post a negative review on Yelp. While companies that receive negative reviews on Yelp can respond with reviewers both publicly and privately, law firm responses to negative reviews may not be practical due to attorney-client confidentiality and other ethics rules. Thus a firm will likely need to make a determination as to whether it wants to create a Yelp account and accept the positive reviews with the potentially negative reviews.

Yelp also provides business account owners with detailed information about the amount of traffic their Business Page is receiving, demographics of users frequenting their page, and an opportunity to create special offers and announcements to share with current and potential clients frequenting Yelp.

SOCIAL NETWORKING ETIQUETTE

Social networking etiquette is really simple – treat others with the same consideration and respect that you wish to be treated. If someone has something nice to say on one of your web pages or blog postings, consider saying something nice back on theirs. Don't treat the opportunity to "write" on someone's wall as an open invitation to market your firm's services (much like you wouldn't appreciate if they did the same thing to your wall).

On Facebook, for instance, if you build a business page for your firm and want to get "fans" for your business, it's perfectly fine for you to post a message on your wall to ask your friends to check out your page and become a fan. If you want your Facebook friends to become fans, in addition to writing on your wall, send them an e-mail through Facebook asking them to sign up.

As noted in the Chapter 17, blogs are a great way to interact with others on the Internet. In order to get traffic to your blog, check out the blogs of others that are on topics that interest you, and if you find ones that have good postings, feel free to ask questions, share opinions, or simply say that you like their posts.

It's also perfectly acceptable to tell a little bit about yourself in your posting ("I appreciate your story; I'm also a personal injury attorney ..."), as well as a link to your blog or website. Don't overdo it though. For instance, it typically wouldn't be appropriate to say something like "I've been practicing personal injury law for 30 years and recovered over $15 million for my clients, I was the attorney of record in ....." – you get the idea.

Also, as mentioned earlier, one of the highest compliments in the blogging world is to be referenced positively (or at least with respect) in the blog of another. An example - "While others, including John Smith [link to John Smith's blog] believe that the court signaled an end to the Johnson doctrine, I'm not so sure that the court is going quite so far because ... ". Here, while you may not entirely agree with Mr. Smith's opinion, you're nonetheless showing respect for his views, and, in addition, you're also promoting both him and his blog simply by mentioning them.

The next chapter provides another avenue for a firm to increase its presence both on the Internet and in the media through public relations.

CHAPTER 19 – PUBLIC RELATIONS PLANS AND PR FIRMS

On a dollar-for-dollar basis, money spent on Public Relations (PR) efforts can often be more effective in generating clients than spending the same amount on advertising. Public relations efforts can position law firms and attorneys as experts in the media, which can lead to the firm and its attorneys as being perceived as the top experts in the minds of targeted clients. To be effective, an ongoing public relations plan should be established; public relations should not be considered a one-time campaign.

WHAT'S SO IMPORTANT FOR LAW FIRMS ABOUT PUBLIC RELATIONS EFFORTS?

Public relations efforts may be thought of as a connection between your law firm and the public, including, most importantly, those who may need your firm's services. While advertising is seen as obvious self-promotion by the advertiser, public relations efforts may be viewed more objectively, especially if it is the news media that is focusing on you or your firm.

HIRING A PUBLIC RELATIONS FIRM AND DEVELOPING A PR PLAN

As with website development, don't try to engage in an extensive public relations campaign yourself unless you have an in-house person with the time and expertise to do so. Good PR campaigns can take a tremendous amount of time to develop and implement, and few law firms have either the experience or available time to do a good job.

PR PROPOSALS AND PR PLANS

PR Firms typically ask for three to six month contracts; and usually bill a set minimum monthly fee plus expenses. To a skeptic, the minimum monthly fees and somewhat long term commitments may seem that the PR firm is trying to ensure that the rent will be paid for the year. Understand that this is not the case.

Solid PR efforts take months to develop and implement. They also require significant work that most lawyers would rather avoid, such as compiling lists of media contacts and making calls to reporters to introduce the firm. Additionally, a good PR plan takes a significant amount of time to develop to both identify the goals to be achieved and to map out a strategy for success. If the law firm is not willing to commit to a certain level of time and expense, the PR firm knows that the desired goals likely won't be achieved, which will lead to dissatisfied clients.

In addition to PR plan development expertise, it's important that the PR firm have (or develop) the necessary relationships with the targeted media in order to effectively implement the PR campaign. Newspaper, television, magazine, and other reporters and writers are busy people. You shouldn't expect that because your firm sends its latest news release to a newspaper reporter that the newspaper will publish an article or even re-print the news release. Your news release will be competing against other stories being considered. This is where the relationships of PR firms prove valuable.

Professional PR firms typically have developed relationships with key news media in local markets, and often also in national markets for specific industries. These relationships are beneficial, as the PR firm will know who to contact and how to best position your law firm in order to have the best chance at getting publicity for your firm.

BECOMING A MEDIA EXPERT

The benefits of becoming a media expert can be tremendous. Imagine that whenever the local newspapers, television stations and radio shows need an expert on an area of law; you're the one they contact. Not only are you potentially featured to thousands or even tens of thousands of people (and perhaps hundreds or thousands of potential clients), you are being held out by the media as an "expert." If the media seek you for expert advice, shouldn't others go to you as well?

Have you ever wondered how certain attorneys become featured on television news programs and in newspapers and magazines? In many (if not most) instances, it's not an accident. Part of the job of a public relations company is to get you and your firm positioned as experts with the media, which also involves cultivating relationships. Understand that becoming an expert with the media usually doesn't happen overnight or with only one call, it's a process that will typically take months to develop (which also factors into why PR firms seek longer-term contracts). Your PR firm may work at contacting newspaper writers and local television media about your firm, and perhaps get a write-up for your firm in a local magazine.

The more exposure you and your firm receive, the easier it is to work your way up the chain to being seen as a legal expert by successively larger and more influential media, until one day you'll be appearing on Nancy Grace.

PRESS RELEASES

ISSUE PRESS RELEASES ON A REGULAR SCHEDULE; PREFERABLY WITH NEWS THAT WILL BENEFIT OTHERS.

As part of a public relations campaign, press releases should be issued on an ongoing, scheduled basis. Often law firms only issue press releases to announce the election of new partners or new lateral or law school hires. Not only is there little interest in these releases outside the law firm community and the people involved, but these releases are done so infrequently that they do not keep law firms in the upper minds of clients.

Instead of these annual or infrequent press releases, establish a regular schedule of press releases, such as one every month or every two months, and stick with this schedule. In determining the subject of the press release, ask yourself what is in it for potential clients or the public? Maybe your firm has developed a new practice area focused on a particular area of law, or has re-developed its website to include information that might be of use to potential clients. Or perhaps announce what your firms or attorneys are doing to make a difference in the community. In any event, it's important to keep your firm positioned in the minds of the community and prospective clients using methods other than advertising.

MAKE SURE YOUR PRESS RELEASES ARE OPTIMIZED FOR SEARCH ENGINES.

Each press release is posted on the website of the company used to issue the press release. Hopefully the press release will be "picked up" or included on other websites. Regardless of the number of websites where the release is published, the press release should be optimized for SEO purposes with links back to the law firm's website. The releases and the anchor text of the links should include keywords that relate to both the release and to keywords around the firm's services. Not only will such links help for SEO purposes, but an optimized release itself will show up on search engines for those using search terms which are included in the releases themselves.

Ideally, in addition to the local media, it would also be beneficial if your press releases are picked up by other legal publications. Your press releases should get to such publications by two separate ways. First, your PR firm should send the release to the publications with a follow-up call to discuss the importance of the release. Second, there's a good chance that legal publications will see the release as part of compilations such as Google Alerts that may be delivered to the legal and other media. Therefore, in addition to making sure that a release is optimized for SEO purposes, you'll also want to make sure that the release is optimized for Google and other types of alerts that may have been created by the media.

TARGETING INDUSTRIES

In addition to general press releases, you may also want to target the release for certain publications that may be influential for your clients, in particular non-legal publications that may be aimed at a specific industry. For instance, if your practice is focused on the construction industry, you may want to issue a news release around new regulations that affect the construction industry, and then target the news release to industry magazines. Your PR firm can then follow up with the industry magazine publication.

The goal in this instance is *not* to get the release itself published; rather it is to convince a writer at the publication to feature an article about the new regulations or other changes in the construction industry, and to feature (and quote) you to explain what the new regulations or changes mean.

In this case, you may wish to have your news release written in the form of an article, with you being quoted about the new regulations or other changes. When the release is sent to the industry publication, it will hopefully convince the publication that they too should publish an article about the new regulations or other changes. With respect to an industry trade magazine, it's much more effective to be quoted and have your firm featured in a two page article about a topic relevant to your clients than to pay for a quarter page ad.

PRESS RELEASE FORMATTING

The formatting of the press release will be dependent upon the goals to be achieved by the press release. The format may be different if the goal is to have an article published in an industry magazine versus a short story in a local newspaper. In addition, the cost to issue the press release may be dependent upon the number of words in the release itself. As a result of these factors, press releases are often written in collaboration between the attorney and the PR firm. The PR firm will be able to advise on the structure of the press release (such as a title and sub-titles, etc.), and how to format the release in a specific manner depending upon the primary audience to whom the release is targeted.

PRESS RELEASE DISTRIBUTION

There are a number of different companies that can be used to distribute a law firm's press releases. Individual press releases on some of the major press release sites typically cost from around $50 or so for the less expensive companies to $350-$500 on the large press release companies that are more national in scope. Here are a few companies to consider.[42]

- **PR Web** (*www.PRWeb.com*): Guaranteed placement on some of the top news websites like Yahoo! News and Topix. Boasts an online distribution to more than 250,000 RSS subscribers. Offers SEO to increase the visibility of press releases. Membership is free and press release distribution packages range from $80 to $360 and include analytics and SEO statistics on releases.

- **Marketwire** (*www.Marketwire.com*): Press releases can be sent to out geographically, or to a specific industry or specialty market such as distributions targeting the legal field. Marketwire can help with optimizing the content of your articles for increased search engine visibility. Call for pricing.

- **Eworldwire** (*www.Eworldwire.com*): Offer a highly targeted distribution list to both online and traditional news media sources, and copywriting services to help your press release get the attention it deserves. Prices for Law and Legal Newsline distribution focusing on lawsuits and class actions are $150.

- **PR Newswire** (*www.PRNewswire.com*): Distributes press releases to mainstream news media or a highly targeted list relevant to your area of law. PR Newswire can help you get your press release noticed and track its performance. Prices range from $125 for an SEO online only posting to $3,750 premium package including video.

- **PR Leap** (*www.prleap.com*): Pricing for PR Leap is per release, not subscription. Prices range from $49 for the Basic Plan to $149 for the Premium Plan. The Premium Plan includes next day service, up to 5 media attachments (embedded video, images, PDFs and MP3s), Associated Press, UPI, Google News, Ask.com News, Moreover, Statistics and Tracking, a 2,000 word limit, and more.

---

[42] Pricing compiled from websites as of October, 2009. The exact pricing for news releases will be dependent upon the scope of distribution, the number of words in the press release, whether the release is optimized for SEO purposes, and other factors.

It should be noted that some of the largest press distribution companies have targeted geographic and industry distributions that firms may wish to consider depending upon their needs.

APPENDIX 1 - REGISTERING YOUR FIRM'S DOMAIN NAMES[43]

THE DOMAIN REGISTRATION PROCESS

The domain name registration process is fairly straight-forward:

> At either www.EsquireInteractive.com or www.GoDaddy.com[44], type the desired domain name in the search box in the middle of the page and click "**GO!**"
>
> On the next page, you'll be informed as to whether your domain name is available. If it is, click on any other extensions to be registered. If the domain name isn't available, use the "**Search Again**" box below the results to search again for another domain name.

> *You may be surprised to find that letter combinations representing the letters of your firm's named partners may not be available. In addition to the domain names being legitimately used, there are literally millions of domain names held by domain name "squatters" – those that register domain names with the sole purpose of reselling them at a significantly higher price.*

If you're having problems trying to find an available domain name, try adding an extension to your firm's name such as shown in the following examples:

www.zollolantzlaw.com
www.zololantzlawfirm.com
www.zololantzlawpc.com
www.zololantzlawyers.com
www.zololantzattorneys.com
www.zololantzlawonline.com
www.zololantzlawweb.com
www.zololantzlawwebsite.com

---

[43] Please note that companies frequently change the exact processes, page information, and other content; thus some aspects may have changed some for the processes described in these appendices.

[44] Esquire Interactive is a domain name re-seller under a GoDaddy affiliate. Regardless of whether Esquire Interactive or GoDaddy is used, the registration steps will look much the same.

Once you have a primary domain name and any extensions, consider registering any common misspellings of your primary domain name. You can continue searching for domain names; the website will keep track of the available domain names near the bottom of the page.

After finalizing the list of domain names, you'll want to check out and pay the registration fees. To do so, click on the "**add and proceed to checkout**" button at the bottom of the page. On the following pages you can make changes to your order if you wish, for example, to remove a particular domain name from being registered. You can also register other domain names later if you wish.

On the next page you will be offered other domain names for sale. To skip these items, click "**No Thanks**".

The next page is the Domain Registration Page, where a new account can be created. As mentioned above, this will be the legal name of the registrant that will thereafter control the domain name as long as the registration does not lapse. **Do not have your domain name(s) registered in the name of your developer**. If you wish for the legal registrant to be your firm, be sure to check the box below the Company Name. After the required information has been filled in, click the orange "**Continue**" button at the bottom of the page. Also, be sure to provide a currently-working e-mail address (don't use an address for one of the domain names that is being registered as your e-mail address).

The next page is called "**Registration and Checkout Options**". This page provides a number of options, as follows:

TOP BOX
Registration Length - Select the number of years for which you wish to register your domain name. If you select one year, for example, you'll need to renew your registration by the end of the year to keep your domain name.

> *At about $10-20/year, the annual domain name registration fee is cheap. Because of the possibility of inadvertently missing a renewal deadline, it's a good idea to pay the $100-$200 to register the <u>primary</u> domain name (the one used to access your firm's website) for ten years. With other less important domains, such as the .net extension or firm misspelling domains, you may wish to register for a shorter period, especially if the name of your firm may change during the next several years. These domain names then can be considered for renewal when they expire, but if they inadvertently are not renewed it won't affect your primary domain name.*

Certified Domain Seal – This really isn't important for law firms unless you like seals (they are cute animals, right?).

Hosting and E-mail – scroll over the "**Learn More**" link if you're interested in these options. Hosting and e-mail accounts are discussed in other sections of this book. Note that you can purchase hosting and e-mail options later if you wish; so don't feel the need to do it now if you're not sure. (To start immediately receiving e-mail under your new domain name, select the purchase e-mail option now.) The e-mail account option can also be cancelled later when your new website is ready.

> *Regardless of whether your e-mail is through Godaddy, another hosting provider, or your own server, if you use Microsoft Outlook, you'll need to create a new e-mail account in Outlook and then associate this account with your new e-mail account after the new e-mail account has been created on the server.*

MIDDLE BOX

Here are the different registration types offered by GoDaddy. Scroll over the blue links on the left hand side to find out more about each of the options.

I suggest choosing at least the Deluxe option, primarily for the Private Registration aspect. With Private Registration, the domain name is registered in the name of a GoDaddy affiliate (Domains by Proxy), although the person or firm making the registration still controls the domain name. With a private registration, the Domains by Proxy contact information is publicly displayed in the WHOIS information, not your registrant information, which may reduce spam. (See *"Using the WHOIS Database to Find Registrant Information"* in Chapter 4 for more information about WHOIS information.)

Godaddy also offers a service called the "Protected Option". With the Protected Option, GoDaddy will renew your domain name for up to one additional year should it expire and not be timely renewed by you. During this time period, the domain name is "parked", and thus will not display your firm's website. Also, you'll still need to pay the registration fee to continue using the name after expiration. However, if the domain name is registered for an extended period, such as ten years, this option is less important.

SMARTSPACE AND OTHER OPTIONS

SmartSpace is essentially a pre-built website with room for blogs and other content. If you plan on having a website built immediately, this option can be ignored.

If you're interested, SmartSpace can be purchased now, and it may reduce the cost of your domain name, or it can be purchased later if you subsequently decide that you want it. SmartSpace can also be cancelled later if you decide not to use it.

After you've gotten through the myriad of options on this page, click "**Continue**" at the bottom of the page. Finally, at last, you'll be taken to the payment page.

But Wait – There's More! – Even after your domain name is registered, GoDaddy will try to sell you more products. (These guys didn't get to be at the top of the business for nothing. They understand that once a person is in the buying mood, the best thing to do is to keep selling). Unless you want to purchase these options, you're done. Congratulations, your domain names are now registered!

You should receive an e-mail from Godaddy (or Esquire Interactive) shortly (in the next ten minutes or so) confirming the registration of your domain name(s).

APPENDIX 2 – CHANGING THE NAMESERVER FOR YOUR DOMAIN NAME (FOR GODADDY OR ESQUIRE INTERACTIVE DOMAIN ACCOUNTS)

By default, your domain name will likely be associated with what is called a "nameserver" at the company where the domain name was registered. If you wish to have your website hosted at another company, the default nameserver must be changed to the nameserver where your website will be hosted. To change the nameserver, four tasks need to be completed:

1. <u>You or your developer will need to create a new account for your domain name with the hosting company.</u> The hosting company may be the same company with whom your domain is registered (Godaddy, for instance, also provides hosting services), or it could be another highly reputable hosting company (Esquire Interactive comes to mind).

2. <u>If the hosting company is not the same company where your domain name is registered, the hosting company will need to provide you with the nameserver information for its hosting facility.</u> Typically two nameserver addresses are provided, such as NS1.GreatestHostingCompanyEver.com and NS2.GreatestHostingCompanyEver.com (the "NS" stands for Nameserver).

3. <u>You will need to login to your GoDaddy or Esquire Interactive account and change the nameserver for your **PRIMARY** domain name (the one where your website will be hosted) to the nameserver specified by your hosting company.</u> Here's how you do this:

    Step 1 – On the GoDaddy Home Page, login to your account with your account number and password. If your domain account is through Esquire Interactive, click on the red "**Go**" button in the "Domain Search" box, and login to your account on the next page. (The Login/Password boxes are at the extreme upper right hand portion of the page).

GoDaddy

Step 2 – Click "**Domain Manager**" on the left hand navigation.

Step 3 – Click on your **PRIMARY** domain name (the one where your website will be hosted).

Step 4 – The next screen will look like this. Click the blue "**Manage**" link in the lower left hand corner under "Nameservers".

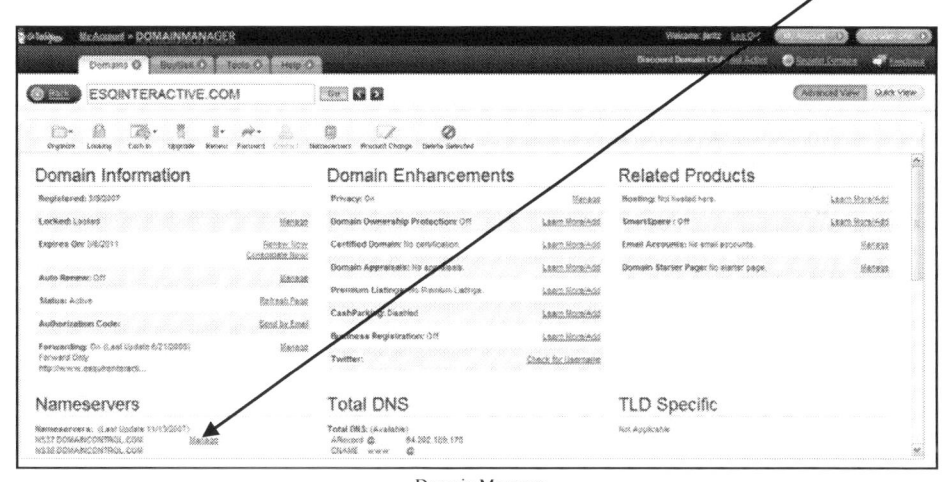

Domain Manager

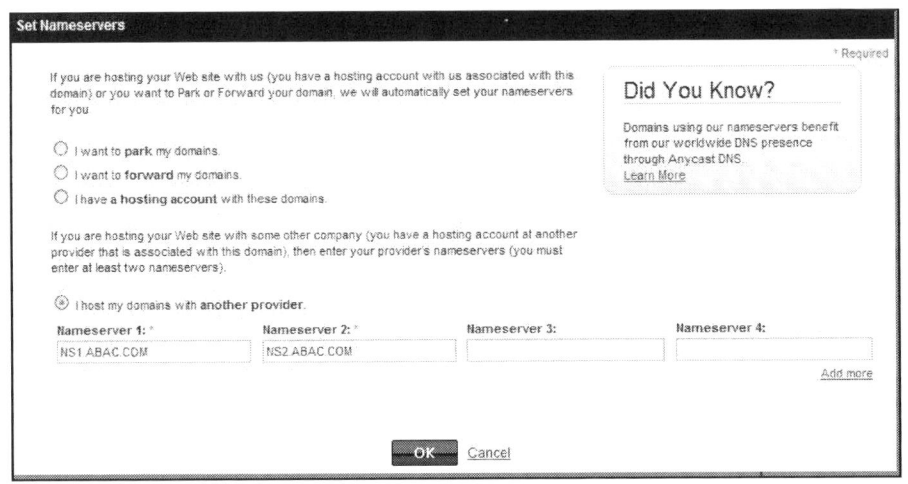

Set Nameserver

Step 5 – You should see a pop-up box with the heading "Set Nameservers". Click on the last option – "**I host my domain names with another provider**", and the pop-up box should look like this:

Step 6 – Type in the new nameserver address(es) that was (were) provided by your hosting company in the boxes (such as ns1.GreatestHostingCompanyEver.com). Your hosting company may have only provided one or two nameserver domain names; if this is the case, just type in the nameserver domain names that were provided and leave the other nameserver boxes empty. Then click "**OK**".

Now wait for up to 24 hours (at least you're not waiting in line for some clerk to wait on you, right?).

*You do **NOT** have to move your other domain names (variations on your firm's name or domain names with ".net" or other extensions) to your hosting company. Instead, a simpler method is used to "point" these domain names to your primary domain name. In other words, if someone types www.zoloandlantz.com, they will be immediately re-directed to the primary domain name – www.zololantz.com.*

To have your other domain names pointed to your primary domain name, do the following:

1. <u>Log back in to your GoDaddy or Esquire Interactive account</u> if you previously logged out.

2. <u>Click "**Domain Manager**" on the left hand navigation.</u>

3. <u>Click in the boxes next to **all** of the domain names that are to be forwarded/re-directed</u> (but ***do not*** click on the box with your primary domain name).

4. <u>Click the green "**Forward**" arrow/link</u> above the list of domain names at the top of the page. You should see a box that looks like this:

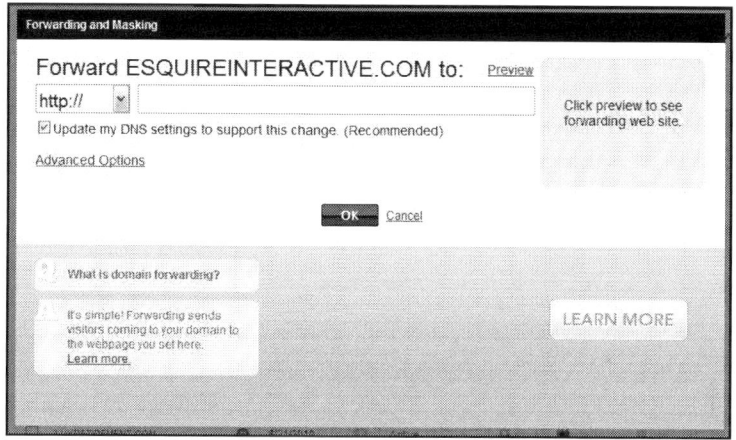

Domain Forward Box

Click on the "**Enable Forwarding**" box and the "**301 Moved Permanently**" box and then click "**OK**". Users typing in any of these domain names will then be re-directed to your primary domain name.

APPENDIX 3 – CREATING A PAY-PER-CLICK ACCOUNT WITH GOOGLE

If you've ever done a search on Google, Yahoo!, or Microsoft, you've seen the ads on the search results pages that often run across the top and the right hand side of the page. These ads are a type of search engine marketing often referred to as Pay-Per-Click advertising or "PPC advertising".

PPC Advertising

With PPC advertising, search engine companies display advertising related to the search terms entered on the search engine results pages (sometimes called "SERPS"). With Google, these ads are displayed on the right hand side and at the top of the search results pages. If a user clicks on the ad, the advertiser is charged a fee, and the user is re-directed to the advertiser's website. If the ad is not clicked no fee is charged.

This section takes you through the process of creating PPC advertising with Google. The steps in the process are as follows:

- Create an Account
- Structure Your Advertising
- Create Campaigns
- Create Compelling Ads
- Create Keywords to Trigger Display of Ads
- Enter Billing Information & Activate Ads
- Manage & Revise Ads as Necessary

CREATE AN ACCOUNT

Creating a Google PPC Account is relatively easy. First go to ***www.Google.com*** and click "***Advertising Programs***". From there you'll be taken to a page displaying Google's two Internet Marketing Programs, AdWords and AdSense.

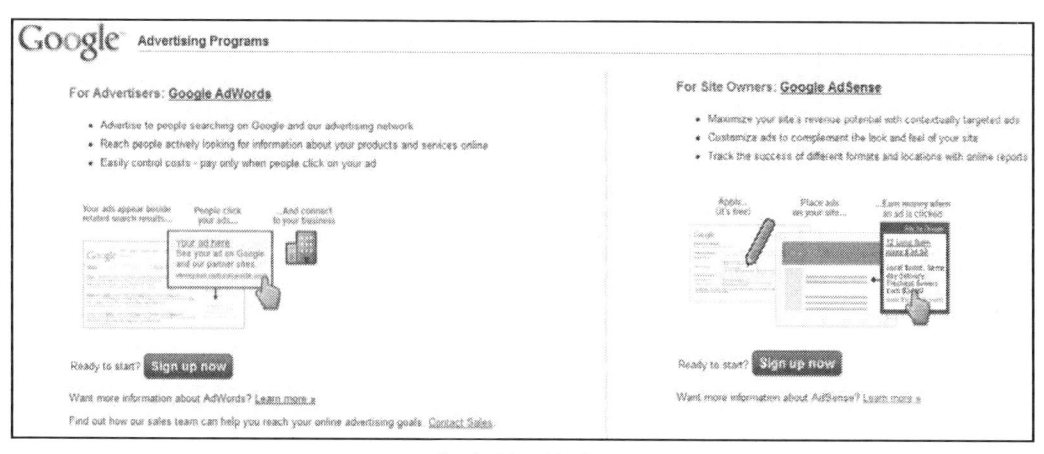

Google Advertising Programs

AdWords is designed for advertisers who want to have their ads displayed with the search results. AdSense is for website owners who want to make money by having Google Ads displayed on their website. Only AdWords will be discussed, as few law firms wish to have Google place advertising on their websites. To go to the next step, click "**Sign up now**" under Google AdWords.

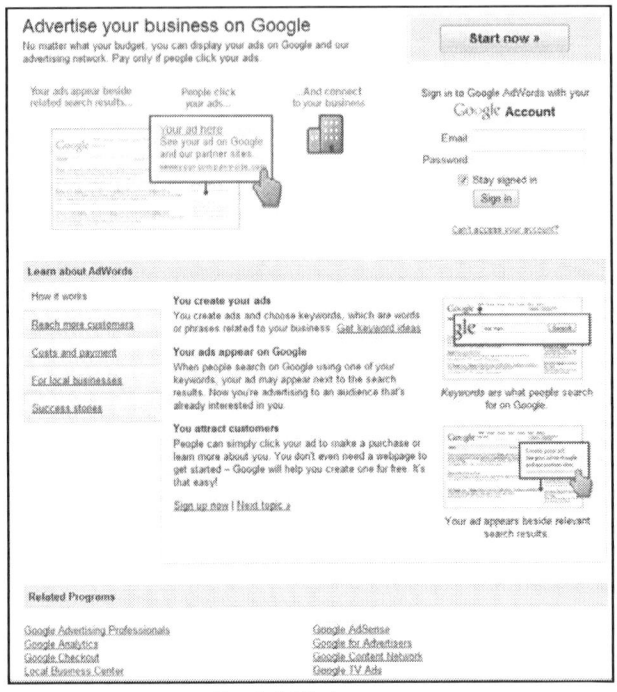

Google AdWords

On the next page you'll be presented with two options for the AdWords program – Starter Edition or Standard Edition. Select "**Standard Edition**". The Standard Edition offers the same features as the Starter Edition but allows multiple campaigns to be created. Multiple campaigns let a firm promote more than one practice area, present ads to more than one geographic location, and see more detailed reports of ad campaign performance.

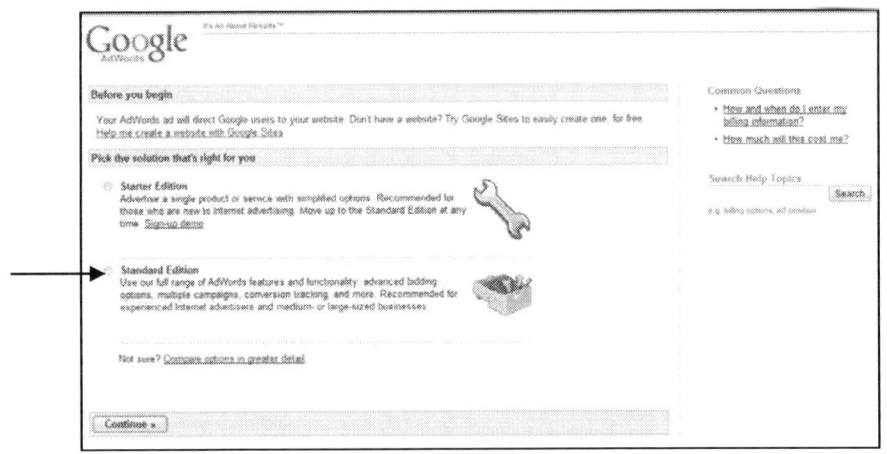

Starter & Standard Edition

Next, you'll be asked if you have a preexisting account with Google services. If you already have an account you can use it; however, you may wish to create a new account, especially if others may be accessing the account to manage campaigns. Either select to use your current account, or create a new one.

You will then be asked to select your currency preference for payment on your account. Select "**US dollars (USD $)**".

Next you'll be asked to verify your account information through an e-mail sent to the e-mail address assigned to the account. Once you've received it, **click on the link** supplied in the e-mail. The next page you will see will say "E-mail Address Verified", **click to continue**.

Click "**Create your first campaign**".

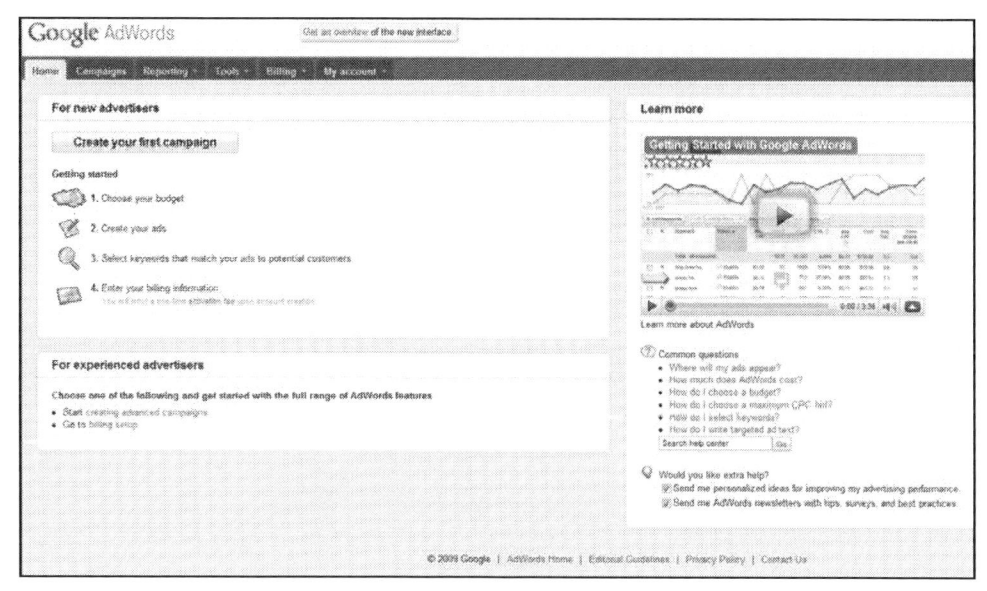

Creating Your First Campaign

STRUCTURE YOUR ADVERTISING

Before creating ads, it's necessary to understand the difference between Campaigns and Ad Groups. With Google, a Campaign may be thought as the top-level organization for your advertising. A Campaign is made up of one or more Ad Groups, each of which can be focused on a specific area to be marketed. Google makes the following distinction with respect to Campaigns and Ad Groups:

Campaigns are used to give structure to the products or services you want to advertise. The ads in a given campaign share the same daily budget, language and location targeting, end dates, and syndication options.

Within each campaign, you can create one or more ad groups. While a campaign may represent a broad product class, the ad groups within that campaign can be more focused on the specific product you want to advertise.

The following example illustrates this concept:
Suppose you practice personal injury law. You wish to create Google PPC ads that will appeal to potential clients who are injured. Two possibilities for structuring your campaigns would be as follows:

STRUCTURE CAMPAIGNS AROUND THE <u>INDUSTRY</u> IN WHICH THE INJURY WAS SUSTAINED OR THE <u>EVENT</u> WHICH CAUSED THE INJURY.

For this type of Campaign, the Ad Groups would consist of the specific body part injured. Campaign examples might look like the following:

        Construction Injuries [Name of Campaign]
            Neck Injuries [Name of Ad Group]
            Back Injuries [Name of Ad Group]
            Leg Injuries [Name of Ad Group]

        Secretarial Injuries [Name of Campaign]
            Neck injuries [Name of Ad Group]
            Carpal Tunnel [Name of Ad Group]

        Non-Industry – Auto/Truck [Name of Campaign]
            Neck Injuries [Name of Ad Group]
            Back Injuries [Name of Ad Group]
            Leg Injuries [Name of Ad Group]
            General Injuries [Name of Ad Group]

Non-Industry – Falls [Name of Campaign]
    Neck Injuries [Name of Ad Group]
    Back Injuries [Name of Ad Group]
    Leg Injuries [Name of Ad Group]
    General Injuries [Name of Ad Group]

STRUCTURE CAMPAIGNS AROUND THE <u>TYPE OF INJURY</u> SUSTAINED.

For this type of campaign, the name of the campaign would consist of the specific body part injured. Campaign examples could include the following:

Neck Injuries [Name of Campaign]
    From Construction [Name of Ad Group]
    From Secretarial [Name of Ad Group]
    From Auto Accident [Name of Ad Group]
    From Falls [Name of Ad Group]
    General [Name of Ad Group]

Back Injuries [Name of Campaign]
    From Construction [Name of Ad Group]
    From Secretarial [Name of Ad Group]
    From Falls [Name of Ad Group]

Carpal Tunnel Syndrome [Name of Campaign]
    From Secretarial [Name of Ad Group]

General Injuries [Name of Campaign]
    From Construction [Name of Ad Group]
    From Secretarial [Name of Ad Group]
    From Auto Accident [Name of Ad Group]
    From Falls [Name of Ad Group]

Either of these structures would work well, or if you have a structure that makes more sense for your practice, that would also work. ***Creating an effective structure for campaigns is important. What you want to avoid is potentially creating ad groups in different campaigns that might use the same keywords.***

As an example, if the structure immediately set forth above was used, you would <u>not</u> want to create the following:

Manufacturing Neck Injuries [Name of Campaign]
From Falls [Name of Ad Group]

Creating this campaign would be problematic, as all "neck" injuries should be set forth under the "Neck Injury" campaign. When keywords are designated (after the ads for each ad group are created), there is the possibility that the same keywords could trigger ads in more than one ad group or campaign, especially when several hundred keywords may ultimately be used.

In this respect, <u>with PPC advertising, the **more specific campaigns** that can be created, **the better**</u>. More directed campaigns allow for more specific ad groups (and ads) to be created. Ideally you would like to have an ad that speaks directly to a prospective client that describes the client's legal need as closely as possible.

AD CREATION

Regardless of how your Campaigns are structured, the same ad can be created. An example of this is as follows:

Example of the Same Ad That Could Be Used in Two Different Campaign Structures

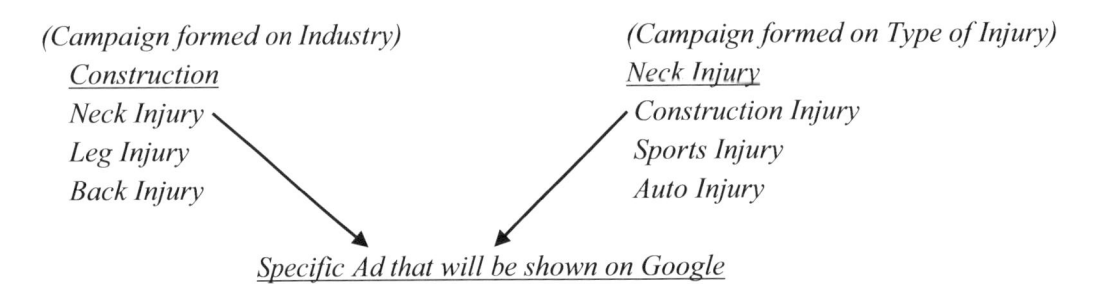

(Campaign formed on Industry)
    Construction
      Neck Injury
      Leg Injury
      Back Injury

(Campaign formed on Type of Injury)
    Neck Injury
      Construction Injury
      Sports Injury
      Auto Injury

Specific Ad that will be shown on Google

Construction Neck Injury?
We've Represented Construction Neck
Injury Cases for 12 Yrs-Free Consult
www.xyzLawFirm.com

CREATE CAMPAIGNS

When setting up a campaign on Google you will be asked to complete the following:

1. **Name your campaign** - In the above example the campaign would be defined as either "Construction" or "Neck Injury"

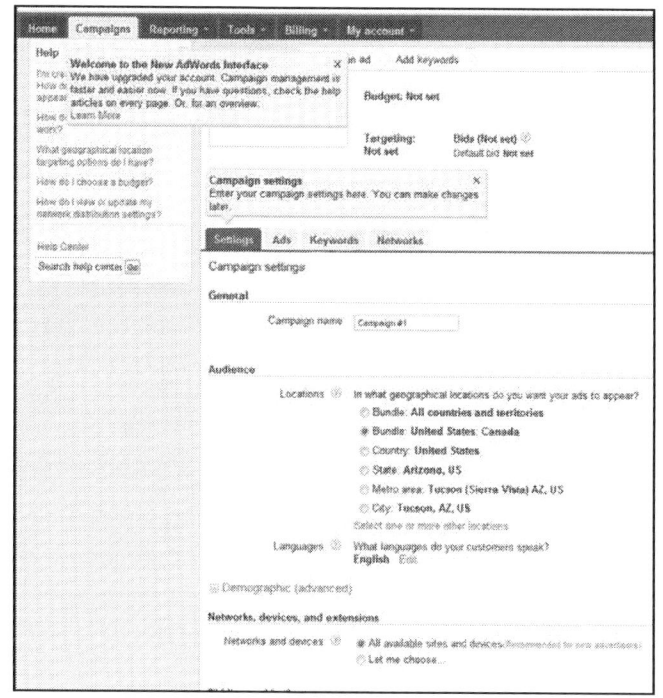

Create a Campaign

2. **Define your audience (geotargeting)** – Geotargeting is the process of selecting the geographical areas where your ads will be displayed. Geotargeting is extremely useful and saves money as your ads won't be shown to (and possibly clicked on) by those unlikely to become your clients.

   When defining your audience, click on the link "**select more than one location**". On this page you can select more than one geographic area for your target audience. To specifically define the areas you want to target, click the tab marked "**Browse.**" Here you'll see a list of countries. Click on the "+" next to the United States to see a list of the states, then click on the "+" next to your state to see a list of the Metro Cities. To further define the search click on the "+" next to the Metro City to see a list of individual cities. Please note, if you click on a major metropolitan city, such as Chicago, the geographic area will include ALL of the cities in the greater Chicago Metro area. But if you prefer to select ONLY some of these cities, click on only the ones you want to target to have them added to your list.

If you wish to make your target group even narrower, click on **"Demographic (advanced)."** Here you have the ability to exclude your ads from showing up on sites targeting a particular group. For example, if you do not want your ads to appear on websites targeting individuals 0-17 and 65+, check these two boxes on the page. This will exclude your ad from appearing on sites within the Google network that target individuals 0-17 and 65+ years of age.

You can define the location of your audience even further by selecting target language(s) for your ads. If your law firm has a large Hispanic clientele, you may want to select both Spanish and English as the designated languages. Google will then place your ads on Google interfaces showing Spanish and English search results.

To select a language in addition to English, click "**Edit**" to see a list of languages; check the languages of your target audience. **Note that Google does not translate your ads into other languages; they only place your ads on Google interfaces representing the languages you have selected.**

Individuals using Google can select their Google interface to appear in the language of their choice. All help options are written in the preferred language, but the ads appear in the language used by the advertiser. When using a language other than English, be sure to include an ad written in that language. For example, if you have selected Spanish as one of your languages, include an ad written in Spanish in your campaign.

Select your location

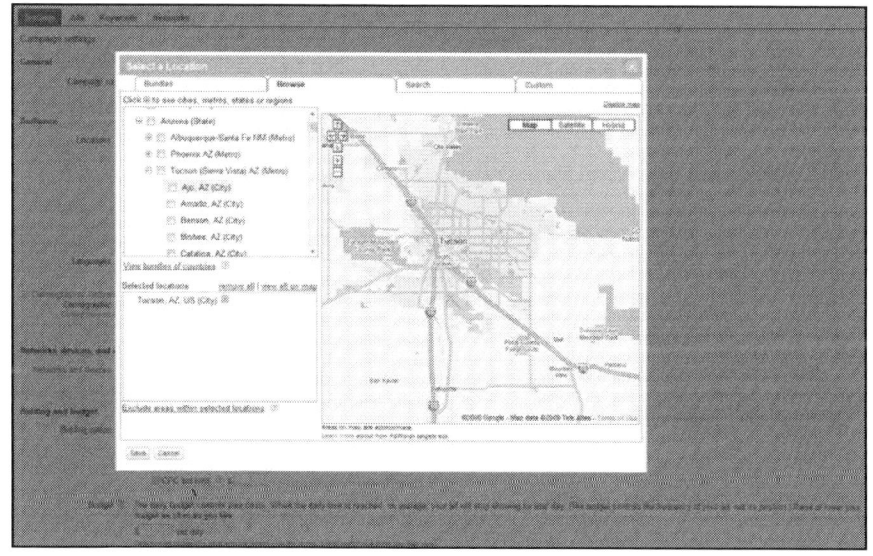

Define Your Location

Select Language

3. **Select your network – Networks, Devices and Extensions – This section has two important aspects – Search and Content.**

   With Google, your ads can be shown on the **Google Search Network** and/or the **Google Content Network**. The following describes the important differences between these two networks. First, however, to see the options for the Google Search Network and the Google Content Network, click the circle "**Let me choose**"; which will cause the page to expand to show the options noted below.

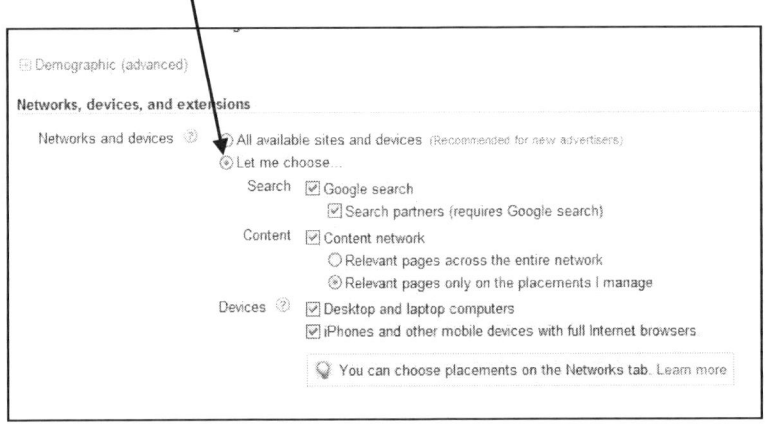

   Networks, Devices, and Extensions

   The Search Network shows ads in connection with search terms typed in by a user. Checking **Google Search** will display your ads only when a user is searching for a particular term on Google; adding **Search partners** will include displaying your ads when a user types in a search term on

Amazon.com and Google search partner websites. For instance, if a user is looking for a book about divorce on Amazon.com and types in "divorce" in the Amazon.com search box, an ad for "Chicago divorce lawyer" might be displayed on the page).

With respect to the Search Network you have two possibilities: (1) have your ads displayed on Google Search **and** the partners in the Google Search Network, or (2) have your ads displayed **only** on Google Search.

With the Content Network, your ad could be shown on any of the hundreds of thousands of websites that have opted to show Google Ads by participating in Google's AdSense Program, or that otherwise have agreements to show Google ads. In most instances ads are shown in a box on a website along with the "Ads by Google" text at the bottom of the ad box.

With respect to the Content Network, you have **three possibilities**: (1) have your ads shown by Google across the whole Google Content Network, (2) have your ads shown across the whole Google Content Network *except* for websites that you have expressly excluded, or (3) have your ads shown *only on websites that you have specified* through creating "site-targeted ads.

For possibilities (1) and (2), Google places ads on the web pages of participating websites in the Content Network that Google deems to be "contextually" relevant. For example, on a web page about divorce, Google may place ads for "divorce lawyers in Chicago." It's up to Google's automated algorithms to determine what websites and web page content are "contextually relevant".

Note that such ads are shown to users that happen to be on the particular web page; the ads are **not** displayed in response to a user-initiated search. Thus a user might be on MySpace visiting the page of a friend; if Google's program interprets the friend's MySpace page to be about divorce in Chicago, Google would then display an ad for "Chicago divorce lawyers" on that page. Such ad may or may not have any relevance to the visitor on the MySpace page.

Because the web page visitor may not be actively looking for the information that may be displayed in the advertising, advertisers should consider having a different (and likely, much lower) bid for clicks on the

Google Content Network than for the **Google Search Network**. An advertiser on the Google Search Network might be willing to pay $.10/click on the basis that a click is more likely to result in a client (because the user is specifically searching for a law firm), and only $.02/click on the Google Content Network (on the theory that the person making the click is less likely to become a client). Separate bids placement is discussed in the next section.

With respect to possibility (2) above, advertisers can "opt-out" of having their ads placed on specific websites. For instance, if an advertiser doesn't want to have their ads placed on MySpace web pages, the advertiser could "opt-out" of MySpace ad placement by first accepting "**All available sites and devices**" or "**Let me choose**", and then "**Relevant pages across the entire network**".

With respect to possibility (3) above, advertisers can alternatively elect to have their ads placed on only the specific websites that they designate. These websites **MUST** be part of the Google Content Network. To choose this option under the **Content** section, click the circle next to "*Relevant pages only on the placements I manage*".

Here's where it gets a bit tricky. Before selecting either the websites that you want to **exclude** (possibility (2)) or the websites that you want to **include** (possibility (3)), you must first complete the remainder of the page with respect to bidding and budgets, and then click **"Save and Continue"** at the bottom of the page. **See Item 4 – "*Bidding and Budget*" below for information on these areas.** The remaining portion of this item discuses opting out or including specifically-designated websites, AFTER the "**Save and Continue**" box is clicked at the bottom of the page.

The middle of the next page that should be displayed should look like the following:

Ad Placements

Here you can add websites that you wish to include or exclude in the placements box, or, if you wish, you can add websites to be included or excluded later. To include or exclude websites and web pages, simply type in the full url in the box (with a "-" sign before the websites or web pages to be excluded).

If you wish to add websites **later** to be included or excluded from showing your firm's ads, the procedure is different.

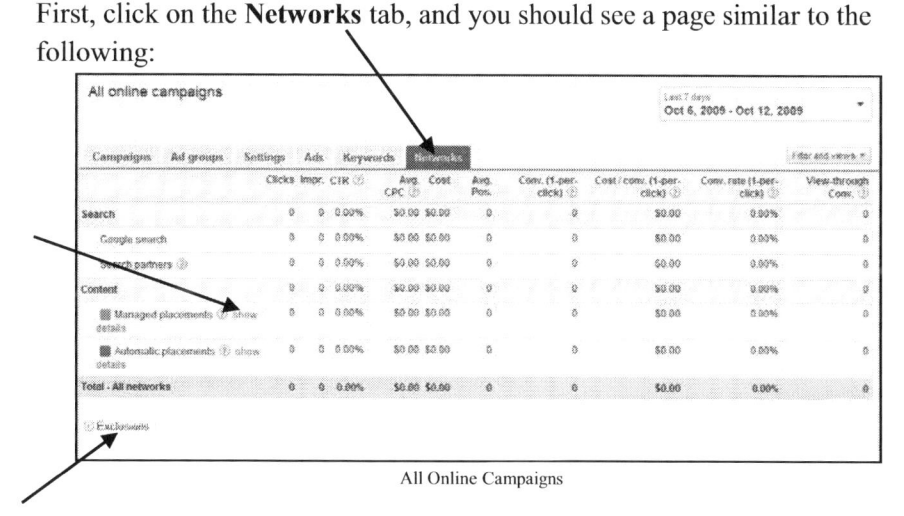

First, click on the **Networks** tab, and you should see a page similar to the following:

All Online Campaigns

To add placements, click on the "**show details**" link.
To add exclusions, click on the "+" sign by "**Exclusions**".

223 | P a g e

To Add Placements (Websites Where Your Ads Will be Targeted) or Exclusions (Where Your Ads Won't Be Shown)

If the "show details" link is clicked to add a placement (website) where ads are to be shown, the page will expand to look like the following:

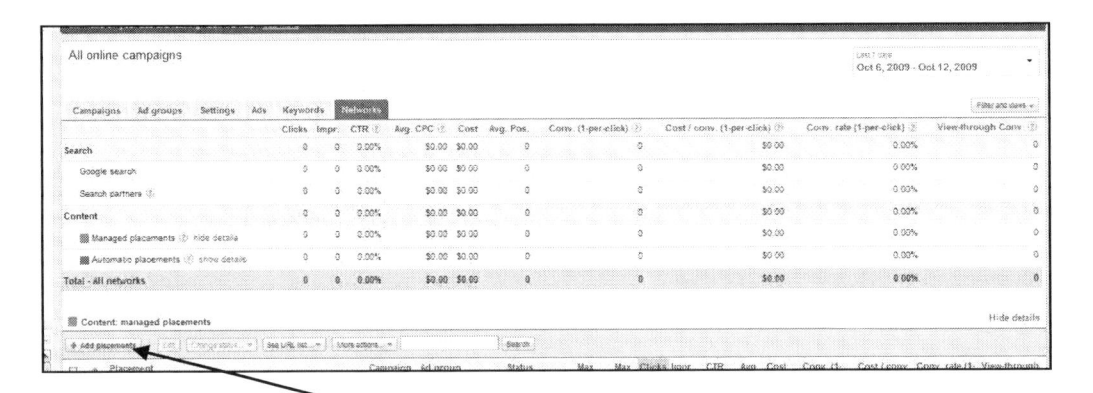

Click on the "**+Add placements**" box. The next box will look like the following:

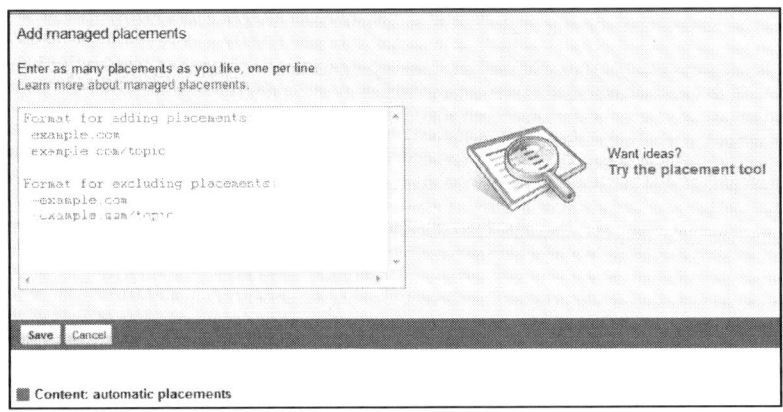

Managed Placements

As you'll note, at this stage you can add websites (and web pages) where your ads WILL be shown, and also websites where your ads WON'T be shown.

224 | P a g e

Special Notes about Managed Website Placements
1. Only websites that participate in Google's AdSense program can be targeted.
2. With some participating websites, it's possible to target specific pages; with other participating websites it's only possible to target the website itself.
3. Different bids can be placed for each website, if desired. To place a bid for a specific website, after entering the website url in the box indicated above, add a space and then the following "**.05"; this would indicate that you wish to bid 5 cents per click for clicks generated from that website.

4. **Bidding and budget** – Bidding involves selecting the maximum amount you are willing to pay each time someone clicks on your ad. Note – the amount bid is NOT necessarily the amount that will be charged. Google generally does not charge more than one cent above the next highest bid, so if your bid is $.50 per click and the next highest bid is $.26 per click, you might only be charged $.27 per click. Google uses other factors to establish the final click price (ads that have higher click through rates, for instance, are charged lower rates); but you'll never be charged more than you bid.

Within a campaign you can set different amounts for different keywords, or all keywords can have the same click amount. In most instances the keywords that would appear to be the most likely to result in a prospective client should get the higher bid.

You will also be asked to set a daily budget for each campaign. Once your daily budget has been reached, Google stops displaying your ads until the following day. Both the keyword bid amounts and daily budgets can be changed at any time, so don't be concerned that the initial settings are permanent. It's better to keep both of the keyword and budgets lower at first and then increase them after monitoring campaign performance.

Bidding and Budget

When determining your bidding and budget, it is important to understand the term Cost-Per-Click.

Cost-Per-Click, or CPC, is the amount you have decided to pay each time someone clicks on your AdWords ad and is taken to your site. Cost-Per-Click is also often referred to as Pay-Per-Click, or PPC.

PPC ad rank in Google is not strictly determined by bid amounts. Google also considers factors such as an ad's historical click through rate, and how closely the words in the ad are associated with the search terms. Note that Google prefers that users click on ads (where it earns money) than on the organic (or free) search results, where no money is earned.

CREATE COMPELLING ADS

Once the campaign settings have been selected, you will be asked to create an Ad Group. An Ad Group consists of one or more ads and the associated keywords. Ads are displayed in response to the search terms entered by a user (assuming the ad bid price is high enough).

Each ad consists of a **headline** (limited to 25 characters), the **first descriptive line** of the ad (limited to 35 characters), the **second descriptive line** (limited to 35 characters), the **URL** of your website (usually the name of your website - limited to 35 characters), and the **destination URL** (where the user will be taken once they click on the ad, possibly a page in your website describing your practice areas – limited to 1024 characters). The destination URL is not displayed.

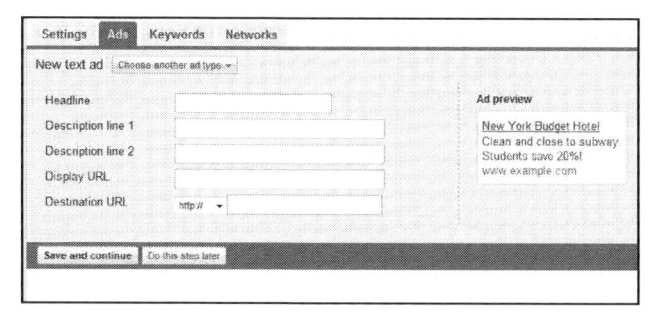

Ad Creation

Creating an ad is not difficult, but it does take some work to create a compelling ad.

A well-written, compelling ad:

- ➢ Triggers an emotional response by the reader
- ➢ Incorporates search terms in the headline as well as the body of the ad
- ➢ Includes only relevant information about the law firm and practice area promoted
- ➢ Elicits a call to action (clicking on the ad, and hopefully contacting the firm)
- ➢ Promotes the law firm's services

BELOW ARE TWO EXAMPLES OF ADS THAT COULD BE FOUND ON GOOGLE:

Good Ad:

Construction Neck Injury?
We handle **Construction Neck Injury**
Cases. 12 yrs - Free Consultation.
www.xyzlawfirm.com

Bad Ad:

XYZ Law Firm
We Represent Clients
Injured On the Job.
www.xyzlawfirm.com

- ➢ The ad on the left represents a well written PPC ad. The bold words correspond to search terms used by prospective clients searching for a law firm handling "construction neck injury" cases. Since the ad uses search terms actually used by prospective clients in a search (in the case of a search for "construction neck injury"), these words are highlighted in bold text, allowing the ad to stand out in the search results.

- ➢ The ad on the right does not use search terms associated with the search placed by the user, thus none of the words are in bold. By not using search terms the ad does not stand out from the others in the search results, limiting the chances of being clicked by potential clients.

- The ad on the left triggers an emotional response by asking the reader a question. The ad on the right does not.

- The ad on the left is more specific, addressing the needs of potential clients. The ad on the right is more general in nature.

- The ad on the left describes the experience of the law firm as well as their area of practice providing the user with more relevant information. The ad on the right does not.

Remember, your ad will be competing not only with other PPC ads but also with the website listings appearing in the general search results. Therefore, your ad needs to stand out from the crowd to get the desired clicks.

Also note that Google does not allow the following:

- Misspelled words and incorrect grammar in ads
- Excessive punctuation
- All capitalization
- Over-Promoting
- Offensive language or racial remarks

For more information on Google Ad Guidelines visit http://adwords.google.com/support/bin/static.py?page=guidelines.cs&topic=&view=all to get the full list of what can and cannot be included in an AdWords ad on Google.

You can (and should) create more than one ad to promote your services to your target audience. Within an Ad Group, when more than one ad is created, Google rotates the display of the ads. Over time, one of the ads may have a higher click through rate, indicating that it is more appealing to search users.

Google has an extensive library (http://adwords.google.com/support/aw/) to help with any questions you might have about writing an ad Pay-Per-Click practices.

CREATE KEYWORDS TO TRIGGER DISPLAY OF ADS

After creating an ad, you'll need to determine the keywords to be associated with the ad. Enter keywords in the box, one line at a time.

Keyword Creation

Keywords are the same as the search words prospective clients are likely to use when searching on Google to find legal services.

When creating a keyword list it's important to think like potential clients. Begin by listing words or phrases potential clients might use. For example, if you're a personal injury attorney creating an ad group for "neck injuries" you may want to include: neck injury, injury to the neck, broken neck, lawyer for broken neck, construction neck injury, on the job neck injury, neck accident, neck pain, neck trauma, and neck problems.

You may also want to include: common misspellings, plurals, words placed in different order (back injury, injury to back), abbreviations, and the substitution of similar words (attorney, lawyer) in your keywords. (Note – Misspellings are allowed in keywords but not in the ads that are shown.)

Additionally, when choosing the appropriate keywords consider using Negative Keywords. Negative Keywords are the words you don't want to be associated with in a search. For example if you're an estate planning attorney and one of your keywords is "estate planning", you don't want your ads to be shown if a user is searching for "real estate". If the term "real estate" is set up as a negative keyword, your ads won't be shown when that search query is used.

To add Negative Keywords to your ad group, place a negative sign (-) before the keyword you do not want associated with your ad group, and add "- real estate" to your list of key words. This may help reduce costs by limiting the number of visitors that come to your site by accident and have no intention of using your legal services.

Another way to target potential clients is to add Exact Match keywords to your list. Exact Match keywords <u>only</u> trigger your ad when the search term exactly matches your keywords. An Exact Match is identified with brackets ([ ]) placed around the keywords. For example, if you want your add shown only when someone is searching for an estate planning attorney you must add [estate planning attorney] to your list of keywords. In this example your ad would not be shown if a user enters "estate planning lawyer".

Google also provides a Keyword Tool to help generate additional keywords based on words or phrases, content found in your website, or an existing keyword. Google does not guarantee the performance of the generated keywords, they are simply an additional resource to use if you prefer.

ENTER BILLING INFORMATION & ACTIVATE ADS

Once you've selected keywords, your ads can be activated. Before doing so, you must add your billing information: preferred payment option, acceptance of the Terms and Conditions of service, and billing address as well as information needed for desired form of payment.

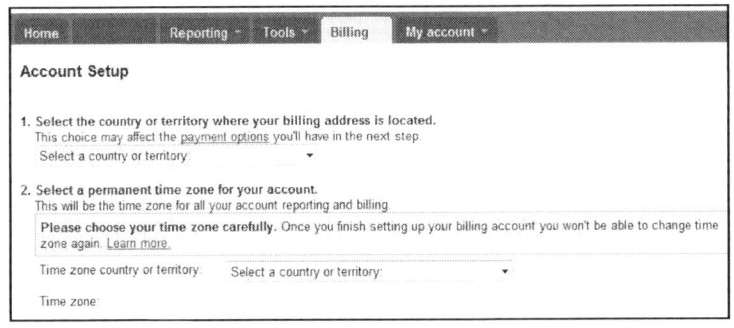

Billing & Activation

Once all of the billing information has been added to your account, Google will activate your ads.

Please note, before displaying your ads Google requires a $5 set-up fee, after that the cost you are willing to pay is entirely up to you.

MANAGE AND REVISE ADS

You can easily manage ad groups and campaigns with the Google AdWords Control Panel. There are six main components displayed on the Control Panel: Home, Campaigns, Reporting, Tools, Billing, and My Account.

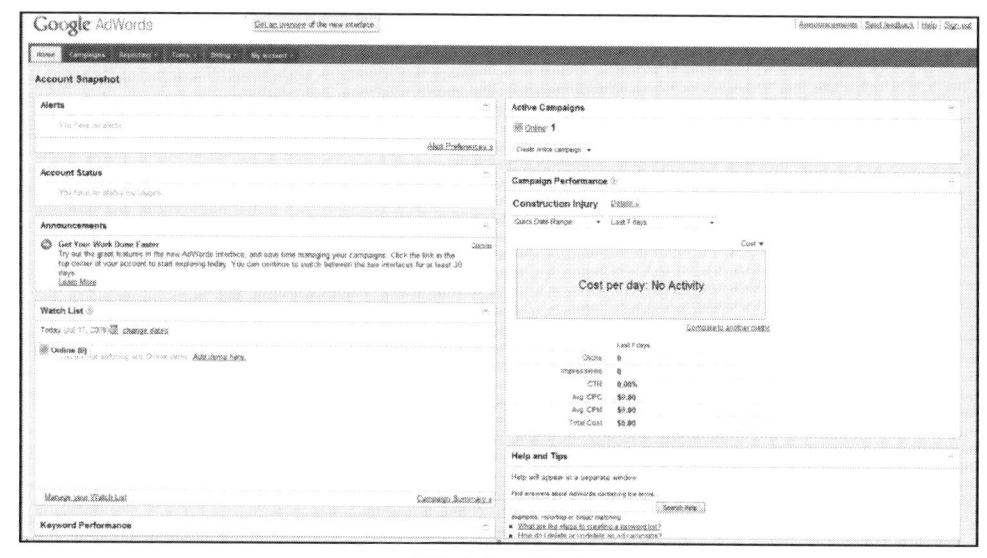

AdWords Control Panel

The **Home** tab allows you to see any notifications from Google, and a brief overview of your account.

With the **Campaigns** tab you have the ability to create a new campaign or ad group within a campaign, pause or stop an ad group or campaign, edit the settings for a campaign or ad group, add or edit keywords for your ad groups and campaigns, and edit the networks your campaigns will be served.

On the left hand side under the Campaign tab is a Help section. The information in this section changes depending on the Campaign function you are using and offers clarification and assistance with common questions associated with the different aspects of creating a campaign.

The **Reporting** tab allows you to create detailed reports about your campaigns. Track and compare your campaigns and ad groups to see how they are performing with reports, Google Analytics, and the Website Optimizer.

Google Analytics is a more precise tracking tool that, with the help of your developer, can easily be added to your website. A small piece of code is imbedded on a targeted page in your website (the conversion page) to track the number of visitors coming to your site and converting to potential clients. When the user visits the conversion page Google Analytics tracks that action. Google Analytics gives you a more accurate view of your ad spend, the click through rate of your campaigns, the conversion rate of visitors to potential clients, and the return on your marketing investment.

The Tools tab allows easy access to tools such as the Keyword Tool, Conversion Tracking, Ads Diagnostic Tool, and Ad Preview Tool.

Under the **Billing** tab you can review your billing summary and edit billing preferences and information.

The **My Account** tab allows contact information to be edited, as well as control who has access to your AdWords account. You can give others access to your AdWords account by inviting them to create their own login information with an email and password.

The amount of time needed to manage your PPC Account is entirely up to you. You can review reports and revise campaigns as little as once a month, or daily to make sure that your ad spend is on target.

APPENDIX 4 – CREATING A PAY-PER-CLICK ACCOUNT WITH YAHOO! SEARCH MARKETING

Note: If you have not done so already, please read "Creating a Pay-Per-Click Account with Google AdWords" included as Appendix 3. There are a number of concepts discussed in that Appendix that will be applicable here, including structuring campaigns, creating effective ads, setting budgets, and identifying keywords for the ads. These concepts will not be repeated in this Appendix, except where Yahoo! differs from Google AdWords.

Creating a Yahoo! Search Marketing account is easy. The steps are similar to creating a PPC account on Google except for one – <u>the keyword list is created before the ad is created.</u> Other than that the terms and procedures used in both Internet marketing programs are similar.

Yahoo!

First, go to www.Yahoo.com and click **"More"** on the navigation bar at the top of the page. On the next page, under the Search box, click **"For Site Owners"**, then click **"Advertising Info"**.

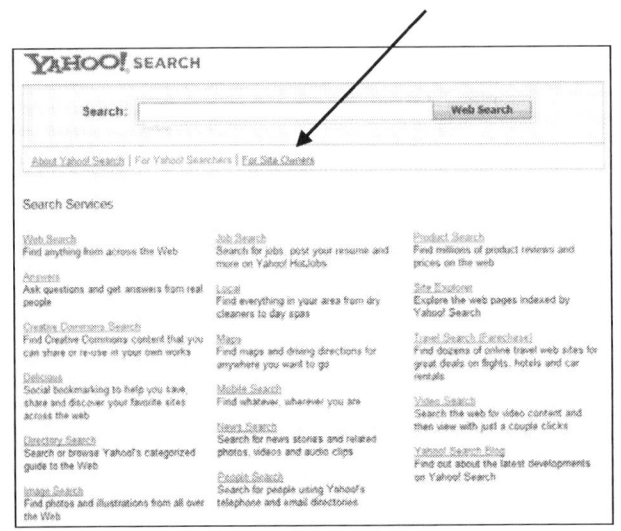

Yahoo! Search

On the next page will be a brief explanation of the Yahoo! Search Marketing program. Click **"Sign Up"**, in the orange box.

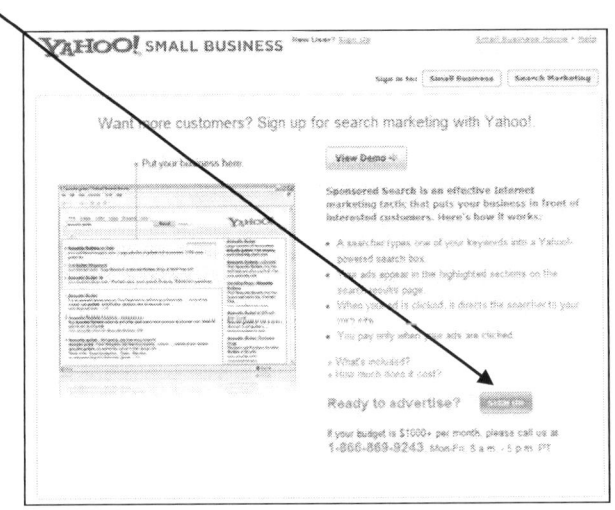

YAHOO! Small Business

There are **5 steps** to creating a Yahoo! Search Marketing account. To get started select **the market and time zone** of your law firm. Make your selection and click "**Get Started**".

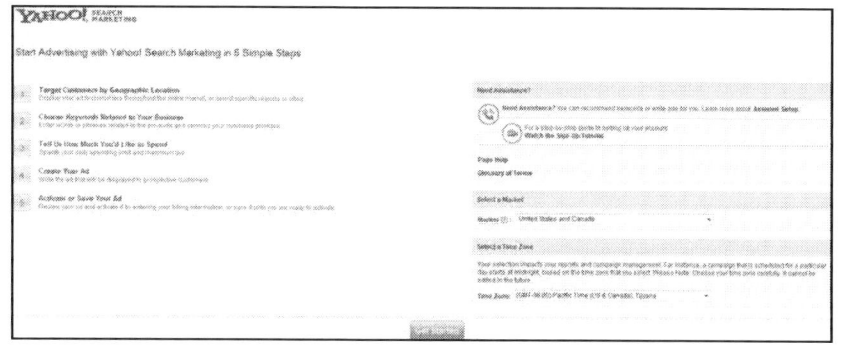

YAHOO! Search Marketing

TARGET CUSTOMERS BY GEOGRAPHIC LOCATION

Now it's time to start creating your campaign. The first step is geo-targeting – deciding where you want your ads to be displayed.

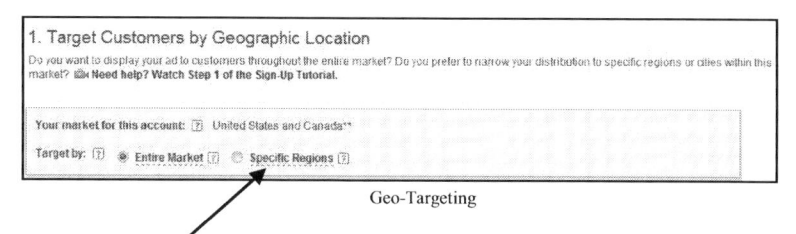

Geo-Targeting

To avoid unwanted clicks by users not living in your practice area potentially driving up costs, click "**Specific Regions**".

You will then be shown two boxes; the one on the left allows you to narrow your search, while the box on the right accepts the geographic locations you want to target. Click **"Search"** to generate locations by entering a city, state, or zip code in the box. Once the geographic location has been defined click "**Next: Keywords**".

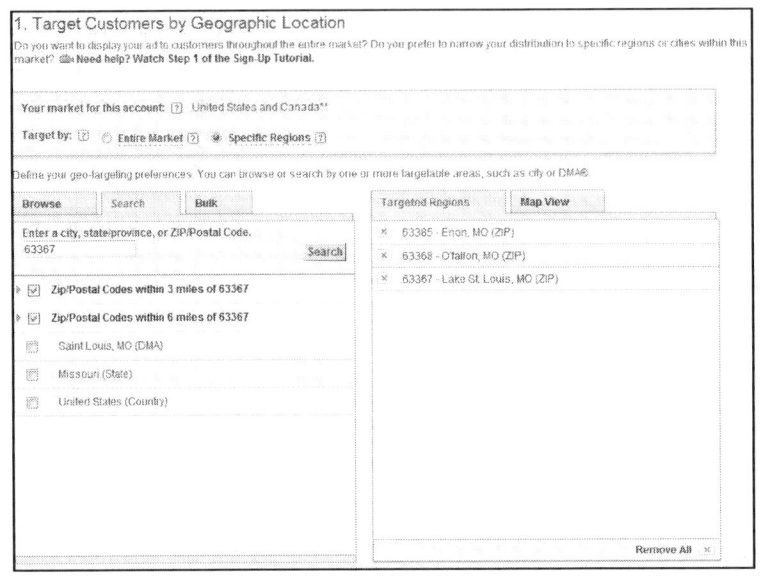

Target Customers by Geographic Location: Specific Region

CHOOSE KEYWORDS

Creating your keyword list on Yahoo! is a two step process. First, enter up to 50 keywords or keyword phrases, one per line, in the box provided. When finished, click "**Next: Related Keywords**".

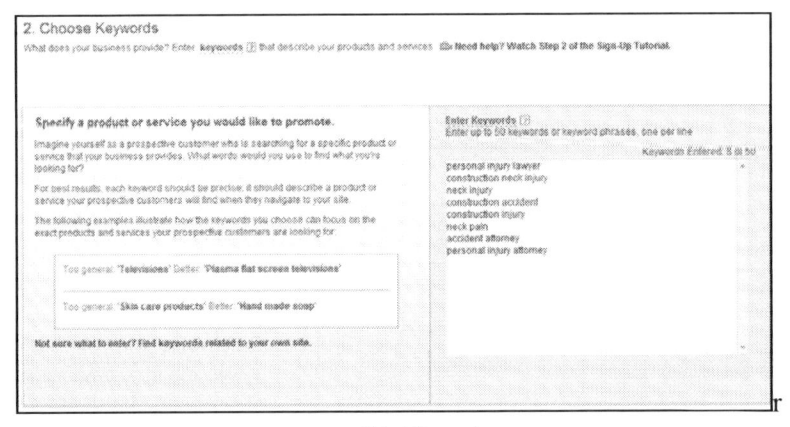

Select Keywords

On the following page notice that Yahoo! has generated additional keywords associated with the ones you previously entered. To add one of their keywords to your list click "**+Add**"; when complete click "**Next: Pricing**".

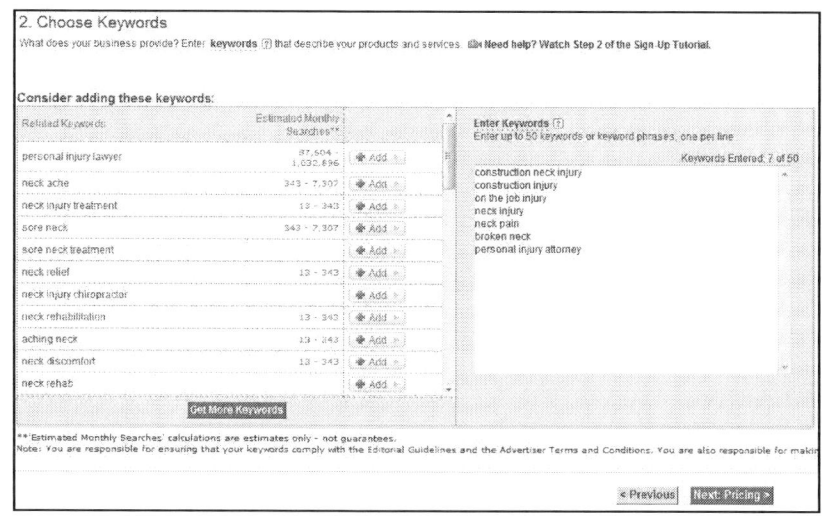

YAHOO! Generated Keywords

TELL US HOW MUCH YOU'D LIKE TO SPEND

After creating the keyword list to be associated with your campaign set your daily spending limit as well as your maximum Cost-Per-Click bid. Click **"Next: Create Ad"**.

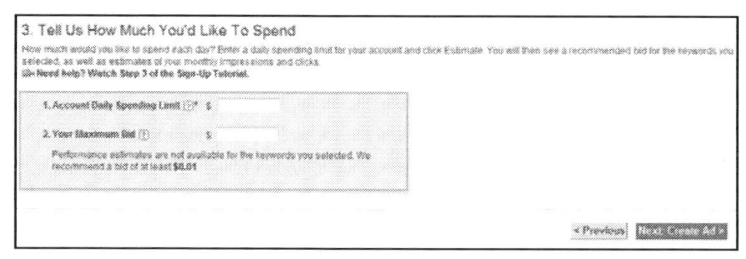

Daily Spend & CPC

CREATE YOUR AD

Creating an ad is simple. Fill in the Title (40 characters max), next add the Description (70 characters max), and finally the URL (1024 characters max). Please note, with Yahoo! there is only one URL associated with your ad, not two as with Google and Bing. Click **"Next: Review"**.

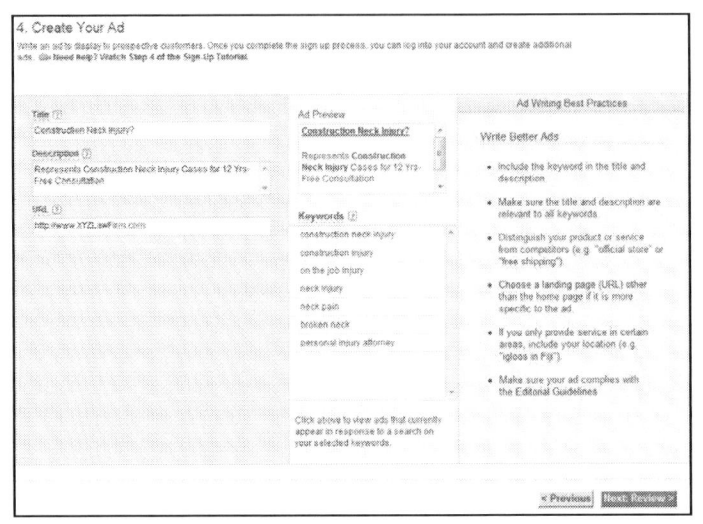

Create Your Ad

REVIEW AND ACTIVATE YOUR AD

On this page you'll review and edit your ad, if necessary. If changes need to be made click **"edit"**. Next, enter your account information (username, password, email address, company name, and enter the security code shown on the page), click **"Activate Now"**, and read and **"Accept"** the Terms and Conditions of use.

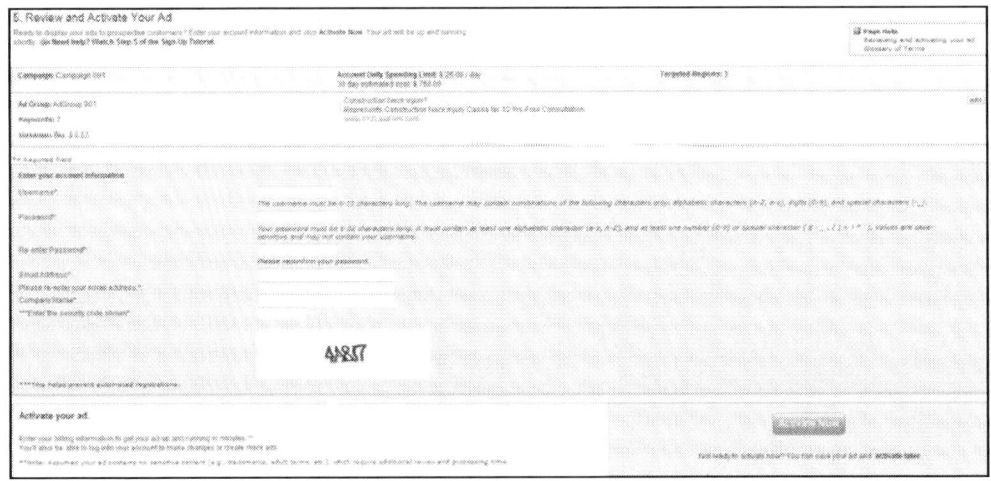

Review & Activate Your Ad

Before your ad is shown, you must enter your contact and billing information.

Please Note - Yahoo! requires that a deposit be charged to your account that is equal to the maximum daily amount previously specified over the course of a month. For example, if you chose $25 as your maximum daily spend, the deposit will be $750. Yahoo! also charges a $30 nonrefundable deposit to activate an account in addition to the individual deposit.

Click "**Done**" when complete.

With Yahoo!, most ads appear online within minutes of submission. If, however, the ad contains any content deemed sensitive (such as ads relating to adult content, online gambling, or pharmacies) the ad will require additional time for review where the ad will either be made active or disapproved.

APPENDIX 5 – CREATING A PAY-PER-CLICK ACCOUNT WITH MICROSOFT BING

Note: If you have not done so already, please read "Creating a Pay-Per-Click Account with Google AdWords" included as Appendix 3. There are a number of concepts discussed in that Chapter that will be applicable here, including structuring campaigns, creating effective ads, setting budgets, and identifying keywords for the ads. These concepts will not be repeated in this chapter, except where Bing differs from Google AdWords.

Before getting started, it's important to go over a few of the terms used in connection with Microsoft's Bing search engine advertising program. Bing is the name of Microsoft's search engine, which replaced the previous Microsoft search engine called "Live". Live is now dead.

Advertising on Bing is sometimes referred to by Microsoft as "Search Advertising" or "Microsoft Advertising". Advertisers may engage in Search Advertising by signing up through Microsoft adCenter (or "adCenter" for short).

Fortunately, creating an adCenter account is easy and involves much of the same concepts that pertain to Google AdWords Accounts.

First, go to www.bing.com and click the "**extras**" link located in the top right corner of the page. Then, on the next page, scroll down and click on the "**advertising**" link, and click the "**sign up**" pink box/link.

Bing.com

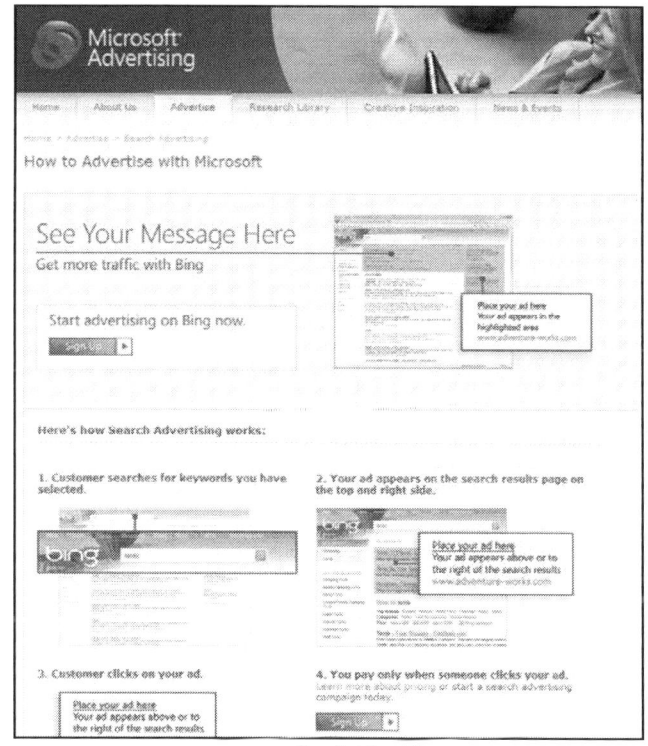

Search Advertising

You'll now be on the page called "Signing Up for Microsoft adCenter is Easy" (see below), which provides an overview of Search Advertising with Bing. After reading this material, confirm your country/region and click "**Sign up now!**"

241 | P a g e

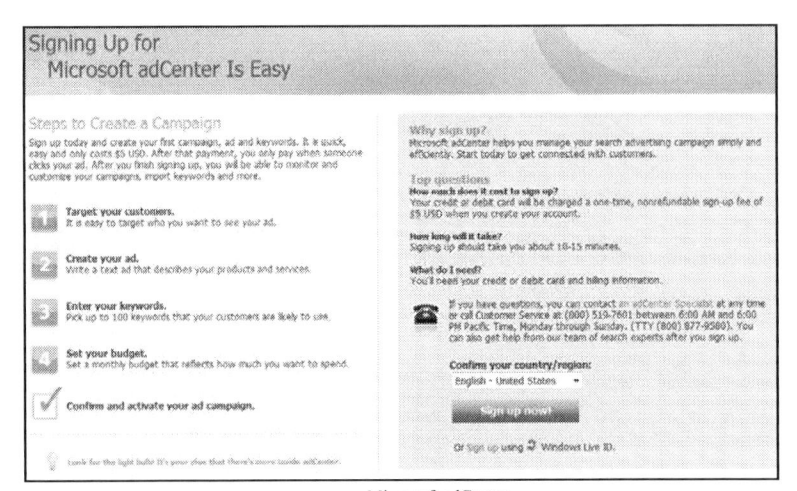

Microsoft adCenter

TARGETING YOUR CLIENTS

On the "Target your customers" page, select the "**language**" your ads will be written in, and target the "**geographical areas**" where your ads will be shown.

Next, select the location of your prospective clients. If you wish to target a specific city, for instance, click "**Specific cities within a country/region**". Click on the name of the city(ies) you would like your ad to be deployed and then click **"Add"** to place it in the box on the right. When finished, click **"Continue"**.

Target Your Customers

CREATING YOUR AD

Now, you're ready to create your first ad. Ad limitations are similar to Google:

>Ad Title (25 characters max)
>Ad Text (70 characters max)
>Display URL (35 characters max)
>Destination URL (1017 characters max)

Once the ad is complete, click **"Continue"**.

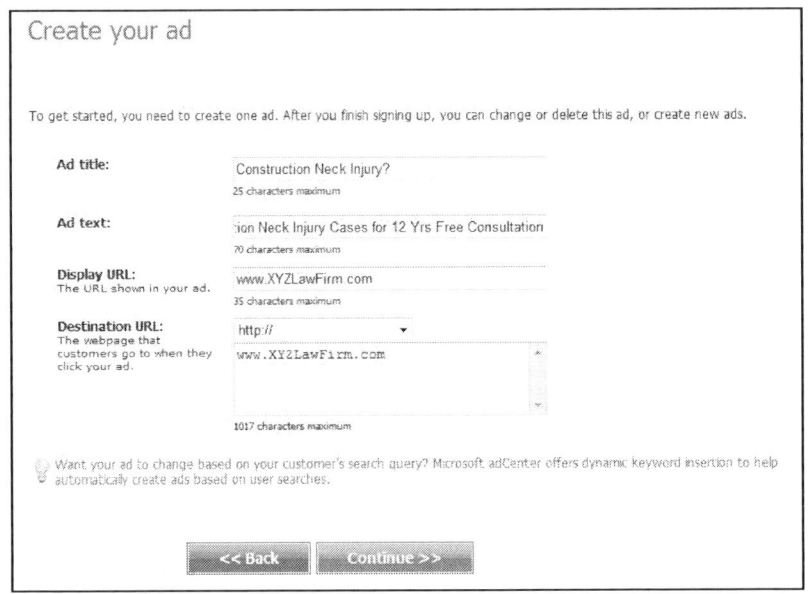

Create Your Ad

ENTER YOUR KEYWORDS

Enter the keywords in the orange box on the left, one keyword per line.

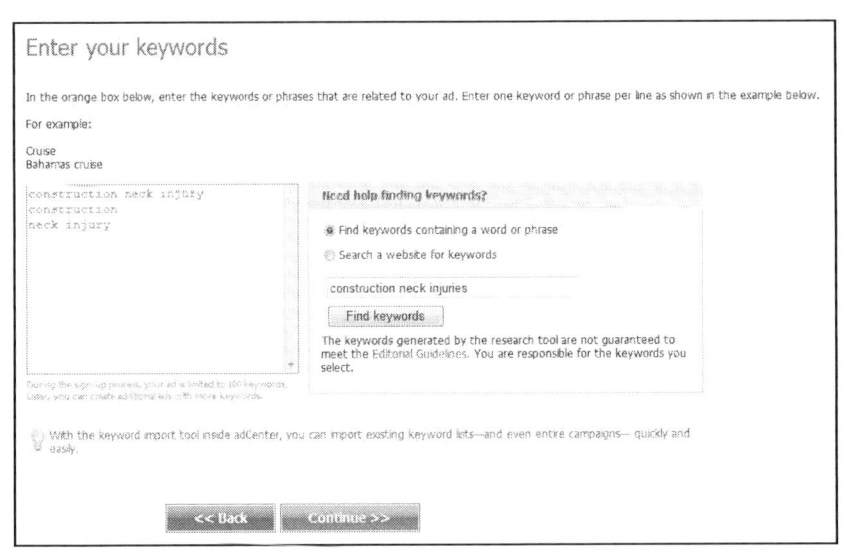

Enter Your Keywords

Bing offers assistance in the development of your keyword list. For help developing your list from a word or phrase click "**Find keywords containing a word or phrase**," type the word or phrase in the box provided and click **"Find keywords"**. Or if you prefer, you can

244 | P a g e

click **"Search a website for keywords"** allowing Bing to examine your website for appropriate keywords for your ad. These features will generate a list of keywords you may, or may not, want to include in your list. To add any of these to your list click **"Add keywords"** on the box located to the right of the keywords.

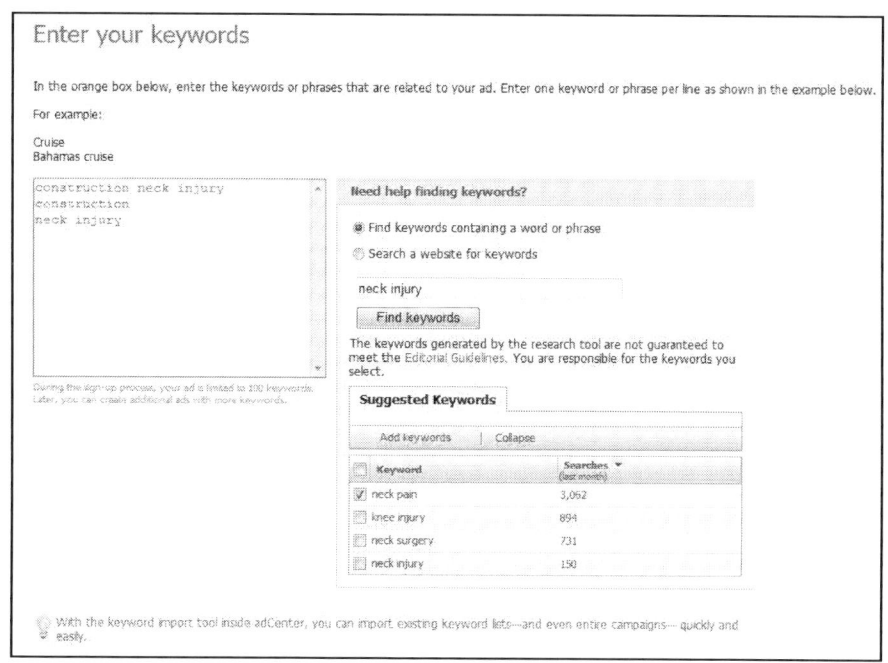

Find Keywords

SET YOUR BUDGET

Determining the monthly budget and cost per click is necessary when setting up an adCenter account with Bing. Fill in the boxes with the desired dollar amounts and click **"Continue"**.

Set Your Budget

CONFIRM YOUR AD CAMPAIGN DETAILS

Once the ad is written, the keyword list is complete, and the budget has been determined, it's time to review your ad campaign details (monthly budget, default bid, language, targeted country/regions, your ad, and keywords), and add your account information (name, user name, password, select a secret question and answer, and E-mail address). When finished, click **"Continue"**.

Confirm Campaign

246 | P a g e

ACTIVATING YOUR AD CAMPAIGN

To activate the account you must provide information about your company (company name, type of industry, company address, city, country, state, zip code and business phone), as well as payment information (name on card, card type, currency, card number, expiration date, and security code). If the billing address is different than the company address it will need to be included. You will also need to provide your contact preferences, type in the word verification, and agree the Terms and Conditions. Click **"Submit"** to activate your account. Note - Bing requires a $5 nonrefundable fee prior to activating your ads. Thereafter the amount you pay for PPC advertising is entirely up to you.

Activate Your Campaign

MAKING CHANGES TO YOUR ACCOUNT

After your account has been activated you will be taken to a "Thank You" page containing a link to the adCenter control panel. With the control panel you can make changes to your account, and edit and create campaigns and ad groups. Click **"Continue to adCenter"**.

Thank You for Signing Up!

The adCenter control panel is similar to the control panel found in Google. Here you can get an overview of your campaign and ad groups, edit account information, create reports, and research keywords for campaigns and ad groups. Once you have access to the adCenter control panel, you may name your ad group.

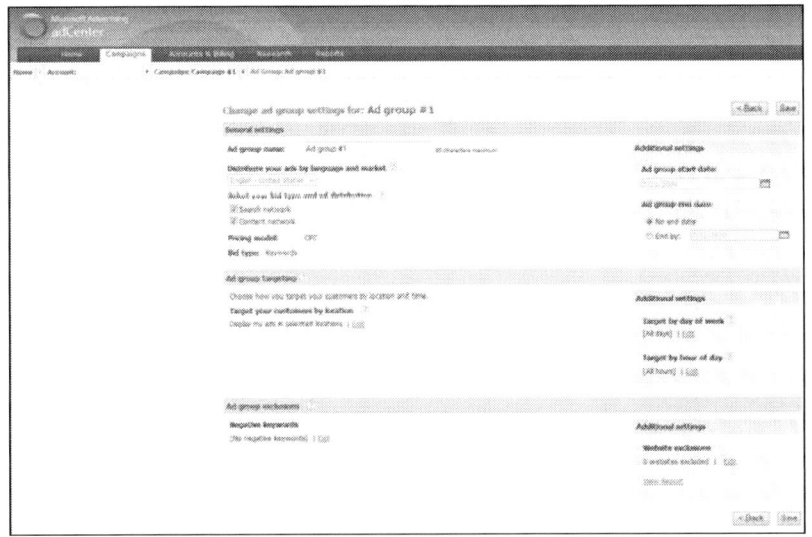

adCenter Control Panel

Changing Ad Group Settings

adCenter Labs is the help and tool center of Bing. To access adCenter Labs, scroll down to the bottom of the page and click **"adCenter Labs"**. Here you'll find information about Microsoft, assistance with your Bing PPC account, Tools to help you with and optimize your campaign and ads, and more.

Bing has a library of innovative and useful tools to help optimize your search engine marketing efforts. The tools have broken down into four main categories for easier use: Audience Intelligence, Keyword Research, Content Analysis, and Video & Interactive Media.

For information on how these tools can help you better understand your target audience, select the most powerful keywords for your campaign, create compelling and commanding content, and strengthen your online marketing presence with video and interactive media visit http://adlab.microsoft.com/Default.aspx.

All ads submitted to Bing must go through an initial review process to make sure that they are in accordance with the Microsoft adCenter Editorial Guidelines. The initial review process is short and should only take a few minutes. If the ad passes review it will be displayed on Bing. However, if the ad does not pass the initial review it will receive an additional review that can take several hours where it will either be activated or disapproved.

IMPORTING CAMPAIGNS FROM GOOGLE

If you have already created a campaign on Google, Bing allows a Google campaign to be imported using an Excel file or comma-separated values (CSV) file once you have activated your account. The files must be saved in a Bing template, or include all of the necessary data required by Bing, before you can import the data. For complete instructions on how to import a campaigns see: http://advertising.microsoft.com/wwdocs/user/en-us/adexcellence/text/Importing.html.

APPENDIX 6 – CREATING YOUR FACEBOOK BUSINESS PAGE

Before creating a business page on Facebook you must first create a personal page. You can set up a personal page on Facebook by going to www.Facebook.com. For a complete explanation of how to create a Facebook page visit http://www.Facebook.com/advertising/FacebookPagesProductGuide.pdf.

Facebook

Once a personal page is established, a business page can be created by first selecting the category you want your business to be associated with. Don't be concerned if the exact business type isn't there; pick the closest match to your law firm. If your firm is primarily a "local" law firm, you may want to select "**Local**" and then "**Professional Service**" as your category. If your firm has multiple offices in a variety of locations, you may wish to select "**Brand, Product, or Organization**", and then "**Professional Service**". By selecting the category that best matches your firm you are helping your chances of appearing in a Facebook search when users are looking for a local law firm or a law firm in general.

Once you've selected your category you'll need to select a name for your business page. When creating a name, make sure that it not only includes the name of your law firm, but also any search terms that you want associated with your firm. For example if you practice DUI defense in Phoenix, you may want your business page to appear as "Phoenix DUI Attorney, The Law Office of John Smith, P.C.

Please note that when creating a business page on Facebook, <u>once a category and business page name have been established, they cannot later be changed.</u> If for some reason you feel that you have mis-categorized your page or did not include a name that clearly identifies your business (and which also is search engine friendly), your only recourse is to delete your current business page and create a new page. In addition to the time that it takes to start over, if you've established a fan base (discussed below), your existing fan base will be lost.

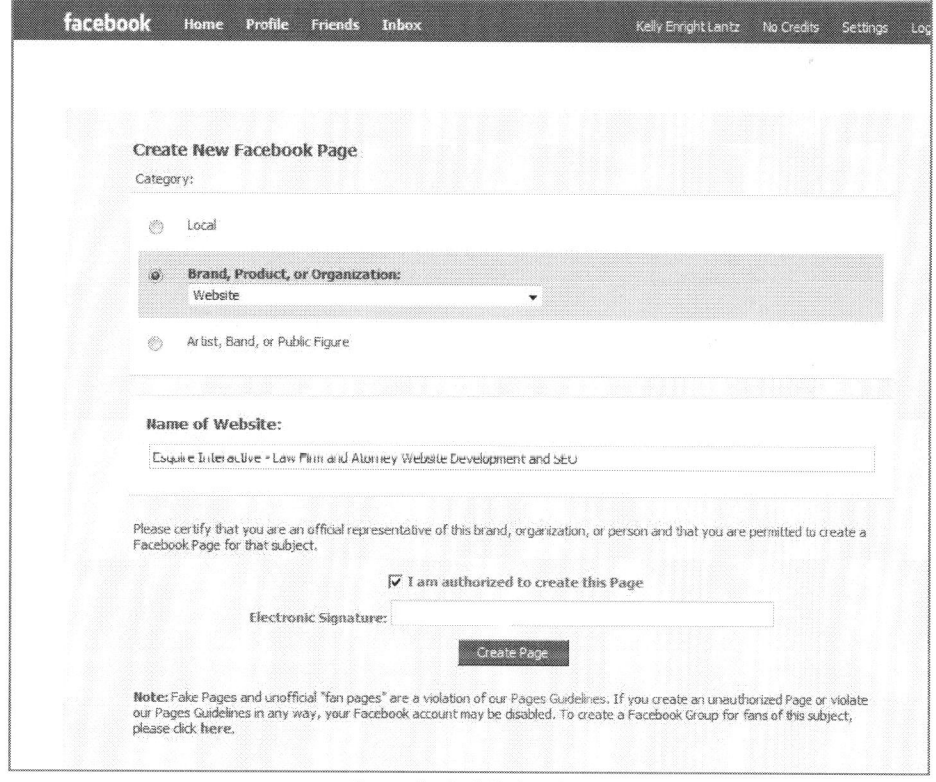

Create a Facebook Business Page

After selecting a category and title for your page you will need to verify that you are authorized to create this page and include your electronic signature (this is your Facebook/real name), and then click the "**Create Page**" button.

The next page will be your new Facebook business page. Before your page can be published, you must add the required business information and upload an image to identify your business page. To add your logo or another image, click on the large question mark "**?**" on the left hand side of the page. From there click "**Upload a Picture**" to add the image you want associated with your business page. This image can be changed at any time. Once an image has been added to your page you can add text describing your law firm and practice by clicking on "**Edit Information**", found on the right hand side of the page next to the pencil icon.

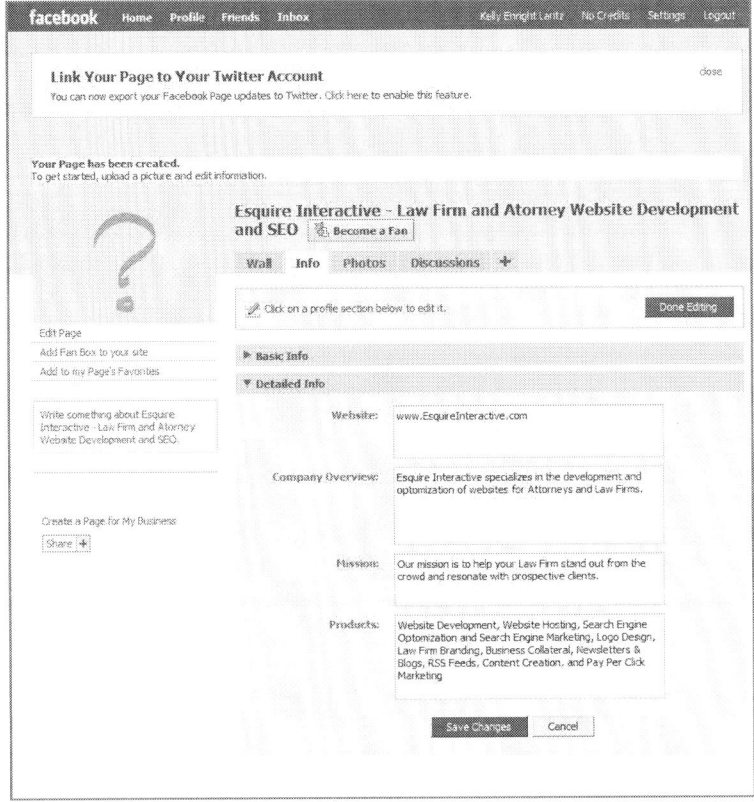

Add and Edit Information

Once your basic information and logo have been added you can activate your page by clicking on the orange text "**publish this Page**?" above the page title.

For a full list of rules and FAQ's on creating a Facebook page for your business visit the Facebook Help Center (http://www.Facebook.com/help.PHP?page=175).

252 | P a g e

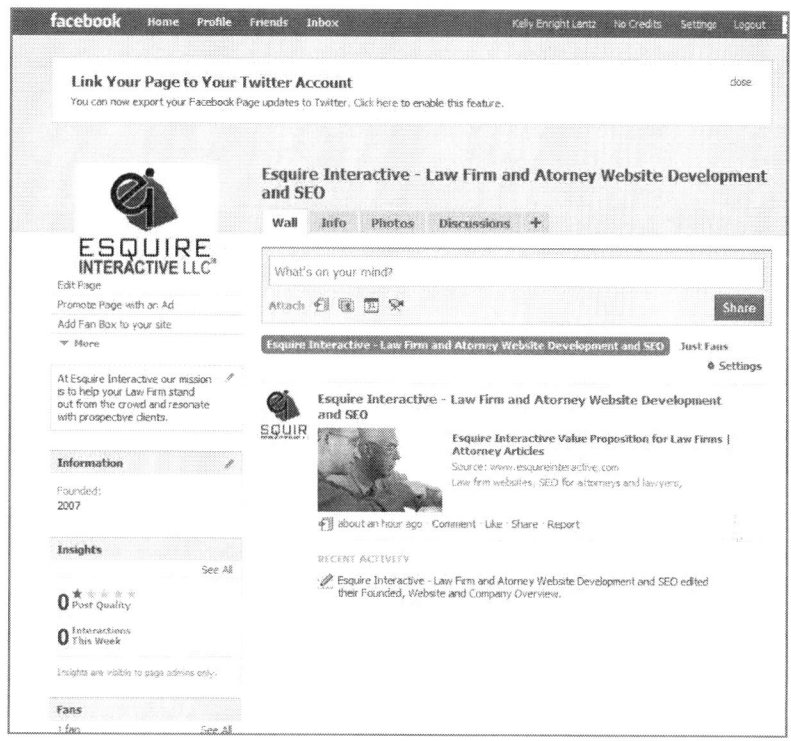

Facebook Business Page

After your page is published you can access it by clicking on "**Applications**" in the lower left hand corner of the page, then click on "**Ads and Pages**".

One easy way to promote your law firm once your business page is published is to invite friends and acquaintances to become fans of your business page. This will help establish a fan base and promote your site to friends of your friends since a users activity on Facebook is displayed on their wall. To do so you must first become a fan of your site (On Facebook, fan invitations must come from registered Facebook users, not sent by a business). Click on the link "**#1 Become a Fan**" to become a fan of your site – then you can invite friends to become fans.

Another free and easy way to promote your law firm and your business page is to add a "Find us on Facebook" banner to your website and blog. To obtain the banner image, visit http://www.Facebook.com/help.PHP?page=175.

ADVERTISING ON FACEBOOK

Placing ads on Facebook is extremely easy. While it's not possible to target users searching for any particular terms, users can be targeted by demographics such as gender, age groups, and city. When an ad is created, it is then shown only to users meeting the selected criteria.

To advertise on Facebook, first go to your business page (Click on "**Your Name**" on your main Facebook page, then click the "**Info**" tab, and then scroll down and click on the image for your business page. From your business page, click on the link "**Advertise on Facebook**"; from there you will be taken to a page where you can design an ad and see the different types of targeting available.

On the advertising page, you'll note that Facebook has already taken information from your business page to create an ad for you; you can either keep the information or change it. It's best to create and upload an appealing image to be shown as well as text that serves as a call to action, such as "Free Divorce Consultation – Open Saturdays. Call Us." Once the text and ad image have been created and uploaded, click "**Continue**" to select the geographic region where your ad will be shown and your target audience.

Next, you'll need to determine a payment basis and budget. On Facebook advertising can be bid on a **CPC (cost per click)** or **CPM (cost per one thousand impressions)** basis. It's not clear which method will be more cost advantageous, but a general rule is that if your prospective clients are likely to make up only a very small number of the targeted group, then CPC will likely be better; conversely, if there are a larger number of prospective clients in the targeted group and if your ad is very appealing, a CPM basis may be better.

To start with, I would suggest using a CPC basis and make a small bid (such as $.20 per click), and see how the ad performs after a few days. Then, when you start receiving statistics, you can increase or decrease the bid, and perhaps also change to a CPM basis. In addition to measuring the statistics from your Facebook account, you'll also want to check out your website statistics to see the number of click-throughs (people clicking to your website from your Facebook business page – see Chapter 14). For a complete list of FAQ's associated with placing an ad on Facebook, visit http://www.Facebook.com/help.PHP?page=864.

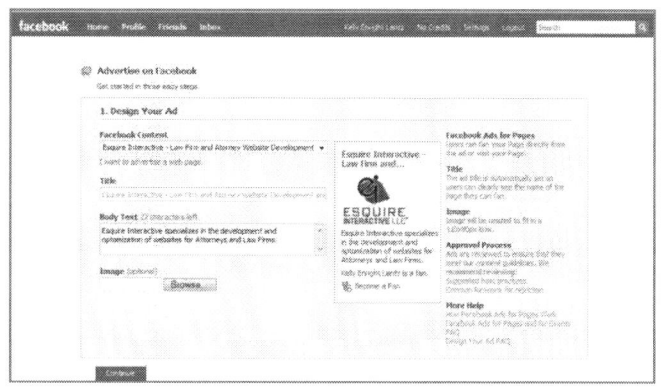

Advertise on Facebook

Additionally, please note that Facebook has established guidelines to follow when promoting your business page. You can view these guidelines and obtain a "Find us on Facebook" banner that can be added to you website by visiting the Facebook Help Center (http://www.Facebook.com/help.PHP?page=175).

APPENDIX 7 – CREATING A TWITTER ACCOUNT

Twitter can be an effective tool for attorneys and law firms to promote themselves and their services to prospective clients. For a complete explanation of how Twitter can help you promote your law firm please refer to the business help guide at http://business.twitter.com/twitter101.

Signing up for a Twitter account is easy. First go to www.Twitter.com and click **"Sign up Now"**.

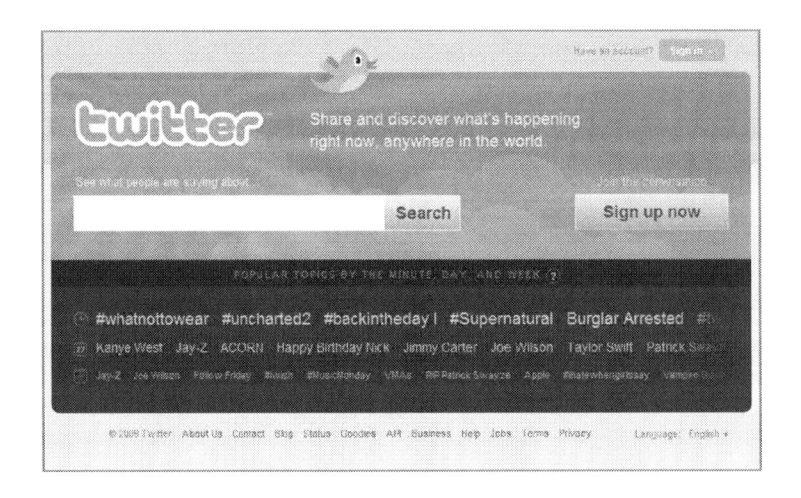

Next, complete the sign up form by supplying the following:

> ➢ Your name – first and last
> ➢ User name – limited to 15 characters. Please note, when selecting your user remember to select one that reflects your law firm or practice area. Your user name is the name associated with your Twitter postings.
> ➢ Your preferred email address

Sign-Up Page

On the next two pages you can locate your friends and acquaintances using Twitter as well as sign up to follow their tweets. Skip these steps and return to them later once your account is set up and you have started tweeting.

This is the page you signed up for, you can now start tweeting. Tweets are limited to 140 characters. Please refer to the business help guide (http://business.twitter.com/twitter101) if you have questions on what makes a powerful tweet. Once you have added your tweet click **"update"** to post.

The next two pages will take you through the final steps - selecting users to follow and setting up your cell phone to receive updates. Don't feel that you must complete these steps now; you can come back to them later you wish or not at all.

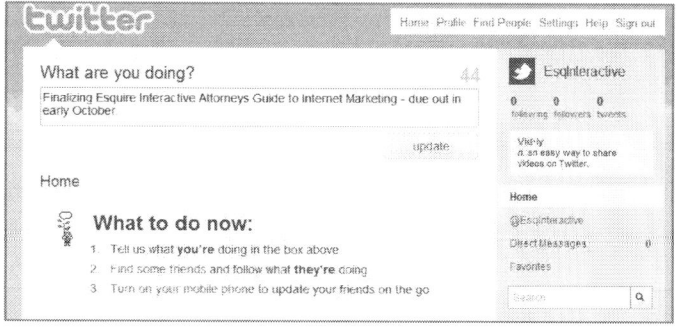

Twitter Account

To make changes to your Twitter account click **"Settings"** at the top of the page. From there you can add information about your Law Firm by clicking **"Account"**, add your Law Firm logo by clicking **"Picture"**, and more.

Twitter Dashboard

Twitter allows you to easily import your Facebook business page updates to your Twitter account. To do this you will need to go to your Facebook business page. At the top of your Facebook page will be a message, "Link Your Page to Your Twitter Account." Click **"Click Here"** to enable this feature.

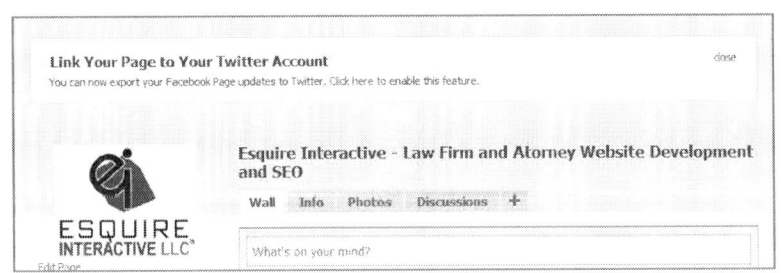

Facebook Business Page

The next page will briefly explain what you can export from your Facebook business page to your Twitter account. Click **"Link a Page to Twitter."**

Link Your Facebook Page to Twitter

On the next page will be an icon of your Facebook business page – click **"Link to Twitter."**

Link to Twitter

The next step will take your from Facebook to Twitter where you will be asked to connect your Facebook business page with your Twitter feed by providing your user name or email address, and your password. Click **"Allow."**

Allow Facebook to Link to Twitter

Next, you will be taken back to Facebook where you can choose which information you want exported from your Facebook business page to your Twitter account. Click **"Save Changes."**

Edit Settings

CHANGES TO FACEBOOK / TWITTER LINK

If you need to make changes to your Facebook/Twitter link, go to your Twitter account page. From there click on **"Connections"**, then click on the Facebook link. You will then be taken back to the page connecting your Facebook business page to Twitter. Click **"edit"** if you need to make changes to the Facebook feeds being sent to Twitter, or if you want to revoke access to Twitter all together.

Made in the USA
Charleston, SC
26 April 2011